International Society after the Cold War

Anarchy and Order Reconsidered

Edited by

Rick Fawn
Lecturer in International Relations
University of St Andrews

and

Jeremy Larkins
Department of International Relations
London School of Economics

in association with
Millennium: Journal of International Studies

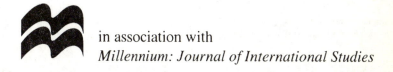

First published in Great Britain 1996 by
MACMILLAN PRESS LTD
Houndmills, Basingstoke, Hampshire RG21 6XS
and London
Companies and representatives
throughout the world

A catalogue record for this book is available
from the British Library.

ISBN 0–333–65955–4 hardcover
ISBN 0–333–65956–2 paperback

First published in the United States of America 1996 by
ST. MARTIN'S PRESS, INC.,
Scholarly and Reference Division,
175 Fifth Avenue,
New York, N.Y. 10010

ISBN 0–312–16104–2

Library of Congress Cataloging-in-Publication Data
International society after the Cold War : anarchy and order
reconsidered / edited by Rick Fawn and Jeremy Larkins.
p. cm.
Includes bibliographical references and index.
ISBN 0–312–16104–2
1. International relations. I. Fawn, Rick. II. Larkins, Jeremy.
JX1391.I6387 1996
327.1'01—dc20 96–7691
CIP

---

10 9 8 7 6 5 4 3 2 1
05 04 03 02 01 00 99 98 97 96

Printed in Great Britain by
Ipswich Book Co Ltd, Ipswich, Suffolk

INTERNATIONAL SOCIETY AFTER THE COLD WAR

Also published in association with *Millennium: Journal of International Studies*

Hugh C. Dyer and Leon Mangasarian (*editors*)
THE STUDY OF INTERNATIONAL RELATIONS: The State of the Art

Lorraine Eden and Evan Potter (*editors*)
MULTINATIONALS IN THE GLOBAL POLITICAL ECONOMY

Kathleen Newland (*editor*)
THE INTERNATIONAL RELATIONS OF JAPAN

Ian H. Rowlands and Malory Greene (*editors*)
GLOBAL ENVIRONMENTAL CHANGE AND INTERNATIONAL RELATIONS

Contents

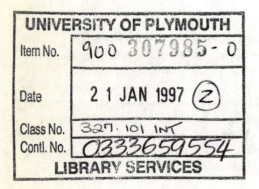

Notes on the Editors and Contributors

Rick Fawn is a Lecturer in International Relations at the University of St Andrews. He is writing a dissertation on 'The Ironies of a Civic Foreign Policy' at the London School of Economics where he was a Tutorial Fellow in International Relations in 1994–95. He has published on Central and East European politics and international relations and has taught at Keele University and the School of Slavonic and East European Studies. He was previously an editor of *Millennium: Journal of International Studies*.

Jeremy Larkins is a Research Student in the Department of International Relations at the London School of Economics. He is writing a dissertation on 'Postmodernism, State Theory and International Relations'. He has recently published on Durkheim and International Relations theory and was previously an editor of *Millennium: Journal of International Studies*.

Chris Brown is the Professor of Politics at Southampton University. He has written extensively on international relations and political theory. His most recent work includes *International Relations Theory: New Normative Approaches* (1992) and the edited collection, *Political Restructuring in Europe: Ethical Perspectives* (1994).

Barry Buzan is Professor of International Studies at the University of Westminster, and a Project Director at the Centre for Peace and Conflict Research in Copenhagen. His recent books include: *An Introduction to Strategic Studies: Military Technology and International Relations* (1987), *The Logic of Anarchy: Neorealism to Structural Realism* with Charles Jones and Richard Little (1992), and *Identity, Migration, and the New Security Agenda in Europe* with Morten Kelstrup, Pierre Lemaitre, Ole Wæver, *et al.* (1993). Work in progress includes *An Introduction to the International System* with Richard Little (1995) and *Military Security and Technology in the Post-Cold War Era* with Eric Herring (1996).

James Der Derian is Professor of Political Science at the University of Massachusetts at Amherst. He has taught at Columbia University, the University of Southern California, and the Gardner and Lancaster State Prisons. He is the author of *On Diplomacy: A Genealogy of Western Estrangement* (1987), *Antidiplomacy: Spies, Terror, Speed and War* (1992), co-editor, with Michael Shapiro, of *International/Intertextual Relations:*

Postmodern Readings of World Politics (1989) and editor of *International Theory: Critical Investigations* (1995).

Robert H. Jackson is Professor of Political Science at the University of British Columbia. During 1993–94 he was Visiting Senior Research Fellow, Jesus College, Oxford. He is the author of *Quasi-States: Sovereignty, International Relations and the Third World* (1990), *Personal Rule in Black Africa* as co-author (1982), and other works. Currently he is completing a normative theory of international relations entitled *The Global Covenant: Power and Responsibility in World Politics*.

Ronnie D. Lipschutz is Assistant Professor of Politics and Director of the Adlai Stevenson Program on Global Security at the University of California, Santa Cruz. He is author of *Radioactive Waste: Politics, Technology and Risk* (1980), *When Nations Clash: Raw Materials, Ideology and Foreign Policy* (1989), and *Global Civil Society and Global Environmental Governance* (forthcoming, 1996). With Ken Conca he has co-edited *The State and Social Power in Global Environmental Politics* (1993), and is editor of *On Security* (1995).

James Mayall is Professor of International Relations and Chair of the Steering Committee of the Centre for International Studies at the London School of Economics and Political Science. His publications include *Nationalism and International Society* (1990); *The Fallacies of Hope*, co-edited with Anthony Payne (1991); and he is editor of *The New Interventionism: The UN Experience in Cambodia, the Former Yugoslavia and Somalia* (forthcoming).

Justin Morris joined the University of Hull in 1990 as a student on the MA in International Law and Politics programme. He remained in the Department of Politics, working as a part-time tutor and research assistant, primarily to Professor Juliet Lodge in the European Community Research Unit based at Hull. In 1993 he was appointed to a Lectureship within the Department, specialising in and publishing on UN affairs and the role of international law in international relations.

N.J. Rengger is Lecturer in Political Theory and International Relations at the University of Bristol. His publications include many articles and chapters on political and international relations theory as well as the co-edited volume with John Baylis *Dilemmas of World Politics: International*

Issues in a Changing World (1992). His *Political Theory, Modernity and Postmodernity: Beyond Enlightenment and Critique* was published in 1995 and a second book, *Duties Beyond Orders: World Order and the Dilemmas of Liberal Politics* is due out in 1996. He is currently working on a co-authored book on the history of international political thought, and on a book on political judgement and public ethics.

Martin Shaw is Professor of International Relations and Politics at the University of Sussex. His publications include *Dialectics of War* (1988) and *Post-Military Society* (1991). He has edited a number of books including *War, State and Society* with Colin Creighton (1984), *The Sociology of War and Peace* (1987) and with Michael Banks, *State and Society in International Society* (1991). He has most recently published a collection of his essays and articles under the title *Global Society and International Relations: Sociological Concepts and Political Perspectives* (1994). His *Civil Society and Media in Global Crises* will appear in 1996.

Ole Wæver is Senior Research Fellow at the Centre for Peace and Conflict Research, Copenhagen, part-time Lecturer at the University of Copenhagen, and member of the board of the Danish Government's Commission on Security and Disarmament Affairs. His recent books include *Introduktion til Studies af International Politik* (Introduction to the Study of International Relations) (1992); *The History of the European Idea,* co-authored with Pim den Boer and Peter Bugge (1993); and *Identity, Migration and the New Security Agenda in Europe,* co-authored with Barry Buzan, *et al.* (1993).

Nicholas J. Wheeler holds degrees from North Staffordshire Polytechnic and the University of Southampton. He was formerly a Lecturer in the Department of Politics at the University of Hull and is currently Lecturer in International Politics, University of Wales, Aberystwyth. He is co-author of *British Origins of Nuclear Strategy, 1945–55* and has written extensively on security issues and international relations theory. He is currently writing books on theories of security (with Ken Booth) and on humanitarian intervention.

Preface

Any book devoted to the concept of International Society must necessarily acknowledge its debt to the Department of International Relations at the London School of Economics. Coming from the site of International Society's birth and early nurturing in the writings of Charles Manning, Hedley Bull, Martin Wight and, all too briefly, R.J. Vincent, this volume hopes to build on their valuable intellectual legacy. However, it is perhaps a testament to the success of International Society that, apart from ourselves, only one of the contributors to the present volume is from the LSE. Chapters have been provided by scholars not only from other departments throughout the United Kingdom but also from Canada, Denmark and the United States. While some of the chapters challenge and critique the tenets and assumptions of International Society, we feel that the book as a whole provides evidence of the continued interest in and vitality of this approach to the study of International Relations.

Although the Department of International Relations at the LSE might not be featured strongly in the chapters in the volume, the assistance of several of its members was instrumental to the undertaking and completion of the project. We wish to acknowledge the assistance of several people. First and foremost we are indebted to *Millennium: Journal of International Studies*. We are grateful to our successors at the journal who have willingly allowed us to use their facilities, and the project itself started life as a special issue of the journal even though the book has evolved considerably from there. Robert D. Newman was our co-editor on that volume of the journal and provided assistance on the book. Several people have provided valuable guidance and support during the project's fruition, notably Michael Banks, Mark Hoffman, Andrew Hurrell, Margot Light, James Mayall, Peter Wilson and James Der Derian. Paul Wilkinson and Bruce Hoffman of the School of History and International Relations at the University of St Andrews kindly offered their support in the later stages of production. Finally, we would like to thank Gráinne Twomey and John M. Smith at Macmillan Press for their assistance on the book.

Rick Fawn
Jeremy Larkins

Part I
Introduction

1 International Society After the Cold War: Theoretical Interpretations and Practical Implications

Rick Fawn and Jeremy Larkins

Within the British International Relations community the notion of International Society gained considerable popularity during the Cold War. At a time when international politics was dominated by ideological division and geopolitical competition, international theorists still managed to discern elements of order and society in the relations among states. While the post-Cold War world order seems, as yet, to lack definition, it is routinely claimed by advocates of globalism and the champions of the victory of liberal capitalism that there is a convergence of beliefs and norms in the international community. Under such conditions we may expect the International Society approach to be all the more valid. This book is concerned with the fate of International Society in a world where the conditions of its intellectual origins and development are no longer as evident but where new possibilities for and challenges to International Society are arising.

It is worth emphasising at the outset that reference to International Society should not be understood either as a synonym for international relations *per se* or as an academic term for what politicians commonly refer to as the 'international community'. International Society is a specific concept, a way of speaking about and theorising international relations. However, at the same time, one of the assumptions of the book is that the notion of International Society has traditionally been limited by its association with the concerns of the so-called English School.[1] Our intention in this volume is to suggest that the International Society perspective can be usefully brought to bear on major issues that confront the discipline of International Relations today. This is especially so in the post-Cold War era when many of the discipline's long-standing explanatory paradigms have been found wanting.

The book is constructed with this aim in mind. In this introductory chapter we outline and elucidate some of the essential characteristics of the International Society approach. Thus, readers who are familiar with this perspective may wish to proceed directly to the second section. In the second, 'theoretical' section our contributors assess, critique and develop International Society in terms of recent theoretical developments both within and outside International Relations. In the third section, the chapters show how the International Society approach can be usefully be applied to the subject matter of international relations: intervention, the global environment, secessionism and state-recognition, security and international institutions in a post-Cold War world.

INTELLECTUAL ORIGINS: FROM GROTIUS TO WIGHT

Although much of his work remained unpublished during his lifetime, Martin Wight is generally considered to be the intellectual forefather of International Society. Indeed for Wight 'the most fundamental question you can ask in international theory is, "What is international society?"'.[2] In response to his own question, Wight undertook a systematic and detailed study of classical works of history, political theory and law. From his research he concluded that international thought could be conceived in terms of three traditions, each of which embraced a distinctive view of the possibility and desirability of international society. These traditions he termed Realism, Revolutionism and Rationalism.

At one extreme is the Realist or Machiavellian tradition. Included among the 'blood and iron and immorality men' are figures such as Hobbes, Frederick the Great and twentieth-century thinkers like Carr and Morgenthau. Representatives of this tradition deny the possibility of international society. International politics consists of international anarchy where the Hobbesian 'war of all against all' proceeds unhindered. In the international realm where conflict between sovereign states guided by their national interests is the norm, questions of morality are largely irrelevant.[3] At the other extreme lie the Revolutionists or Kantians, the 'subversion and liberation and missionary men'. For those in this tradition, embodied by the advocates of the Protestant, French and Communist Revolutions, the primary actor in international relations is not the state; the ultimate reality is the potential, if not real, community of mankind. Morality therefore concerns the imperatives that drive all men to revolutionary brotherhood. Like the Realists, those in this tradition are opposed to the notion of a society of states, for whom it amounts to 'a complex of legal fiction and obsolescent diplomatic forms which conceals, obstructs and oppresses the *real* society of individual men and women, the *civitas maxima.*'[4]

In between these two extremes Wight locates the Grotian or rationalist tradition. This approach is derived from natural law thinkers such as

Suarez, Pufendorf and in particular Grotius, and also includes the classical international lawyers and such figures as Locke, Burke, Castlereagh, Gladstone, Roosevelt and Churchill. For those in this tradition, to the extent that international politics is an anarchy, it is an anarchy mitigated by international intercourse; a relationship between states characterised not only by conflict but also cooperation. States exist in a society whose functioning can be seen in institutions such as diplomacy, international law, the balance of power and the concert of great powers. Common codes, norms and rules regulate international behaviour. This tradition thus constitutes a middle road between the Machiavellian and Kantian approaches: while it accepts the centrality of the state as an international actor, it rejects the Hobbesian account of violence as the natural state of international affairs.[5]

Wight acknowledged that each of the traditions offers important insights for understanding the complex nature of international relations. He also pointed out that during different periods of European history different traditions best describe the prevailing state of affairs. For instance, he suggested in *Power Politics* that the history of international society since 1492 has been fairly equally divided between revolutionary and non-revolutionary international politics.[6] Nevertheless, it is perhaps with the Grotian tradition that Wight felt most affinity and from which his own conception of International Society is primarily derived:

> International society...can be properly described only in historical and sociological depth. It is the habitual intercourse of independent communities, beginning in the Christendom of Western Europe and gradually extending throughout the world. It is manifest in the diplomatic system; in the conscious maintenance of the balance of power to preserve the independence of the member communities; in the regular operations of international law, whose binding force is accepted over a wide though politically unimportant range of subjects; in economic, social and technical independence and the functional international institutions established latterly to regulate it. All these presupposes an international consciousness, a world-wide community-sentiment.[7]

The relationship of International Society to the 'Grotian tradition' is certainly central to the self-identity of the International Society school. For Benedict Kingsbury and Adam Roberts, both Wight and Bull's conceptions of international society are solidarist, namely that 'states or other members of the society share a common commitment to the maintenance of the society and its institutions against challenges to them'.[8] Such solidarist principles are also, they suggest, implicit in Grotius's work, which they read as being 'concerned with the principles applicable to a society of states, and thus with an international society'.[9] Grotius's classic work *De Jure Belli ac Pacis*, a legal tract written in response to the turmoil and chaos of early-seventeenth-century Europe, set out a normative framework for the emerging state system, and he was perhaps the first theorist to attempt a comprehensive treatise on international law on the basis of state sovereignty. Although his immediate concern was with war and the conditions for peace and order – the work outlines the laws limiting the conduct of war – in effect he produced an account of the law of nations rooted in the laws of nature, which has defined many of the concerns of the International Society perspective.[10]

It is worth highlighting two aspects of Grotius's intellectual legacy to the International Society tradition. First, although Grotius accepts that sovereign states are the primary actors in international relations, he also accords rights and duties in international law to individuals. Grotius's recognition that states are composed of individual human beings and that the individual is the ultimate subject of all law reappears, for instance, in Bull's discussion of world order, which he suggests is 'more fundamental and primordial than international order because the ultimate units of the great society of all mankind are not states…but individual human beings'.[11]

The second legacy derives from Grotius's conclusion that while it is true that the most significant actors in the international realm are sovereign states, there is no logical necessity for international relations to be characterised by disorder and perpetual conflict. States, like individuals, are for Grotius essentially sociable. As A. Claire Cutler observes, for Grotius, '[t]hrough the reciprocity of mutual needs a "great society of states" develops, characterised by common norms and customs…[which] are embodied in the law of nations and in natural law and are binding upon all nations.'[12] Law observance is not just based on self-interest but in a deeply-rooted sense of obligation deriving from man's nature as a rational and social creature. Bull suggests '[t]he central Grotian assumption is that of the solidarity, or potential solidarity, of the states comprising international society, with respect to the enforcement of the law.'[13]

BULL AND THE INSTITUTIONS OF INTERNATIONAL SOCIETY

In his classic work *The Anarchical Society*, Bull developed Wight's concern with the institutions of international society in terms of a general theory of order in International Relations. Subtitled a *Study of Order in World*

Politics, the book's primary concern is with how order can be maintained in international society which, in the absence of a Leviathan, is necessarily 'anarchic'. Although Bull did not prioritise order over other values such as justice, he did maintain that order is fundamental for social life as it is the pattern of human activity that sustains elementary, primary or universal goals: the security of life against violence, the sanctity of promises and stability of possession.[14] At the level of the society of states, Bull saw order being obtained, as R.J. Vincent suggests: 'by seeing the goal of limitation of violence represented by such rules as those associated with the just war tradition; by seeing the goal of keeping promises represented by the principle *pacta sunt servanda*; and the goal of stabilising possession represented by their recognition by states of each other's sovereignty.'[15]

The common acceptance of such rules and norms provided the basis for Bull's argument for the existence of a society of states or an international society, which he defined accordingly:

> A *society of states* (or international society) exists when a group of states, conscious of certain common interests and common values, form a society in the sense that they conceive themselves to be bound by a common set of rules in their relations with one another, and share in the working of common institutions.[16]

Having emphasised the existence and importance of order to International Society, Bull set out to show how order is maintained in international politics by means of five institutions: balance of power, international law, war, diplomacy and the great powers. For him, the institutions of International Society not only serve to indicate the presence of these common rules but also in practice regulate interstate behaviour. It is the fact that states do cooperate, implicitly if not explicitly, on the operation and functioning of these institutions which provides evidence of the existence of International Society. This section provides an overview of the institutions, their relationship to International Society and offers some tentative conclusions regarding their role in the post-Cold War era.

The Balance of Power

The term balance of power is a contested concept. It can be considered as an objective phenomenon, one that operates as a natural law, as the invisible hand of the free market does for liberal economists. It can be an analytical tool to assess the distribution of power. Or, it can be an objective of state-policy, as when a leader or country consciously undertakes a policy in order to influence their assessment of the distribution of the balance of power. Bull was explicit in his interpretation. He defined the balance of power in reference to Vattel's definition of 'a state of affairs such that no one power is in a position where it is preponderant and can lay down the law to others'.[17] Its functions were (i) in terms of the system as a whole, to preclude the mastery of one power and the conversion of the system into a universal empire; (ii) on a local or regional level to maintain the independence of states; and (iii) on both levels to allow for the functioning of the other institutions of International Society.[18] Following the collapse of the bipolar superpower structure, the post-Cold War balance of power has yet to take on a definable form. However, in his treatment of the concept, Bull makes allowances for various types of balances of power, including membership and geographic distribution. The principal question regarding the balance of power after the Cold War is, in Bull's terms, whether any one power can in fact lay down the law to others.

International Law

The above discussion of the Grotian tradition emphasised the importance of international law to the concept and existence of International Society. International law is an attribute of International Society which is not only rather abstract, but has also perhaps received less focused attention than the other institutions of International Society, even though it is germane to all of them.[19] After all, as Bull pointed out, the first function of international law was to recognise the idea of a society of sovereign states.[20]

Bull acknowledged that his definition of international law would not necessarily receive universal acceptance, but nevertheless demarcated it as 'the body of rules which binds states and other agents in world politics in their relations with one another and is considered to have the status of law'.[21] He differentiated between abstract laws and those that could be identified as influencing conduct in international relations as 'a part of social reality', as well as acknowledging that principles of comportment need not derive exclusively from existing laws.[22] As Bull observed, 'respect for the law is not in itself the principal motive that accounts for conformity to law'. States observe international law for several reasons: because of 'habit or inertia'; because the state deems the law to be valuable; from a fear of coercion; or, out of the desire for reciprocity from other states.[23] Even when a state abrogates international laws, it continues to respect others and generally attempts to justify its actions.[24]

International law, then, underpins much of the rest of International Society, in particular the management of the balance of power and war.[25]

This raises a number of questions, especially in the Cold War context. If a legal order does exist, then we can expect to identify a 'force monopoly of the community'. This might be said to be developing, with the examples of the use of collective force against Iraq and the clumsy but nevertheless significant efforts to redefine collective military presence and action in the form of UN operations in former Yugoslavia. There is, therefore, a need for empirical exploration of the connection between international law and the balance of power after the Cold War. To the extent that a balance of power does not exist, or is only nominal, is there a substitute at work with greater respect for universality of international law?

Diplomacy

So central is diplomacy to the International Society tradition that for Bull, diplomacy 'presupposes that there exists not only an international system but also an international society'.[26] In diplomacy is to be found both the objective evidence and the operational rules of international society. This is not to say that diplomacy in the International Society perspective need be uniform. Indeed, Wight differentiated between European diplomacies and 'old' and 'new' forms and showed how its functions can be interpreted differently according to the premises of the three traditions.[27] Nevertheless, a clear core of diplomacy exists, if only in the form of the exchange of representatives and the opening of embassies; these practices operate on the basis of continuous and mutually-recognised principles. It was the use of recognised symbols of diplomacy which made Bull define diplomacy as official, although, as with the system in general, he acknowledged that non-state actors could be players as well.[28]

The study of the institution of diplomacy in terms of International Society has benefited considerably from Adam Watson's *Diplomacy: The Dialogue Between States*. Watson explored further the central role of diplomacy in International Society, emphasising that diplomacy could only be comprehended 'in its particular context of a number of independent states closely involved with one another to form an institutionalized international society or at least a system of states'.[29] Der Derian's chapter in this volume can be seen as proceeding along similar lines in arguing that Bull's conception of diplomatic culture helps to explain the totality of the International Society approach.

War

Bull justified war as an institution of the society of states on the grounds that it is 'a settled pattern of behaviour, [and is] shaped towards the promotion of common goals'.[30] He also defined it as an instrument of the sovereign state. War is a means of enforcing international law; it allows for the maintenance of the balance of power; and can even serve as an agent of positive change. War can, for Bull, be viewed as a social act in the society of states.[31] While war serves other institutions of International Society, it is also shaped and conditioned by them. This is particularly true of international law, which in the Grotian tradition, dictates both when and how war can be conducted.

Bull had already contemplated how the role of war had changed with nuclear weapons, both as a practioner and in his early written work.[32] He acknowledged that their use endangered the survival of the system but resolved that the threat or use of war were not fully devoid of political application.[33] This debate is all the more relevant to post-Cold War international society. War clearly has not been extinguished either as a threat to or an instrument of International Society. The danger of nuclear war has assumed new, if different proportions with the official and unofficial proliferation of nuclear weapons. Furthermore, post-Cold War international society faces significant challenges in the form of low-intensity, premodern ethnic conflict, as witnessed in the Caucasus and the Balkans.

The Great Powers

For Bull, the term 'Great Powers' carried three connotations. The first was that there had to be two or more states possessing significant resources and capabilities in the international order, and that those attributes allowed them to constitute an exclusive club. Even with the recognition of the importance of technological innovation, Bull maintained that the second defining characteristic of a great power was military power. The third characteristic, for Bull, of a great power was that they are 'recognised by others to have, and conceived by their own leaders and people to have, certain special rights and duties'.[34] The great powers maintain international order in two ways: first, by managing their mutual relations; and, second, by employing their disproportionate influence to contour international society. The first is achieved by maintaining the general balance of power and by averting or managing crises and outright wars between or among them; the second by the individual exercise of regional preeminence, respecting spheres of influence, and by joint action. For Bull these practices were mutually reinforcing: the management of relations between great powers necessarily influences the general course of world politics; while their efforts to use their preponderant influence on international society requires some regulation of great-power relations.

It is perhaps in the area of Bull's conception of the institution of the great powers that the end of the Cold War can be seen to challenge the notion of International Society most fundamentally. The demise of the Soviet superpower opens the debate as to the number and nature of contemporary 'great powers'. Power is now seen as increasingly based on economic and technological prowess rather than military capacity. Thus, the question arises as to whether contemporary international society is dominated by one hegemonic power in the form of the US or by, for example, a series of new great powers assuming the form of trading-blocs centred on North America, Western Europe and East Asia. Ole Wæver in his contribution to the book suggests that we are witnessing the possible re-emergence of zones of influence, a thesis which may reinforce Bull's characterisation of the great-power management of international relations.

CONCEPTS, THEMES AND ISSUES

The previous section discussed the intellectual history of the International Society approach, in terms of the writings of Wight and Bull and outlined some of its principal characteristics and institutions. This section considers how the International Society perspective deals with traditional concepts, themes and issues in International Relations. It opens with a discussion of the complex relationship between international society and international system. This leads on to a consideration of the broad macro-historical agenda relevant to International Society. The rest of the section will briefly indicate how some of the perennial themes of international relations are theorised from an International Society perspective. These include: the state, the question of sovereignty, nationalism, intervention, and human rights and international morality.

International Systems and International Societies

Much International Relations theory, especially North American strands of Neorealism, portrays the environment of states as a system.[35] International Society, by contrast, introduces another dimension to holistic theories of the international realm. Bull, for instance, took care to distinguish between international system and international society. In an often-cited passage, he wrote: '[a] *system of states* (or international system) is formed when two or more states have sufficient contact between them, and have sufficient impact on one another's decisions, to cause them to behave – at least in some measure – as parts of a whole'. However, '[a] *society of states* (or international society) exists when a group of states [already forming a system], conscious of certain common interests and common values, form a society in the sense that they conceive themselves to be bound by a common set of rules in their relations with one another and share in the working of common institutions.'[36]

The conceptual distinction between international system and international society raises a number of important theoretical debates. The first concerns the precise nature of the distinction. Alan James has argued that rules, communication and common interests, which for Bull distinguish international society, are integral to the functioning of any international system.[37] Second, while International Society seems to presuppose the existence of an international system, international systems can exist without international societies. Third, and related to the previous point, the question arises as to the circumstances that favour the emergence of international societies. Much of Wight's work on systems of states – thereby meaning international societies – was centred on this question. Wight restricted his understanding of a system of states to groups of sovereign states without a superior and having permanent relations with each other by means of the institutions of messengers, conferences and congresses, a diplomatic language and trade. On the basis of such criteria Wight argued that only three states-systems have ever existed. His research into two of these, the modern Western states-system and the Greco-Roman system, lead him to conclude that a states-system (international society) presupposes a common culture especially in terms of religion and language.[38]

More recently, Buzan has suggested that an understanding of how international societies develop from international systems can be elucidated by drawing upon Tonnies's distinction between *gemeinschaft* and *gesselleschaft* societies. *Gemeinschaft* societies are seen as organic and traditional with bonds of common sentiment, experience and identity, whereas *gesselleschaft* societies are viewed as contractual and constructed consciously by an act of will. *Gemeinschaft*, or 'civilisational' international societies occur where the units in an international system exhibit a significant degree of cultural unity or common identity. Alternatively, *gesselleschaft* or 'functional' international societies arise where the mutual self-interest of avoiding anarchy forces units to construct an international order. Contemporary international society is, in these terms, a hybrid as it originally arose from the *gemeinschaft* international society that developed in Europe and expanded globally by means of imperialism, but also partly reflects a *gesselleschaft* process in that the different cultures within today's global international society have managed to come to terms with each other.[39]

Historical Systems of States and the Expansion of International Society

The theoretical debates concerning the distinction between international system and international society have acknowledged a large body of historical sources. This sensitivity to history, characteristic of International Society, contrasts with the behaviourism characteristic of much social science analysis of International Relations. However, the emphasis on history has opened up at least two important research agendas for International Society.

First, histories of International Society have shown that different international orders have had significantly different characteristics. Wight differentiated two distinct types of systems of states: international states-systems, namely systems of sovereign states, and 'secondary' or suzerain state systems where one political unit is paramount, such as in Imperial China, Byzantium and the British Raj.[40] Such suzerain state-systems are based not on the institution of the balance of power as in Bull's modern international society, but on divide-and-rule tactics. In extending Wight's agenda, Adam Watson's wide-ranging historical survey of the evolution of international society has shown that international systems and societies have embraced an even wider spectrum of political units. At the extremes are independent sovereign units and empires but also possible are hegemonies, suzerain and dominion systems.[41] Apart from the obvious importance that such historical research has for understanding the distinctiveness and evolution of modern international society, this work is suggestive in terms of understanding post-Cold War international relations where the sovereign states-system is increasingly beleaguered. Wæver, for example, in this volume employs Watson's understanding of Empires as a metaphor to describe the emerging political order within Europe. International societies need not, for Wæver and Watson, be limited to societies of sovereign states, as in Bull's conception but can be international societies of empires or suzerains.

A central driving force behind this historical research is the concern to understand the conditions that produced and enabled the emergence and expansion of the modern global international society. This is the subject of one of the classic works in the field, *The Expansion of International Society*.[42] The book explores the many dimensions of the expansion of a European-based and defined set of norms and rules, their imposition on other cultures and societies over five hundred years, and the nature of the resulting global international society mirrored on the European model. Familiar themes reappear in this account of International Society. First, Bull again emphasises the primacy of system over society when he claims that the expansion of Europe, which started in the fifteenth century, created an international system long before an international society came into existence.[43] Second, the expansion of modern international society connects with the earlier discussion of Grotius. For, despite his concern for the rights of the individual and his place in the international system, Grotius identified and defined these values exclusively in terms of European and Christian values. Unlike Vitoria, Grotius was not concerned with the relations between European and non-European cultures, and for idealists, he laid 'an early foundation for an older order, characterized by state sovereignty and European expansion into the extra-European world'.[44] Third, while for Gerrit W. Gong it is only possible to talk of a truly global rather than European international society by late in the nineteenth century, Buzan's highlighting of the *geselleschaft* element in modern international society reminds us that the globalisation of international society has not been a unidirectional process.[45] Many in the International Society school have argued that values have been shaped by non-Europeans, particularly in recent decades. This theme, often termed the 'Revolt Against the West', has caused some concern for adherents of International Society who fear that International Society which is dependent one set of norms, rules and values may not survive in an increasingly pluralistic world which, using Samuel P. Huntington's term, may be progressing towards 'the clash of civilizations'.[46]

States and Sovereignty

The perspective on the modern state adopted by the International Society tradition rejects the Weberian view of the *Maachstaat* based on a legitimised order of domination, in favour of an 'associative' view of the state as *Rechstaat*. States are the 'creations of laws, customs and practices' and the autonomy of the state is a legal creation or attribute of sovereignty.[47] The primacy accorded to law in International Society, in view of the centrality of the Grotian tradition, is thus re-emphasised by the favoured theory of the state. States though primarily legal constructions must, however, also possess territory, have populations and be in possession of a government. For Bull, states are 'independent political communities, each of which possesses a government and asserts sovereignty in relation to the human population. Similarly, for James, states have three defining features: frontiers enclosing people, some form of government and a clearly defined territorial identity or reach.[48] Finally, for Robert H. Jackson, 'A sovereign state...consists traditionally of a bordered territory occupied by a settled population under effective and at least to some extent civil – that is "civilized" – government'.[49]

While government, people and territory are necessary, but not sufficient conditions for participation in the society of states, sovereign status is emphasised as *the* determinate criteria for membership. Indeed, for one observer '[s]overeignty is...the ground rule of interstate relations in that it identifies the territorial entities who are eligible to participate in the game'.[50] Sovereign status necessitates both internal sovereignty – supremacy over all other authorities within a defined territory and population – and external sovereignty – independence from outside interference. Recognition of the right to participate in International Society on the basis of sovereignty is traditionally accorded by the UN. Some of the problems with the emphasis on sovereignty have recently been made explicit by Bosnia-Hercegovina. For despite having received recognition as a sovereign state by the US and the EC on 7 April and membership in the UN on 22 May 1992 it enjoyed neither internal sovereignty – the Bosnian government at best could be said to control only a part of its territory – nor external sovereignty – Croatian and Serbian troops have invaded and occupied significant parts of its territory. Thus legal recognition of sovereign status does not always mean sovereignty in practice. One attempt to overcome such conceptual distinction has been made by Jackson who has suggested that it may be useful to conceive of many Third World states as 'Quasi-states'. These are states which possess only 'negative sovereignty' or formal legal freedom from outside interference. This is in contrast with the positive sovereignty of fully-developed Western states which enjoy not only the rights of non-intervention and other international immunities, but also the ability to provide political goods for their citizens thorough the organisation of alliances and other international arrangements.[51]

Nationalism

The post-Cold War world has witnessed the dramatic resurrection of nationalism in many guises and numerous locations. For nationalists, the aim is a sovereign political community in the form of the modern national state. For many, however, nationalism poses a serious threat to international society in that it threatens the rational orderly conduct of affairs based on shared values, customs and principles.[52] The complexities of the relationship between international society, the sovereignty principle and nationalism has been a primary concern of James Mayall.[53] While sovereignty and other constitutive principles of international society were, he suggests, established before the emergence of nationalism, the modern period has witnessed considerable modification of International Society by the 'national idea'. For example, the nationalism of the French Revolution substituted a popular for the traditional prescriptive principle of sovereignty. Likewise, the principle of national self-determination favoured by nineteenth-century liberal nationalists provided an important incentive and legitimation for state creation. While these developments may have strengthened the society of states, nationalism has also had a detrimental impact. Secession, as recently demonstrated by Eritrea's 'liberation' from Ethiopia and in many cases throughout post-Communist Eastern Europe, constitutes a significant challenge to international society based on the sanctity of the sovereignty principle. Likewise the failure of so many 'nation-building' experiments following decolonisation has done little to reinforce the principle of state sovereignty, as is graphically illustrated by the collapse of Somalia into factions of embattled warlords.

Intervention and Human Rights

The intervention by the United Nations forces UNISOM in Somalia as a response to the humanitarian hardship that resulted from the collapse of the state illustrates another distinguishing feature of International Society which is the concern with intervention. Debates within International Society over the right of sovereign states to intervene in one another's affairs cut to the heart of its normative dimension. There is, as Nicholas J. Wheeler has pointed out, a crucial tension in the International Society tradition between those like Bull and Wight who subscribe to a 'pluralist' position which holds that states are the principal bearers of rights, and those like Grotius and Vincent who favour a 'solidarist' position which asserts the duty of collective humanitarian intervention in cases of extreme human suffering such as genocide.[54]

For the pluralists there are no universal human rights, as individuals only have rights accorded to them by states. The rights of states are, however, largely determined by the principle of sovereignty and its legal corollary – the norm of non-intervention. Bull favoured this position in that he argued that non-intervention is the minimal requirement for order in the society of states. Noting that there is little, if any, sympathy for collective let alone individual intervention on humanitarian grounds in the world of state practice, Bull argues that, 'Proposals to abandon the rule of non-intervention...are in effect proposals to abandon the principle that states have rights to independence and to construct world order on a quite different basis.'[55] Indeed, while he could recognise the possibility of collective intervention if agreed by the society of states, he was clear that, '[u]ltimately, we have a rule of non-intervention because unilateral intervention threatens the harmony and concord of the society of sovereign states.'[56]

The solidarists, by contrast, are more receptive to the notion that there are basic universal human rights; such as freedom from violence and basic subsistence rights to which all humans are entitled by virtue of their common humanity. Vincent detected an increasingly cosmopolitan sentiment that he felt would encourage citizens of states to force their states to act on behalf of individuals mistreated by other states.[57] However, Vincent, like Bull, recognised that in practice there was little sympathy for intervention on the part of states. Nevertheless he did advocate a minimal duty of intervention in cases where state which subverted the basic requirements of decency forfeited the right of non-intervention. However, he was also aware of the threat that a generalised practice of intervention could pose for order in International Society, as intervention would 'issue a licence for all kinds of interference claiming...to be humanitarian, but driving huge wedges into international order. The large number of recent post-Cold War cases of intervention including Iraq, Bosnia, Somalia and Rwanda have provided fresh empirical evidence for reconsideration of these positions and some of their implications are drawn out by Wheeler and Morris in Chapter 7.

INTERNATIONAL SOCIETY AFTER THE COLD WAR: THEORY AND PRACTICE

Having introduced the fundamental tenants of the International Society approach, this final part of the introduction explains how the chapters of the volume relate to the study of International Society. The volume aims to consider both theoretical and practical concerns raised by International Society's exposure to the post-Cold War order. Accordingly, each is pursued in a section of its own. However, in terms of international society, theory and practice cannot be separated and indeed have a mutually-enforcing relationship. Thus, our intention is that the two sections should complement each other. Some chapters lend themselves predominantly to one section, as with the contributions by N.J. Rengger and James Der Derian. However, others such as those by Wæver, and Morris and Wheeler are deeply rooted in aspects of the theory but use it to analyse contemporary developments.

In terms of the theoretical agenda, the objective is to submit the concept of International Society to critical discussion both from within and without the tradition. A considerable time has elapsed since some of the paradigmatic works of International Society were written. *The Anarchical Society,* for example, is approaching its third decade, and since its publication, social, political and international theory has undergone significant changes, including the revival of Realism in its neorealist form, the resurgence of normative theory, and the emergence of a critical agenda in the guise of 'the post-positivist revolution'. The chapters in this section attempt to expose the established concepts, theories and intellectual assumptions of International Society to critique and to offer analysis on the basis of their readings of these and other recent developments in international theory.

In the third section, the concept of International Society is used to explain major issues and developments in international affairs since the end of the Cold War. The section thereby shows the utility, as well as perhaps the limitations, of the concept by applying it to empirical and policy concerns. At the same time, it also hopes to elucidate contemporary developments and to allow the reader, irrespective of any primary interest in the theoretical nature of international society, to gain additional insights into the nature of the post-Cold War order. It might be expected that the book should logically follow the institutions of International Society as laid out either by Wight or Bull. This would be an easy approach, one that might have served as an addendum to their own writings. In preparing this volume, however, we felt that changes resulting from the end of the Cold War have, at least for the moment, changed the emphasis of the institutions. It is not clear in the post-Cold War era whether, for example, institutions such as the great-power concert, war and the balance of power have been superseded or that international law and its related institutions have gained further, if not even universal, pre-eminence and respect.

Theoretical Interpretations

As the start of this chapter indicated, some observers have interpreted the end of the Cold War in terms of a convergence of beliefs in some broad form of liberal markets and democracy. This thesis reinforces the argument that there is a cohesion of common norms, rules and values in contemporary international society. Chris Brown, in '"Really Existing Liberalism", Peaceful Democracies and International Order', begins with the question of the potential ideological cohesion of international society. He contends that even if the 'end of history' is not in sight, it seems that liberalism in one form or another is likely to be the dominant political ideology for the foreseeable future. He asks what kinds of international relations will result, arguing that Kantian accounts of the international relations of 'Liberal' states have failed to take into account the gap between their models and 'really-existing' liberalism in that they underestimate the importance of non-liberal enemies of liberal states. However, he concludes that simple, cost-benefit analysis may incline liberal regimes towards peaceful international relations. Taking his argument one step further, it could be suggested that a convergence of norms and values in international society will remove the need for the institution of war, or at least its presence among its core members.

International Society is a theory of a social construct: the arrangements of members in an international grouping. Logically, it is therefore rooted in the broader concerns of sociology. In 'Global Society and Global Responsibility: The Theoretical, Historical and Political Limits of "International Society"', Martin Shaw argues that the International Society approach attempts to describe the consensual tendencies within the international system in terms of the development of international society. Thus it erroneously abstracts international relations from social relations in general. He submits the concept of international society to a critical socio-political analysis and argues that trends towards normative integration in inter-state relations are better understood as components of the general trend towards globalisation.

In terms of the Three Traditions it can be argued that International Society offers a totalising explanation of international relations in that while each tradition illuminates different aspects of international politics, taken together they amount to a general theory. In another substantive challenge to International Society, N.J. Rengger asks if it can be considered 'A City Which Sustains all Things?' He contends that the concept of International Society, as developed by Bull, Wight and Watson, cannot sustain the intellectual weight they wish to put on it. It can neither add very much to the explanation or understanding of world politics, nor serve as a useful normative guide to action in world politics. The primary explanation for this weakness lies in the communitarian liberal form the argument takes, a form unable to provide it with the conceptual resources necessary for such a task. Rengger suggests that, 'reflexive' thinking about world politics must develop different strategies to examine and evaluate the contemporary situation.

In a chapter that is more sympathetic to the International Society tradition, James Der Derian, argues in 'Hedley Bull and the Idea of Diplomatic Culture', that Bull's concept of diplomatic culture, although rarely discussed in the literature, is central to his understanding of international society as a whole. Employing some of the methods and research strategies of contemporary critical theory, the chapter suggests that Bull's notion of diplomatic culture permits an understanding of the relations between the institutions of international society, including states, not as one of interdependence but alienation. Diplomatic culture is to be understood as the symbolic mediation of estrangement and, as such, entails the 'becoming' of international society.

While the International Society approach accorded a central role to the state and to relations among them, some authors, particularly Bull and F.S. Northedge, did acknowledge the role and importance of transnational actors. Ronnie D. Lipschutz in 'Reconstructing World Politics: The Emergence of Global Civil Society' builds on this concern by exploring how the role of the state has been changed and challenged by the emergence of non-institutional, transnational political networks. Developed enough to merit the appellation of 'global civil society', the phenomenon has its origins in: the growing role of liberal principles as an overarching set of global norms; the state's declining competence and willingness to undertake welfare functions; and the growing capabilities of elites, fostered by the mobilisation of societies during the Cold War. These assertions are supported empirically, allowing him to conclude that global civil society is not a replacement for the state system, but that it may be seen in terms of a challenge to the Gramscian hegemony of statist world politics.

Practical Implications

The end of the Cold War has, at best, given way to an ambiguous new order. The nature of power distribution began to be questioned during the Cold War as some states gained global prominence without the traditional prerequisite of military power. The question of what constitutes a state's power is all the more relevant, if also more difficult to define, after the Cold War than before. The existence and strengthening of an international society of common norms and values seemed evident as much of the world, from liberal democratic market states to Ba'athist regimes to the (moribund) USSR could agree on the imposition of collective sanctions and then collective security against Iraq. Even if such a convergence of values has been achieved, which seems increasingly unlikely, a number of significant practical challenges to International Society have also emerged. While in some form they can all be said to pre-date the end of the Cold War (the ecological issue existed before 1989; the state-system has been predicated on national self-determination since 1919; and intervention, humanitarian and otherwise has occurred irrespective of the Cold War), nevertheless, all of these issues have assumed heightened relevance or urgency in recent years.

The post-Cold War era has witnessed many cases of what, in name if not in fact, have been termed humanitarian intervention. In 'Humanitarian Intervention and State Practice at the End of the Cold War', Nicholas J. Wheeler and Justin Morris establish the arguments for and against humanitarian intervention. They consider the extent to which state practice during the Cold War recognised the legitimacy of such a right, and then study the responses of the international community to the Kurdish, Somali and Rwandan crises. They conclude that while we should be wary of assuming that state leaders are now imbued with a post-Cold War ethic of humanitarian responsibility, there is perhaps an increase in public pressure on state leaders to challenge the non-intervention norm in cases of extreme human suffering.

The brief depoliticisation of world affairs following the end of the Cold War allowed the global environmental agenda to establish itself in International Relations. In 'Can International Society Be Green?', Robert H. Jackson argues that theories of international society can confront the normative problems that environmental problems present to world politics. The chapter contends that International Society is characterised by 'international normative pluralism' and the diplomatic and legal practices from which it springs are flexible and adaptable enough to accommodate environmental norms. Contrary to those who argue that state sovereignty precludes effective and responsible action on environmental problems, the International Society perspective, which claims that states have duties and responsibilities to other members of international society, can accommodate environmental norms within a sovereignty-based normative order.

While national self-determination has become an organising principle of modern international society, at the same time nationalism threatens to undermine that order. Whereas the Cold War constrained nationalism generally and secessionism in particular, the collapse of Communism has resulted in the destruction of three federations, and has led to the creation of 22 new states with secessionist pressures threatening still more. Some of the norms of International Society that dictate behaviour determine how a state can behave towards its citizens. As a secessionist movement can only gain statehood and sovereignty through the consent of other states, this allows for the constituting norms of state behaviour to be applied. National self-determination is based, in principle, on a democratic test; statehood has conditions attached to it as codified by such agreements or institutions as the CSCE or the Council of Europe; and exacting standards of internal and external behaviour have been made by the EC following the London

Conference on Yugoslavia. These norms determine the test of the conditions that International Society applies to prospective members. In light of the ambiguous resolution of these problems in the past, it is not surprising to find that these rules have been contorted, the explanations for which are discussed by Rick Fawn and James Mayall in 'Recognition, Self-Determination and Secession in Post-Cold War International Society'.

The institutions of International Society have, as has been mentioned in the discussion of the balance of power, been exposed to new dynamics in the Post-Cold War world. Ole Wæver's contribution, 'Europe's Three Empires: A Watsonian Interpretation of Post-Wall European Security', focuses on the fate of post-Cold War European security institutions. The chapter begins with a presentation of the International Relations theory developed by Martin Wight and Adam Watson which emphasised that international systems need not be based on sovereign states. Wæver builds on this thesis to suggest that empire-like concentric circles characterise the emerging post-Cold War European economic, political and security structures. The chapter argues that the European Union, and to a lesser extent both Russia and Turkey, constitute quasi-empires. Security, at least in Europe, is provided by ways and institutions that cannot be accounted for by the traditional categories and vocabularies of security systems.

Developing further the concern with post-Cold war security, Barry Buzan in 'International Society and International Security' suggests it is necessary to interpret security more broadly than in terms of the traditional focus on war. The chapter first establishes its understanding of International Society, and then proceeds to divide International Society into three sectors: the sociopolitical, the military and the economic. Stemming from a discussion of the inclusive and exclusive nature of International Society, the chapter employs a framework which identifies insiders and outsiders, and argues that the existence of a fully fledged international society is not a blessing. Outsiders such as revolutionary and pariah states discover that minimal membership is preferable to the dangers inherent in being absolute outsiders. At the same time, insiders face social threats from the growth of internationalism which undermines local cultures and their ability to reproduce themselves. In conclusion Buzan suggests that, although the relationship between international society and security is complex, there are considerable theoretical insights to be gained from blending the two.

The chapters in this volume certainly do not exhaust all the possible lines of enquiry as regards the state of International Society in the post-Cold War World. However, it has been possible to attempt at least a preliminary diagnosis of the approach's endurance in a world radically different from that of its inception. As a tentative conclusion, the contributions as a whole suggest two things. First, that International Society still offers substantial insights of international relations in a world still searching for the appropriate concepts and theories with which to render it understandable. Second, however, International Society cannot be complacent: adherents of International Society must continue to recognise and engage with the radical changes, both theoretical and practical, that currently engulf the discipline of International Relations if it is to continue to play a central and significant role in it.

NOTES

1. For discussion of the 'English School', see Roy E. Jones, 'The English School of International Relations: A Case for Closure?', *Review of International Studies* (Vol. 7, No. 1, January 1981), pp. 1–12; Sheila Grader, 'The English School of International Relations: Evidence and Evaluation', *Review of International Studies* (Vol. 14, No. 1, January 1988), pp. 29–44; and Peter Wilson, 'The English School of International Relations: A Reply to Sheila Grader', *Review of International Studies* (Vol. 15, No. 1, January 1989), pp. 49–58.
2. Martin Wight, 'An Anatomy of International Thought', *Review of International Studies* (Vol. 13, No. 3, July 1987), p. 222.
3. For a useful introduction to Wight's understanding of the three traditions, see Hedley Bull, 'Martin Wight and the Theory of International Relations: The Second Martin Wight Memorial Lecture', *British Journal of International Studies* (Vol. 2, No. 2, July 1976), pp. 101–16. For Wight's own accounts, see Wight, 'Anatomy of International Thought'; and Wight, *International Theory: The Three Traditions*, Gabrielle Wight and Brian Porter (eds), (Leicester: Leicester University Press, 1991).
4. Martin Wight, 'Western Values in International Relations', in Martin Wight and Herbert Butterfield (eds), *Diplomatic Investigations* (London: Allen & Unwin, 1966), p. 93.
5. See Bull, 'Martin Wight', for a critique of these categories.
6. Wight writes in a footnote that 'If, taking the conventional dates, we regard 1492–1517, 1643–1792 and 1871–1914 as unrevolutionary, and 1517–1648, 1792–1871 and 1916–60 as revolutionary, there are 256 years of international revolution to 212 unrevolutionary'. See Martin Wight, *Power Politics* (London: Penguin, 1966), p. 92.
7. Wight, 'Western Values', pp. 96–7.
8. Benedict Kingsbury and Adam Roberts, 'Introduction: Grotian Thought in International Relations', in Hedley Bull, Benedict Kingsbury and Adam Roberts (eds), *Hugo Grotius and International Relations* (Oxford: Clarendon Press, 1990), p. 8.
9. Ibid., p. 12.

10. A good account of the connections between the work of Grotius and the International Society tradition is to be found in A. Claire Cutler, 'The Grotian Tradition in International Relations', *Review of International Studies* (Vol. 17, No. 1, January 1991), pp. 41–65.
11. Hedley Bull, *The Anarchical Society: A Study of Order in World Politics* (London: Macmillan and New York: Columbia University Press, 1977), p. 22 .
12. Cutler, 'Grotian Tradition', p. 47.
13. Hedley Bull, 'The Grotian Conception of International Society', in Butterfield and Wight (eds), *Diplomatic Investigations.*
14. For some of his views on justice, see Hedley Bull, *Justice in International Relations: The Hagey Lectures, 1983–84* (Waterloo, Ont.: University of Waterloo Press, 1984).
15. R.J. Vincent, 'Order in International Politics', in J.D.B. Miller and R.J. Vincent (eds), *Order and Violence: Hedley Bull and International Relations* (Oxford: Clarendon Press, 1990), p. 43.
16. Bull, *Anarchical Society*, p. 13.
17. De Vattel, *Droit de Gens*, cited in ibid., p. 101.
18. Ibid., pp. 106–7.
19. The leading influences on international law in International Society were Sir Hersch Lauterpacht and Lassa Oppenheim. The works of the former coincide choronologically with Wight's; the latter precede them. Bull also considered the legal origins of International Society. See, for example, 'The Grotian Conception'.
20. Bull, *Anarchical Society*, p. 140.
21. Ibid., p. 127.
22. Ibid., p. 128.
23. Ibid., p. 139
24. Ibid., pp. 137–8.
25. Ibid., p. 131.
26. Ibid., p. 167.
27. See, especially, Wight's third chapter on diplomacy, 'Theory of Diplomacy: Diplomacy', in his *International Theory*, pp. 180–205.
28. Bull, *Anarchical Society*, p. 163. In his discussion of international law, Bull made clear that not only were states international actors but also individuals and international governmental and non-governmental organisations. Ibid., p. 145.
29. Adam Watson, *Diplomacy: The Dialogue Between States* (London: Eyre Metheun, 1982), p. 13.
30. Bull, *Anarchical Society*, p. 185.
31. Paraphrased from Michael Donelan, 'Grotius and the Image of War', *Millennium: Journal of International Studies* (Vol. 12, No. 3, Autumn 1983), p. 233.

32. Hedely Bull, *The Control of the Arms Race: Disarmament and Arms Control in the Missile Age* (London: Weidenfeld & Nicholson for the Institute for Strategic Studies, 1961).
33. Bull, *Anarchical Society*, p. 190.
34. Ibid., p. 202.
35. For the paradigmatic neorealist account of the workings of the international system, see Kenneth N. Waltz, *Theory of International Politics* (Reading, MA: Addison-Wesley Publishing Company, 1979).
36. Bull, *Anarchical Society*, pp. 9–10 and 13.
37. See Alan James, 'System or Society?', *Review of International Studies* (Vol. 19, No. 3, July 1993), pp. 269–88. As well as offering a critique of Bull's distinction, James also offers a number of other reasons for preferring international society over international system.
38. Martin Wight, *Systems of States* (Leicester: Leicester University Press, 1977). See also the introduction by Hedley Bull, 'Martin Wight and the Study of International Relations' pp. 1–20, for an incisive analysis of Wight's contribution to International Society theory.
39. See Barry Buzan, 'From International System to International Society: Structural Realism and Regime Theory meet the English School', *International Organization* (Vol. 47, No. 3, Summer 1993), pp. 326–51, esp. pp. 330–6.
40. See ch. 1, *'De systematibus civitatum'* in Wight, *Systems of States*, pp. 21–45, for his distinction between sovereign and suzerain systems.
41. See Adam Watson, *The Evolution of International Society: A Comparative Historical Analysis* (London: Routledge, 1992), esp. pp. 13–8 for his discussion of the spectrum.
42. See the collection of essays in, Hedley Bull and Adam Watson (eds), *The Expansion of International Society* (Oxford: Clarendon Press, 1984), especially the introduction, pp. 1–9.
43. Hedley Bull, 'The Emergence of a Universal International Society' ch. 8, in ibid., pp. 117–26.
44. Kingsbury and Roberts, 'Introduction', p. 42.
45. Gerrit W. Gong, *The Standard of 'Civilization' in International Society* (Oxford: Clarendon Press, 1984).
46. See the essay by Bull, 'The Revolt Against the West', ch. 14, pp. 217–28 in *Expansion*. For Huntington's thesis, see Samuel P. Huntington, 'The Clash of Civilizations?', *Foreign Affairs* (Vol. 72, No. 3, Summer 1993), pp. 22–49.
47. Cornelia Navari, 'The State as Contested Concept in International Relations', in Navari (ed.), *The Condition of States* (Milton Keynes: Open University Press, 1991), p. 12.
48. See Alan James, *Sovereign Statehood: The Basis of International Society* (London: Allen and Unwin, 1986), p. 13; and James, 'Sovereignty: Ground Rule or Gibberish', *Review of International Studies* (Vol. 10, No. 1, January

1984), pp. 1–18.

49. Robert H. Jackson, *Quasi-States: Sovereignty, International Relations, and the Third World* (Cambridge: Cambridge University Press, 1990), p. 38.
50. James, 'Sovereignty', p. 2.
51. See Jackson, *Quasi-States*, especially p. 29.
52. It certainly contributed to Bull's concerns over the 'Revolt against Western Dominance' in Bull and Watson (eds), *Expansion.*
53. James Mayall, *Nationalism and International Society* (Cambridge: Cambridge University Press, 1990).
54. See Nicholas J. Wheeler, 'Pluralist or Solidarist Conceptions of International Society: Bull and Vincent on Humanitarian Intervention', *Millennium: Journal of International Studies* (Vol. 21, No. 3, Winter 1992), pp. 463–87.
55. Hedley Bull, 'Conclusion', in Hedley Bull (ed.), *Intervention in World Politics* (Oxford: Clarendon Press, 1984), p. 185.
56. Ibid., p. 195
57. R. J. Vincent, *Human Rights and International Relations* (Cambridge: Cambridge University Press, 1986. The 'solidarist' position Vincent advocates in this work may be contrasted with the more 'pluralist' position he took in his earlier work, *Nonintervention and International Order* (Princeton, NJ: Princeton University Press, 1974).

Part II
Theoretical Interpretations

2 'Really Existing Liberalism', Peaceful Democracies and International Order'

Chris Brown

> The triumph of the West, of the Western Idea, is evident first of all in the total exhaustion of viable systemic alternatives to Western liberalism.
>
> Francis Fukuyama[1]

> At the end of the eighteenth century Immanuel Kant suggested that the only states which would not necessarily go to war with each other, sooner or later, were those in which the 'civic constitution' was 'republican'; that is with limited government, the rule of law, and kings who listened to philosophers like him. The insight remains fundamental. In twentieth century terms liberal democracies don't fight liberal democracies.
>
> Timothy Garton Ash[2]

Francis Fukuyama's essay and subsequent book on the 'end of history' have been much criticised and much abused.[3] The abuse seems to be based on the assumption that, given his theme, his work must be written in a tone of complacent triumphalism – an assumption that could not survive a close reading of what are, by no stretch of the imagination, triumphalist texts. More legitimate criticism can be levelled at his Hegelian assumption that the forms of Western liberalism constitute a realisation of freedom that is non-transcendable. The notion that 'history' has a message which has been, as it were, delivered will not convince those who do not share the first premise of the argument, and who thus will be sceptical of the idea that any set of events, however dramatic, can conclusively and for all time set in place one ideology and dispose of another – let alone preclude the emergence of future hypothetical alternatives to the *status quo*. The idea of the 'end of history' will only make sense to those for whom history has a coherent story to tell – a story with a beginning, a middle and an end.

If Fukuyama's position is reformulated in non-Hegelian terms and within more limited frames of reference – of time and space – it does seem to convey quite accurately an important feature of contemporary world politics. For the time being, and as far as the advanced industrial societies are concerned, it does indeed seem as if there are no viable 'systematic' alternatives to one variant or another of Western liberalism – always assuming that 'social democracy' (or even 'democratic socialism') is no more than one such variant. For the time being most of the successor states of the Soviet Union are, in form at least, liberal democratic; it would be optimistic to think that this will uniformly remain the case, but where liberal democracy fails it seems more likely to be replaced by some form of *ad hoc* authoritarianism than by a return to communism. Where systematic alternatives to liberalism do exist – for example, in 'Islamic Republics' such as Iran – they assume forms which have little attraction for the inhabitants of industrial societies, and indeed may actually be incompatible with such societies in the long run. Clearly not all states are or will be 'liberal' in the foreseeable future, but it does seem likely that most of the major centres of power in the world will, one way or another, fit this description, while those that do not will be illiberal in an unsystematic way rather than offering a conscious alternative to the prevailing political form. It does make some kind of sense to talk of the triumph of Western liberalism.

For theorists of international relations this raises an interesting question. If liberalism is indeed, in this sense, triumphant, then what kind of international relations can we predict will accompany this triumph? Putting the matter differently, is there any reason to think that these changes in the world will produce radically different patterns of international relations? The logic of Fukuyama's Hegelianism would suggest not. From his perspective the ideological dimension that has enlivened international relations since 1917 (or before) will disappear, but the underlying patterns of inter-state conflict – deriving from the projection of potentially conflicting state interests on to the world stage – are unaffected by this shift; such at least seems to be Fukuyama's message, and it is certainly the conclusion one would draw from the relevant sections of Hegel's *Philosophy of Right*.[4]

Indeed, international relations theory generally is resistant to the idea that changes in domestic politics can produce significant changes in the international order. Kenneth Waltz in *Theory of International Politics* characterises such a position as 'reductionist' as opposed to the correct, systemic perspective.[5] This much is, perhaps, predictable. What is rather less so is that the 'English School' of international theorists – led by Martin Wight and Hedley Bull, who are certainly more open to the creative role of diplomacy than the structural realists – is equally hostile to the notion that uniformity in domestic regimes can make much difference to international order. Characteristic here is Wight's description of international relations as a realm of 'recurrence and repetition' and not susceptible to a progressivist interpretation.[6] Bull, in *The Anarchical Society*, acknowledges that ideological uniformity might remove some sources of conflict, but points to the others that would remain; in any event, he regards the continuation of ideological confrontation to be so likely that the best source of order remains the toleration of ideological differences that he believes are characteristic of the present state system.[7]

There is, however, another tradition – given contemporary expression in the above quotation from Timothy Garton Ash – which suggests that, in one crucial respect, there is good reason to think that, because of the nature of the new consensus, a major change in the nature of international relations is on the cards. 'Liberal democracies don't fight liberal democracies' – if this is so, and if liberal democratic forms are coming to dominate, then we can indeed expect quite dramatic changes in the nature of international relations.[8] Garton Ash calls in support of his position the authority of Kant – he could equally have drawn on the arguments of Manchester School liberals of this and the last century, and some modern theorists of 'interdependence', as well as on the empirical evidence presented by Michael Doyle and others. However, there is another view of the war propensity of liberal democracies – or, at least, of the capitalist economic forms with which they are associated. Marxist theorists of imperialism deserve to have their view that the logic of capitalism (and thus liberalism) creates conflict between states taken seriously. The fact that Leninism has proved to have disastrous consequences when applied to the running of a country does not mean that Lenin's (or, more accurately, Hilferding's) account of the nature of international relations is not worthy of attention.

The purpose of this chapter is to reflect on some of the arguments and empirical findings that pertain to the proposition that there are characteristically liberal patterns of international order. It will be suggested that the arguments are not compelling in either direction – that is, that liberalism is conducive to either peace or war – and that the empirical evidence is equally inconclusive when read in its proper context, the history of the twentieth century. One reason for this inconclusiveness lies in the gap between the 'liberalism' described in the various theoretical studies that will be examined here, and the 'really-existing liberalism' found in the states that actually make up international society.

Der real existierende Sozialismus (really, or actually, existing socialism) was a term used officially by the German Democratic Republic (GDR) to describe the nature of that regime. It conveyed three separate but linked ideas: that the regime was in a meaningful sense socialist; that, however, it was not socialist in quite the way that the great socialist writers had had in mind; but that, nonetheless, it existed and, after a fashion, functioned, which is more than could be said for the sort of socialism that could be found in those classics. Given the fate of the GDR, the last of these points has lost its force, but the basic notion remains fruitful and applicable to contemporary liberal societies which, equally, are in some sense 'liberal', certainly do exist, but do not function in the manner anticipated by the classics of liberalism.

My argument will be that Garton Ash's Kantian insight is by no means as fundamental as he takes it to be. However, he is right to think that Kant's position is central and it will be with Kant's argument that we will begin, moving on to some economistic variations on his themes, to the Leninist alternative, and to the empirical evidence. The conclusion, at least, will offer some comfort to those who would like to think that Kant and Garton Ash are right, by arguing that Kant's philosophy of history does actually offer some good reasons to think that a more peaceful world will gradually come about – even if his argument about the peacefulness of liberalism *per se* is not convincing.

PERPETUAL PEACE?

Leaving aside for the moment the important and difficult transition from 'republican civic constitution' to 'liberal democracy', what reasons does Kant offer for his fundamental insight that republican states would not go to war with one another? The principle location of Kant's argument is in *Perpetual Peace: A Philosophical Sketch*, where the first (of three) Definitive Article of *Perpetual Peace* states that 'The Civic Constitution of Every State shall be Republican.'[9] However, the context makes it clear that this is a necessary, not a sufficient, condition for peace, and the thrust of his argument undermines any attempt to pull apart and treat separately any of the three Definitive Articles. Kant's argument is that peace requires constitutional relations of the proper kind at all levels – constitutions for the civil rights of individuals within a nation, the international right of states in their relationships with one another, and the cosmopolitan right which follows from the effect of states and individuals exerting mutual influence and coexisting as citizens of a universal state of mankind.[10] Without the second and third of these constitutional relationships (covered in the next two definitive articles of *Perpetual Peace* establishing a federation of free states and a limitation of cosmopolitan right to conditions of universal hospitality), the republican civil constitution is powerless to produce peace. Indeed, far from republicanism guaranteeing peace in the absence of these external constitutions, it is the latter that make possible the survival of free, republican states.

For Kant, the basic reason for a republican civic constitution is that it is the only form of government compatible with freedom and legal equality, the only constitution derivable from the idea of an original contract. But Kant also believes that this constitution would produce the desired result of perpetual peace. His reasoning is simple, indeed too simple. Where the people decide on war or peace they will tend to decide for peace because they will have to bear the costs of war – of fighting and paying for it – whereas a monarch who is not faced with these costs can make the decision to go to war frivolously, knowing that no sacrifices will be required of him.[11] It should be stressed that this argument does not play a major role within Kant's work – fortunately, in view of its thinness. It is noteworthy that Kant does not suggest that the citizens of a republic will decide for peace because they think of themselves as part of a wider, interdependent world society created by the growth of peaceful mutual relations. In the third article of a Perpetual Peace he gives credence to this view, arguing that a universal community has 'developed to the point where a violation of rights in *one* part of the world is felt *everywhere*', but even in this context he argues that for the time being, cosmopolitan right must be strictly limited to a right of hospitality.[12]

The costs that Kant hopes and believes republican citizens will take into account are the costs of warfare in a direct sense, and do not include the opportunity costs of war – such as benefits forgone by the loss of trade and the collapse of an interdependent world economy. This distinguishes Kant's argument from that of the Manchester School 'peace movement' of the mid-nineteenth century,[13] from pre-1914 theorists such as Norman Angell whose *The Great Illusion* was devoted to an elaboration of the point that the losses of war would always exceed potential gains,[14] and from modern 'functionalists' who see peace as the by-product of the emergence of networks of interdependence and the undermining of state sovereignty.[15]

There are two points to be made here. First, a major difference between Kant and what one might term the 'economistic' variety of liberal – from Richard Cobden to Friedrich Von Hayek – is that the latter have been able to draw on developments in trade theory not available to Kant. Crucial here is David Ricardo's *Principles of Political Economy and Taxation* of 1817 which set out the theory of comparative advantages – a theory which nearly two centuries later remains at the heart of liberal thinking on international economic order.[16] The point of Ricardo's work is to show that trade will almost always lead to welfare gains, even in circumstances where one trading partner could produce all goods at a lower cost than another. All that is required for there to be a general gain from trade is that the structure of comparative costs within each economy be different, and this is a condition that will almost always be met. Hence the belief of Manchester School liberals – past and present – that free trade is in the interests of all.

Kant obviously could not have seen things in this light. His writings seem to suggest that commerce was a 'good thing' in so far as it promises mutual understanding, but he combines this with (sensible) doubt as to whether this is its usual effect. He refers specifically to the inhospitable conduct of the commercial states of Europe 'which they display in *visiting* foreign countries and peoples (which in their case is the same as *conquering* them)'.[17] An underlying assumption of the eighteenth century was that trade was unlikely to be beneficial except in circumstances where each partner possessed resources unavailable to the other. This attitude can be found in Rousseau's belief that economic relations between political communities would be a source of conflict, and hence that autarchy would be the ideal.[18] Perhaps this notion also lies behind Hegel's belief that the 'inner dialectic' of civil society would push it towards colonialism and expansionism as a way of meeting the subsistence needs of the people.[19] In any event, the idea that international trade could produce an increase in general welfare needed the work of Ricardo before it could be expressed with any confidence.

More fundamental, however, is a second point, which is that Kant's conception of the role of the state differs in important respects from that of the liberal economists. For the latter, the state has an important but essentially negative role; whenever it tries to perform positive functions problems will follow. This is not how Kant sees the matter. There is an apparent point of contact between Kant and the economists in so far as he would have agreed with them that attempts on the part of the state to develop a positive programme of economic welfare would be counter-productive. However, beyond the realm of the economy, Kant does see the state as performing a positive role of providing the context within which it is possible for individuals to live moral lives.[20] The state cannot make men moral and is not an unqualified good, but it is only in a properly constituted state that men can at least try to live lives in accordance with categorical imperative. Because the state has this role – a role which on pragmatic grounds a world state could not perform – Kant does not want to undermine its sovereignty. The 'federation of free states' set out in the second Definitive Article of a Perpetual Peace simply involves a treaty obligation not to go to war; no organisation is mandated.[21]

Kant's state is much closer to an Oakeshottian 'civil association' in which free citizens converse upon the general arrangements of society than it is to the 'nightwatchman' state of the economic liberals, which, albeit limited, is limited for a purpose – to enable free economic activity to promote the general good.[22] Kant's state comes close to the Oakeshottian ideal of not actually doing anything, even in a negative way. Returning to Kant's citizens who, if given the choice, will decide for peace rather than war, it can now be seen why the argument that they will make this choice is so thin, and, more important, why it does not need to be any thicker than it is. Only the direct costs of war are considered because only these costs are relevant. In their capacities as citizens the people have no common projects that could be disrupted by war, nor have they any reason to think that war could conceivably bring benefits to them. In the circumstances the simplest calculation only is required to produce a decision for peace. Once this is clear, it can be seen why Kant holds that republican states would not fight each other. Obviously, two sets of citizens approaching the decision for war or peace would each separately decide for peace – indeed it is difficult to see how between two republics the issue could arise in the first place. What would be the nature of a conflict liable to cause war? Republican states might find themselves having to face non-republican aggressors, but among themselves no plausible cause for war could emerge.

What is unfortunate here is that the very position that makes sense of the view that states with republican constitutions will not fight each other, undermines the translation of this proposition into the twentieth-century formulation that 'liberal democracies don't fight liberal democracies'. Modern liberal democracies come in all shapes and sizes, but all have some kind of welfare scheme for the poorest and most disadvantaged, all engage to some extent in economic management, and, most important, all are characterised by the existence of concentrations of economic and bureaucratic power alongside democratic institutions. On each of these counts modern 'really existing' liberal democracies are to be distinguished from the republican civil associations described by Kant – and from the equally unreal state structures desired by other classical liberals.

How would these differences factor into consideration of the war-proneness of modern liberalism? In a variety of ways that do not all point in the same direction. First, it is now possible to see how conflicts might arise between liberal democracies in a way that was not possible with Kantian republics. To take a very simple example, if unemployment is seen as a legitimate political issue, and not something that is of relevance only in the private sphere, and if there is, in the medium term at least, surplus capacity in the world economy, then it will indeed be the case that there will be no guaranteed harmony of interests between the peoples of different, competitor countries.

On the other hand, if decisions on war and peace are in the hands of the people, and if these decisions are made on cost-benefit lines, then it would surely be the case that in the modern world the presumption in favour of peace would be even stronger than it was two centuries ago. Even if there are today genuine grounds for conflict between peoples, and not simply between frivolous monarchs, the direct and indirect costs of war are so great that it is puzzling to see how a decision for war could ever be the result of a calculation. And yet, nonetheless, there are still wars – Susan Strange suggests quite plausibly that the attempt to theorise international relations began with the puzzle of why nation-states continue to go to war when it is clear that economic gains will never exceed economic cost.[23]

As we have seen, one possible explanation for this apparent paradox would be that there are structural features of the international system which contribute more to the causes of war than the domestic structures of its component states. But before accepting this conclusion, there are still unexplored features of modern liberal democracies to be taken into account. In particular, as already noted, there exist within these states concentrations of bureaucratic and economic power which put in question the Kantian vision of the citizenry collectively deciding on issues of war and peace. Perhaps wars come about because interest groups generated by these concentrations of power hijack the decision-making process and calculate costs and benefits on a different basis from that employed by the people? Some such explanation was and is, popular with radical liberal democrats and democratic socialists, but has been argued most effectively by another tradition altogether – namely, by Marxist theorists of imperialism – and it is to this tradition that we now turn.

LIBERAL IMPERIALISM?

Marx and Engels were bitterly critical of the international political positions of the Manchester liberals on, for example, the Eastern Question, but seem not to have contested the underlying theoretical notion of international relations upon which these positions were based.[24] Somewhat oversimplisticly, it can be said that the founders of Marxism accepted Ricardo's view of trade and the more general point about the pacific nature of liberal societies – their objection to the Manchester School's view of international politics sprang from the peculiar circumstances of the Eastern Question in the nineteenth century, on which more below. In any event, the mid-nineteenth century was a relatively peaceful time and it was not too implausible for Marx and his liberal opponents to see this relative peacefulness as the product of increasingly republican political systems.

By the end of the century and in the run-up to 1914 things were very different, with the growth of militarism and expansionism, and the 'marxist theory of imperialism' was one response to this difference.[25] This period produced a number of different Marxist theories, but the most influential, perhaps because of its popularisation by Lenin, was that of the Austro-Marxist Rudolf Hilferding. Hilferding characterised the changes that had taken place since the mid-century as the emergence of 'finance capital' – the fusion of financial capital and industrial capital to create new giant concentrations of economic power.[26] An assessment of the validity of this characterisation is beyond the scope of this chapter; what is important is that these new economic concentrations have both the wherewithal to dominate the political process, and the need to do so. The ability of these business concerns to dominate political processes came from the scale of the new enterprises which allowed them to exert direct influence over the government machinery in a way that the smaller economic concerns of the past could not.

The key point here is that finance capital has a foreign economic policy in a way that older forms of capitalism did not. The formation of giant corporations leads to cartelisation and monopoly (in the Marxist sense of the term which more or less corresponds to the 'bourgeois' economist's notion of oligopoly) and the assumption is that no monopoly could be strong enough to dominate world markets; international capitalism thus consists of a series of national capitals. Each national concentration of capital requires a 'national economic territory' within which it can gain the benefits of monopoly pricing, and this requirement generates two imperatives. First, the national territory must be protected from foreign competitors – which means protective tariffs are the basis of commercial policy. Second, the national economic territory must be continually expanded to keep pace with the rate of capital accumulation (the alternative being falling profits); thus the 'economic policy of finance capitalism' is imperialism. Expansionism is a requirement of the system in order to provide outlets for surplus capital – it is, of course, a matter of dispute whether there actually was 'surplus capital' at this time (or, for that matter, whether the term is at all meaningful). Leaving this aside, from Hilferding's perspective, national monopolies would be bound to export capital rather than increase domestic production because the latter would undermine their pricing policy as effectively as would foreign competition.[27]

Thus modern capitalist states – and this means all modern liberal democracies – are necessarily in conflict with one another, struggling to expand their own economic territories and penetrate those of others. This is not a matter of special interests exerting an undue and illegitimate but contingent influence on foreign policy – an interpretation that could be made of the work of even as radical a liberal as Hobson – it is rather a necessary feature of the operation of finance capital. From within the Marxist framework, Kautsky in 1914 argued – with consummately bad timing – that 'ultra-imperialist' arrangements could be made between national capitals given the common interest that capitalists generally shared in the face of anti-capitalist forces.[28] As argued in the next section, this was a rather perceptive argument, but in the realm of Marxist theory it was much denounced. The basis of Lenin's polemical denunciation of Kautsky, found in *Imperialism: Highest Stage of Capitalism*, was the 'Law of Uneven Development'. This states that any arrangement between national capitals to divide the world up among themselves will be undermined by the passage of time since different countries grow at different rates, and what is at time t a satisfactory deal will be unsatisfactory to some by time $t + 1$.[29] Hilferding's basic position, restated by Lenin, Trotsky and Stalin, remains central to much modern Marxist international political economy and can be found, for instance, in the work of the Belgian Trotskyite Ernest Mandel.[30]

If the orthodox Marxist position is that capitalist states are bound to be permanently in conflict with one another, the most popular neo-Marxist alternative conception removes the element of intra-capitalist conflict by underplaying the significance of individual national capitals. Arguments concerning the internationalisation of capital and a world-system of metropolitan and satellite economies posit the existence of clear hierarchies and patterns of dominance in such a way that arguments over the proneness to conflict of different domestic regimes become irrelevant. As with their structuralist cousins, the 'neorealist' writers of this persuasion shift the location of conflict away from the domestic nature of regimes, and thus beyond the scope of this chapter.

Marxist writers on imperialism can be criticised at a number of levels, but what is crucial here is the extent to which it makes sense to replace the characterisation 'liberal democracy' by some such term as 'monopoly capitalist state'. Really-existing liberal democracy is characterised by the presence of great concentrations of economic power which clearly do exercise political power and cannot simply be wished away in the style favoured by some neo-liberals. The Marxist determination to point this out is salutary. Not so the dismissal of the genuinely democratic element within really-existing liberal democracy. The United States Constitution, for example, may not be a reliable guide to the distribution of power in that country, but respect for the rule of law is a reality, and the determination of the United States Senate to exert its constitutional rights in the area of foreign policy has been a feature of United States politics since the 1960s. Economistic accounts of United States foreign policy that fail to take this into account, however sophisticated in other respects, simply fail to hit the mark. The point is, of course, more general; just as the Kantian republic is nowhere to be found today, nor could it be revived without a wholesale (and implausible) change in the expectations of ordinary people that their governments should take at least some responsibility for the general welfare, so the view of the state as simply a reflector of the interests of monopoly capital bears very little relation to reality by virtue of its assumption that these same expectations can be continually disregarded or finessed by the representatives of capital. Both views are defeated by the complexity and indeterminacy of modern politics.

IS THERE USEFUL EMPIRICAL EVIDENCE?

Up to this point, the alleged anti-war tendencies of liberal democracies have been investigated by examining the arguments of a number of theorists taken as representatives of different views on the matter. This is, of course, not the only way that a question of this kind can be examined. In principle it would seem possible to construct a systematic, non-anecdotal, empirical test of the question – and thus the indeterminate nature of the conceptual analysis may be overcome by hard (or hardish) fact. A good attempt to devise such a test has been made by Michael Doyle.[31]

Doyle's work explicitly addresses Kant's formulations, but is sensitive to the distinction between old and new liberalism. He examines in detail the realist critique of accounts of the origin of war which are based on features of domestic regimes, and gives proper attention to the difficulties liberal regimes have in dealing with non-liberal regimes. However, for all this sophistication, the beauty of his work lies in its simplicity. Its centrepiece is a simple juxtapositioning of two tables; one (of his own devising) lists the liberal regimes that have come into existence since the eighteenth century, the other (borrowed from Small and Singer)[32] lists international wars since 1816. On the basis of this juxtaposition Doyle identifies the existence of a 'Pacific Union' of the kind envisaged by Kant. Thus:

> Even though liberal states have become involved in numerous wars with non-liberal states, constitutionally secure liberal states have yet to engage in war with one another.[33]

Moreover, the Pacific Union has grown over the years – at Doyle's time of writing (1983) it had, by his count, reached 49 states but the figure by now would be considerably larger.[34]

On the face of it, it would seem that this simple exercise has made redundant the rest of this chapter, and that Kant's and Garton Ash's optimism has been vindicated. However difficult it may be to pin down the mechanism by which liberalism avoids war, Doyle's empirical evidence seems compelling. As far as the evidence is concerned, it is possible – as Doyle acknowledges – to question some of the judgements he makes about the point of entry of particular states to the Pacific Union; in some cases this could make a difference to the intuitive plausibility of the argument, but without affecting the basic quantitative point.[35]

For all the compelling nature of this evidence, however, the matter of causation cannot be simply set aside, because the possibility remains that the Pacific Union is a by-product of some other factor in world politics. A key issue here is the relationship between liberal and non-liberal states. On this Doyle is without illusions:

> The very constitutional restraint, shared commercial interests and international respect for individual rights that promote peace among liberal societies can exacerbate conflicts between liberal and non-liberal societies.[36]

He might also have made the point that at times things can go the other way. Marx's objection to the Manchester Peace Movement in the 1850s was that liberal non-interventionism *vis-à-vis* Tsarist Russia was allowing the greatest enemy of both the revolution and Britain's economic interests to triumph. Still, whether excessively bellicose or excessively pacifist, it can be agreed that liberal states have difficulty in putting themselves in a right relationship with non-liberal states. In this Doyle is realistic in the best sense of the term.

However, Doyle's handling of the impact of non-liberal states on the relationships of liberal states with one another remains unconvincing. Put simply, the existence of powerful enemies of liberal states, and perhaps especially of liberal capitalist economies, may have the impact of causing the conflicts which might otherwise flare up between these states to be damped down. Two examples can make the point. First, Doyle refers to the various conflicts between Britain, France and the United States in the decades before 1914, remarking, with respect to the first two, that 'despite their colonial rivalries, liberal France and Britain formed an entente before World War I against illiberal Germany', and adds that in spite of a commitment to neutrality the United States joined with the liberals in 1917 against the non-liberal state.[37] This is obviously true, but it tells us nothing of the dynamics that would have been operative in the absence of a non-liberal common enemy – not to mention the further point that it is not clear that it was its 'illiberalism' as such that was the threatening feature of German power.

The point is that counter-factuals are crucial. This is even more clearly the case with a second example, which returns to the polemics of Kautsky and Lenin. Kautsky argued that monopoly capitalist countries could divide the world up between themselves in such a way as to preserve peace, while Lenin contended that any such deal would collapse as a result of changes in the distribution of world economic power. Who was right? In the interwar period the issue is ambiguous because it is not clear whether Nazi Germany can be regarded as a capitalist imperialistic state for purposes of the discussion, but in the post-1945 era it looks pretty much as if Kautsky has the best of the argument. Major changes have taken place in the distribution of power among capitalist states in this period without leading to violent conflict – relatively speaking, the adjustment process has been smooth, and Kautsky's notion of ultra-imperialism seems plausible. But what neither Kautsky nor Lenin could have envisaged was that the rise of the USSR would have changed the structure of world power so dramatically as to throw into confusion any account of the dynamics of intra-imperialist relations based on the assumption that all the major powers would be monopoly capitalist. In the post-1945 era where one of the two superpowers was (in principle at least) dedicated to the overthrow of capitalism, it is hardly surprising that the capitalist countries rallied behind the leadership of the other. Lenin's political achievement of 1917 undermined his conception of how the world worked.

This is not to say that Lenin's account of imperialism was correct. The point is that we have no empirical basis for answering this question, because we have no experience of a world in which all the major power centres are liberal democratic/monopoly capitalist. This is what subverts Doyle's optimistic account of the spread of the Pacific Union – we simply do not know whether the states of this Union would have remained pacific in their relations with one another had they not been faced with common threats from outside the zone of peace. The only way we can approach this problem is by conceptual analysis because a self-contained world of liberalism has never existed.

The reason this point is so important is that we may be about to find out how such a world operates. Russia may remain a major power, and, quite possibly an anti-capitalist power, but it is unlikely to pose the sort of threat to the major liberal capitalist countries that the Soviet Union did in the past. The era of 'forced ultra-imperialism', if such is the appropriate way of describing the last half-century, is coming to a close. For the first time the dominant political perspective will be liberal/capitalist, with no major competing ideology; the world is entering new territory, and suggestive though empirical studies based on the old world may be, they cannot provide conclusive evidence as the potential shape of the new.

CONCLUSION

The basic conclusion of this chapter is that it is not possible to be confident that a world order dominated by liberal states would necessarily have as its core a Pacific Union. That 'liberal democracies don't fight liberal democracies' is a proposition the empirical evidence for which is tainted by the circumstances of the last century, and the conceptual basis of which only stands up on a very implausible account of how decisions are actually made in liberal democratic polities. The existence of powerful state bureaucracies and of concentrations of economic power in really-existing liberal democracies breaks the chain of argument that links this form of society to perpetual peace – although whether these features of liberalism lead in the direction of war and conflict is, again, a question that cannot be answered empirically, nor does conceptual analysis point unambiguously in one direction. No clear answers seem to appear.

Yet the basic proposition that liberal democracies do not fight liberal democracies remains intuitively very appealing. Why? Another argument of Kant's may be relevant here. Doyle calls it Kant's 'international track' to a Pacific Union.[38] It is not simply Kant's argument that republican states will not go to war with each other. In *The Idea for a Universal History with a Cosmopolitan Purpose* and in *The Contest of Faculties* as well as in the First Supplement to *Perpetual Peace*,[39] Kant offers a different line of reasoning: the increasing horrors of war will gradually produce both republican states and perpetual peace. Human beings will find themselves

> compelled to ensure that *war*, the greatest obstacle to morality and the invariable enemy of progress, first becomes gradually more humane, then more infrequent and finally disappears completely as a mode of aggression.[40]

The hidden plan of nature makes men amenable to reason by continually upping the costs of not being amenable to reason.

Kant and Doyle see this as a further argument in favour of the link between liberalism and peace, but in fact all that is required for the point to be made is that states are governed in such a way that their rulers – whether as representatives of people, classes, estates, or simply themselves – are capable of working out the consequences of action and not in the grip of some kind of death wish. It may be that liberal democracies are the systems most likely to produce such rulers, but no exclusivity need be assumed. Certainly in the 1980s, and even allowing for the political motivation behind its 'Peace Offensive', the Soviet system seemed capable of articulating and acting upon a genuine fear of the consequences of nuclear war. The horrifying possibilities of modern warfare – conventional as well as nuclear – may be in the process of rehabilitating Angell and the older generation of peace theorists. War between advanced industrial liberal democracies is unthinkable not because they are liberal democracies but because they are advanced and industrial and therefore, probably by definition, have political systems that meet the minimum standards of rationality required to preclude war as an instrument of policy among themselves.

Stating the matter this way makes it clear why war will remain a distinct possibility between advanced industrial and other societies. As the Gulf War demonstrates quite clearly, given the right circumstances, 'peace through mutual terror' calculations simply do not apply; the coalition partners were able to achieve at least their immediate ends at little cost to themselves.[41] At the same time the apparent irrationalism of the Iraqi regime makes the point in a different way – a minimal ability to work through the consequences ought to have shown the Iraqi leadership that the invasion of Kuwait would provoke a violent response. It committed this act of aggression not because Iraq is an illiberal state – although it obviously is – but as a result of its irrationality and ignorance.[42]

In summary, it is not necessary to envisage restricting membership of an emerging Pacific Union to liberal democracies; a basic ability to make cost-benefit calculations is a sufficient reason to presume a generally peaceful outlook. Given that liberal democracy is, and will remain, a fragile plant, whereas some kind of minimum rationality is probably a functional requirement for a successful advanced industrial society, this is a more optimistic conclusion than that warranted by Garton Ash's 'fundamental insight'. We do not need universal liberalism to create a more peaceful world – although there are, of course, other reasons for hoping that liberal democracy will drive out its remaining competitors.

NOTES

Earlier versions of this chapter were presented at the XV World Congress of the International Political Science Association in Buenos Aires, July 1991 and at the British International Studies Association Annual Conference at Warwick University, December 1991. I am grateful to Dick Arneson, Brian Barry, Rajeev Bhargava, Michael Donelan, Robert Jackson, James Mayall, Hidemi Suganami and my former colleagues at the University of Kent, Stephen Chan, Krishan Kumar, David McLellan and Richard Sakwa for their comments.

1. Francis Fukuyama,'The End of History', *The National Interest* (Summer, 1989), p. 3.
2. Timothy Garton Ash, 'Ten Thoughts on the New Europe', *New York Review of Books* (Vol. 27, No. 10, 14 June 1990), p. 22.
3. Francis Fukuyama, *The End of History and the Last Man* (London: Hamish Hamilton, 1992). For hostile comments on the original article see, for example, Ralf Dahrendorf, *Reflections on the Revolution in Europe* (Chatto and Windus: London, 1990), pp. 33 ff., and most of the contributions to the Symposium on 'The End of History' in *Marxism Today* (November 1989). Reactions to the book have been, if anything, slightly more sympathetic – see, for example, Harold James in *The Times* (20 February 1992); Norman Stone in *The Sunday Times* (1 March 1992); commentary in the *New Left Review* (No. 193, May/June 1992) predictably rejects Fukuyama's conclusions, but Fred Halliday, at least, is quite sympathetic to his project.
4. *Hegel's Philosophy of Right*, trans. and notes by T.M. Knox (London: Oxford University Press, 1967), pp. 208–16.
5. Kenneth Waltz, *Theory of International Politics* (Reading, MA: Addison-Wesley, 1979), ch. 4 'Reductionist and Systemic Theories'.
6. Martin Wight 'Why Is There No International Theory?', in Herbert Butterfield and Martin Wight (eds), *Diplomatic Investigations* (London: Allen and Unwin, 1966), p. 26.
7. Hedley Bull, *The Anarchical Society* (London: Macmillan, 1977), pp. 243–8.
8. Garton Ash, following Kant, uses 'fight' in the literal sense, i.e., to refer to war between liberal democracies; the rest of this chapter will employ the same language, but rather more loosely – thus, 'fight' will be taken to be shorthand for 'engage in extreme conflict behaviour' which need not necessarily be violent.
9. *Kant's Political Writings*, trans. by H.B. Nesbit, Introduction by H. Reiss (Cambridge: Cambridge University Press, 1977), p. 99.
10. This is a summary of a long footnote at the beginning of the section of *Perpetual Peace*, devoted to the Definitive Articles. *Ibid.*, p. 98.
11. Ibid., p. 100.
12. Ibid., p. 108. Emphasis in the original.

13. For example, see Richard Cobden 'The Balance of Power', in M.G. Forsyth *et al.* (eds), *The Theory of International Relations* (London: Allen and Unwin, 1970), p. 306.
14. Norman Angell, *The Great Illusion* (London: Heinemann, 1910).
15. For example, see David Mitrany, *A Working Peace System* (Chicago, IL: Quadrangle Books, 1966).
16. David Ricardo, *Principles of Political Economy and Taxation* (London: Dent, 1955), Ch. 7.
17. *Kant's Political Writings*, p. 106. Emphasis in the original.
18. See Stanley Hoffmann, 'Rousseau on War and Peace', in *The State of War* (New York, NY: Praeger, 1965); and Christine Jane Carter, *Rousseau on War and Peace* (New York, NY: Garland Publishing, 1987).
19. Hegel, *Philosophy of Right*, Sections 246–8, p. 151.
20. For a fuller discussion see, for example, P. Riley, *Kant's Political Philosophy* (Totowa, NJ: Rowman Littlefield, 1983); and H.L. Williams, *Kant's Political Philosophy* (Oxford: Basil Blackwell, 1983).
21. *Kant's Political Writings*, p. 102.
22. There is no scope for extending this comparison here; for 'civil association' see Michael Oakeshott, *On Human Conduct* (Oxford: Clarendon Press, 1975).
23. Susan Strange, *States and Markets* (London: Pinter Publishers, 1988), p. 11.
24. See, for example, Marx's writings collected in *The Eastern Question*, ed. by E. Marx Aveling and E. Aveling (London: Cass Reprints of Economic Classics, 1897/1969).
25. The best account is Anthony Brewer, *Marxist Theories of Imperialism* (London: Routledge and Kegan Paul, 1980).
26. Rudolf Hilferding, *Finance Capital*, ed. by Tom Bottomore (London: Routledge and Kegan Paul, 1981).
27. See ibid., Part V in general, and ch. 22 in particular.
28. Karl Kautsky, 'Ultra Imperialism', *New Left Review* (No. 59, 1970).
29. V.I. Lenin, 'Imperialism: Highest Stage of Capitalism', *Selected Works* (Moscow: Progress Publishers, 1968).
30. Ernest Mandel, *Europe vs. America* (London: New Left Books, 1970); and *Late Capitalism* (London: New Left Books, 1975).
31. Michael Doyle, 'Kant, Liberal Legacies and Foreign Affairs' (Parts 1 & 2) *Philosophy and Public Affairs* (Vol. 12, Nos. 3 & 4, 1983), pp. 205–35 and 323–53. Other relevant studies of this period include R.J. Rummel, 'Libertarianism and International Violence', *Journal of Conflict Resolution* (Vol. 27, No. 1, 1983); and J. David Singer and Melvin Small, *The Wages of War 1816–1965* (London: J. Wiley, 1972) Part D, ch. 11. More recently, following the collapse of communism, studies of the 'democratic peace' have become a major sunrise industry; for the current state of play see Bruce Russett, *Grasping the Democratic Peace* (Princeton, NJ: Princeton University Press, 1993); and special issues of *International Interactions*

(Vol. 18, No. 3, 1993); *Journal of Conflict Research* (Vol. 35, No. 2, 1991); and *Journal of Peace Research* (Vol. 29, No. 4, 1992). Most of these studies confirm Doyle's rather rough and ready correlation – which suggests that, in this instance, we are not simply dealing with a statistical artefact. Also valuable is D. Lake, 'Powerful Pacifists: Democratic States and War', *American Political Science Review* (Vol. 86, No. 1, 1992).

32. Melvin Small and J. David Singer, *Resort to Arms: International and Civil Wars, 1816–1980* (Beverly Hills, CA: Sage Publications, 1982).
33. Doyle, 'Kant, Liberal Legacies', Part 1, p. 213.
34. Ibid., Part 2, p. 352.
35. Although it is possible to challenge some of Doyle's judgements, he always errs on the side of a premature identification of 'liberalism', which means that he is, in effect, making things more difficult for himself by overstating the size of the Pacific Union. A more restrictive definition of liberal states would make his basic point less subject to nit-picking, and more intuitively plausible. In any event, recent studies have confirmed the 'robustness' of his propositions. See footnote 31.
36. Doyle, 'Kant, Liberal Legacies', Part 2, p. 325.
37. Ibid., Part 1, p. 216.
38. Ibid., Part 2, p. 351.
39. *Kant's Political Writings*, pp. 41–53, 176–90 and 108–14 respectively.
40. Ibid., ('The Contest of Faculties'), p. 189. Emphasis in the original.
41. The stress here is, obviously, on 'immediate'. The Gulf War also demonstrates how difficult it is to convert overwhelming military superiority into effective political power.
42. Samir-al-Khalil, *Republic of Fear* (Berkeley, CA: University of California Press, 1989) and *The Monument* (London: André Deutsch, 1991) makes the point that the Iraqi regime has characteristics which distinguish it from other authoritarian systems in the region.

3 Global Society and Global Responsibility: The Theoretical, Historical and Political Limits of 'International Society'

Martin Shaw

The fates of theoretical concepts in the social sciences are intertwined with the development of historical reality. Concepts which are developed in an attempt to understand, even predict, a changing world are necessarily subject to the frequently unpredictable twists and turns of history. Concepts with an apparent mission to explain action are also often both articulations of how actors actually understand their actions, and intended as guides to how they might act in the future. Social-scientific concepts are a part of what they try to explain, and their relevance, validity and indeed success is conditional on the part they play.

Another way of putting this argument, which might have been more favoured in the recent past than it will be today, is to say that social-scientific concepts have an 'ideological' character. Such a presentation of the case will meet with misunderstandings, associated as it is with Marxist attempts to explain away the mainstream of Western social science.[1] It is not, however, necessary to adopt a Marxist stance in order to utilise the concept of 'ideology'. Nor is it necessary, even in the Marxist conception, to impute complete, let alone deliberate, falsehood to a theory because of its ideological character.

On the contrary, to suggest the ideological aspect of a theory is, first of all, to stress its historical *significance*. An ideology has a role in relation to the world of social action which a 'purely' academic theory would lack. An ideologically important theory will also be valid, at least in that it will express important truths and a major viewpoint of a historical period, and probably in that it will articulate more lasting knowledge in the context of its time. The implication of an ideological critique is, however, that theory is limited by its time and viewpoint, and its aim is to explicate its contradictions so as to develop a more historically adequate theory. (Such an approach need not necessarily imply, as it would in a Marxist schema, a concept of historical progress; it is also compatible with a discontinuist concept of historical change since it is the fact of change which is important rather than its content or sequence.)

The theory of International Society can be understood, it is argued here, as a central ideology of the international system in the Cold War period.[2] This argument is presented not in order to deny the relevance of the theory, but to identify how the important insights into the system which it provides were connected to the nature of the period in which the theory was developed, and represented one position on it. Nor is this argument put forward to deny the continuing relevance of these same insights; it does, however, suggest that we have reached the moment of their maximum validity, that the contradictions of the perspective are now unfolding, and that its theoretical foundations can now be seen to be fundamentally lacking.

The argument may seem paradoxical in that, at first glance, the international society perspective does indeed seem to have gained a coherence in the post-Cold War era which it previously lacked; indeed, as we shall see, a central weakness of its case has been removed by the end of the Cold War. It is at the moment of its greatest success that we can see the decisive importance of its contradictions and the need to move beyond the limited theoretical foundations which it provides.

THE CRISIS OF 'INTERNATIONAL SOCIETY' THINKING

The concept of international society has been put forward by its advocates as a 'central' position for international studies, a modal alternative to the extremes of brutish Hobbesian realism and utopian Kantian idealism.[3] It incorporates the dominant realism of the subject in its recognition of the dominance of independent sovereign states as actors in the international system; yet it makes a nod to idealism (as well as to social-scientific functionalism) in the role it assigns to consensus among actors as the basis for 'society'-like elements in the way this system develops. As Nicholas Wheeler has shown, this theoretical balancing act is a source of tensions in the theory.[4]

The international society position has, of course, its own (Grotian) philosophical antecedents; but it is essentially a modern theory, a product (like most of the discipline of International Relations) of the unique international situation of the third quarter of the twentieth century. On first approach, the context of a bipolar conflict between rigidly ideologically opposed powers is hardly the most apposite one for a stance which stresses a consensual framework of relations between states. However, Hedley Bull argued that even in the depths of the Cold War, the idea of international society 'survived as an important part of reality'.[5]

It is perhaps the major achievement of writers like Bull, and the great strength of the largely British-based International Society school, to have recognised the elements of cooperation which underlay the apparently irreconcilable Cold War opposition. Much more than the school of strategically-oriented International Relations dominant in the United States which stressed technological rivalry, the notion of international society has been vindicated by the outcome of the Cold War. To a greater extent than even Bull seems to have thought likely, a shared set of expectations and understandings dominated the behaviour of the political elites in the United States and former USSR. This led – after the crisis of the 'second Cold War' – to a relatively orderly unwinding (at the level of superpower relations at least) of the Cold War.

That the international society perspective stressed the framework of common understandings among states (despite the unpromising Cold War context) is testimony to the strength of broader historical understanding which it brought to the study of the international system. Bull, Martin Wight and others were able to see the Cold War system in the context of a longer historical development and to ask many of the right comparative questions, pointing to the strengths as well as weaknesses of contemporary international society in the light of past models.[6]

It might be thought perverse, in this light, to see the international society position as framed by the Cold War era. In so far as it has political implications it was clearly never a Cold Warrior stance in the narrow partisan sense. While its emphasis on the possibilities of the balance of power might have pointed to the long-term maintenance of the Cold War system, it also opened possibilities of a critical interpretation which promised to transcend the Cold War. For so long as entrenched Cold War hostilities rendered the society element uncertain, there was a strong argument to be made for moving beyond this to a more stable basis of international society.

The case for seeing the international society approach as an ideology of the Cold War period – at its best a historically sophisticated and potentially critical ideology with much to offer to any understanding of the international system – lies elsewhere. Essentially it lies in a weakness which is common to virtually all schools of international relations, as the discipline has developed in the 'postwar' period. Like most International Relations literature, the writings of the International Society school operate with a fundamentally state-centric approach. They are concerned with the international system first and foremost – Bull presents society as an element in that system – and with other realities only as they impinge on that system. Thus, although Bull presents world society and world politics as logically and morally prior to international society, he does not provide a coherent perspective on these in his account of the international. Indeed, writing in 1977, he regarded world society as at best an emergent reality.[7]

It might be thought obvious that the international system forms a relatively discrete order of reality, distinct from, even as it interacts with, world politics, world economy, culture and society. Certainly, modern states behave as though this is the case in most of their dealings with each other which make up the international system, and empirically it seems correct to describe the development of the framework of self-regulation among modern states, which is called international society. This self-evident separation of the international system, and within it of international society, is however something which needs to be explained and critically examined.

Just as discussions of international society have their favourite historical periods, such as that of the early-nineteenth-century Concert of Europe, they have their rather noticeable absences. It is rather difficult, as even Bull himself acknowledges, to see Hitler's Germany and Stalin's Russia as bound by common norms of international society. What such questions raise is the issue of whether the Cold War period was itself special in any way – apart from the bipolarisation and ideologisation of international conflict already mentioned, or its nuclearisation, which obviously had specific effects – which is pertinent to the theory.

The case which can be made is that the Cold War was unique in the twentieth century in so far as it resulted in the predominance of international relations over domestic politics and society. The first half of the century saw a dialectic of national and international politics in which neither could be said to be obviously dominant. The First World War initially subsumed the social tensions and political divides in the industrial societies which had developed in the nineteenth century; it then regenerated these in the revolutionary and counter-revolutionary movements of the interwar years; these movements (notably fascism and communism) in turn fed into international tensions polarising Europe and the world between ideologically polarised states.[8]

The Second World War not only destroyed fascism and turned Stalinism into a ruling ideology in the East but also produced a domesticated oppositional form of labour politics in the West. Its outcome left the single ideologised confrontation between the Soviet Union and the West dominating the politics of all states in the northern hemisphere. Uniquely in modern history outside wartime, the international unequivocally dominated society and domestic politics. The bipolar conflict neutralised –

even froze – many minor international conflicts, but it also froze national politics into Cold War variants (Christian democracy, social democracy, Stalinism), and had many corresponding effects in society and culture.

It was in this atypical predominance of international over national politics, with a corresponding reduction of the influence of politics in the wider sense over the international, that international relations grew as a discipline. Theories such as that of international society emphasised the coherence of relations among states as distinct from other political and social relations. In this context, too, distinguished sociologists who turned their attention to these issues emphasised the completeness of nation-states' 'surveillance' of societies (Anthony Giddens) and the 'geopolitical privacy of states' in relation to their populations (Michael Mann).[9]

All this, as the saying goes, is now history. The Cold War period itself contained major prefigurations of the re-emergence of national revolt and social protest as factors in international politics: the revolts of Eastern European peoples, from Berlin in 1953 to Gdansk in 1980, and the peace movements in Western Europe in the early 1980s. All of these were, in their time, defeated, and hence could be seen as ultimately unimportant to the East-West conflict. The crisis of 1989, however, involved a dialectic of superpower detente and Soviet reform with the mass democratic movements in such countries as East Germany and Czechoslovakia, which ushered in the most fundamental change in the international system since 1945.[10]

The years since have seen an escalation of the role of sub-international politics in the international system. Nationalist and ethnic politics in the parts of the former Soviet Union and Eastern Europe have led to an instability of the state system in Europe not seen since the 1940s, with wars in the former Yugoslavia (threatening a general Balkan war), and between Armenia and Azerbaijan, and in Moldova and Georgia (all of which threaten to involve Russia and a range of other states, both ex-Soviet republics and others). The dialectic of political movements and international relations, so apparently virtuous in 1989, has become much more vicious in its aftermath. The revival of nationalism may be seen, following James Mayall's discussion, as a normal part of the renewal of international society – even Bosnian Serbs seek a place in the community of states for their ethnic mini-state, suitably 'cleansed' of their former neighbours – but it also raises issues of the *extent* to which sub-national developments dictate the international agenda.[11]

As European Community and United Nations mediators scurry after the minor ethnic warlords of the fragments of Bosnia, Croatia and other ex-Yugoslav republics, as UN troops wobble uncertainly between peacekeeping and peacemaking, as the major powers trade the dangers of intervention against the dangers of a public outcry at (mass-mediated) civilian misery and death, it is obvious that something has changed. 'Turbulence in world politics' is not new, but its intensity has been increasing, and in the post-Cold War era is breaking up the insulated categories of international theory in a way which fulfils Rosenau's prophetic view of 'post-international' politics.[12]

In this situation, international society seems both more surely founded and more problematic. The proponents of the concept can take heart from the removal of the Cold War ideological fracture which centrally threatened the cultural coherence of a 'society'. It is now manifest that the major players are the Western powers, among whom the rules and underlying assumptions are widely shared; Russia and other ex-Communist states are eager to avow their allegiance. It is possible, as Barry Buzan has argued, to see the emergence of a gigantic Northern 'security community'.[13] This could stretch from North America and Western Europe, to the major states of the former USSR and Eastern Europe, and to Japan, the newly industrialising states of East Asia, and Australasia. China, as a regional great power and permanent member of the Security Council, is partially implicated, although its democratisation would consolidate its membership and underline the growing implicit connection between international society and political democracy. Other powers, from India to Egypt to Brazil to (a reformed) South Africa, may be involved in regional extensions of this community.

At the very moment, however, when such developments seem to strengthen what is referred to as international society, other changes bring it into question.[14] Increasingly, it is the interactions between the international system and wider social and political changes which command our attention. International relations between states are increasingly about issues within societies, as the crises of 1991–92 have shown. The British-French-American intervention in northern Iraq was a direct response to media and political pressure in Western societies resulting from the plight of the Kurdish people, even if their migration was an indirect consequence of the war in Iraq. The Western powers' intervention, under UN auspices, in Bosnia has increasingly been under the impetus of humanitarian concerns resulting from similarly mediated pressure, even if there are more traditional international issues at stake.[15]

These changes are increasingly modifying what have been seen as the assumptions and institutions of international society. The principles of sovereignty and non-intervention are increasingly problematic. The assumption that international policing is a matter for the major powers, while it still holds a good deal of force, is nevertheless qualified by the enlarged role of the UN in coordinating as well as legitimating intervention. No doubt it will be argued that in none of these respects has anything fundamental changed, but this is to ignore the corrosive effects of *ad hoc* modifications to international practice now occurring at a rapid rate. All these changes raise the question of the adequacy of the theoretical perspective of international society.

INTERNATIONAL SOCIETY AND GLOBAL SOCIETY

The concept of international society is seen by its proponents alongside that of international system. The concept of system is the more fundamental and less problematic: it simply requires us to recognise patterns of interaction between states as possessing a coherence which, at least in part, determines their actions and possibly those of others. Bull, whose account of the relationship of system and society is the most careful, recognises the nebulous character of 'society' by proclaiming it no more than an 'element' in the international system.[16] At the same time, however, he very definitely writes as though international society has a capacity for action, as when it acts in common to assure its goals, seeming to ascribe to it a greater degree of reality than that of a mere element in a system.

The concept of an international society is unusual, in a way that that of a system is not, in that societies are usually defined in terms of social relations among individual human beings. International relations as a discipline has a general problem, viewed from the perspective of the social sciences in general and sociology in particular, in its state-centredness, its treatment of states as actors akin to individuals, and its neglect of the complex social relations which bind individuals and states.[17] Bull recognises this in a discussion, rather curious to the sociological eye, of the similarities and differences between the self-regulating society of states (lacking a central state) and the primitive stateless societies described by anthropologists.[18] Formally, such a comparison may be quite possible, but Bull ignores the substantive difficulties which arise when we discuss a society composed of what are 'already' (as a result of 'domestic' characteristics not considered by international theorists) social institutions.

What is apparent here is that the concept and terminology of international society only work providing that the insulation of international studies from theoretical discourse with other social sciences is maintained. Such an insulation cannot be justified in the name of a division of labour in the social sciences. Certainly there is a case that states are a very distinctive and important kind of social institution, the interactions among which are equally distinctive, and in this sense require a specific mode of understanding which implies a discipline. There is no case which can be sustained, however, which denies the common features between the state and other social institutions or the connections between state-society and state-state relations. In this sense, international relations must be theoretically integrated with the mainstream of the social sciences. Its concepts should be developed not just by analogy with other social sciences – as in Bull's discussion of a stateless society – but consistently with them. The substantive connections between the concepts of international relations and of other social sciences must be clear.

Bull's discussion of international society lays bare a crucial problem in the way he ascribes a particular meaning to society. By defining society in terms of a consensus between its members, he gives a great deal of weight to its normative coherence. There are, of course, approaches in sociology and anthropology, normally described as functionalist, which have adopted precisely such an approach – although Bull hardly acknowledges the connection.[19] These approaches are widely discredited, however, not just because they tended to underrate social conflict, but because they define society in terms of one of its dimensions. Precisely the same could be said of Bull.

Society, among human beings, can be defined by the existence of relationships involving mutual expectations and understandings, with the possibility of mutually oriented actions. In this sense, society can be said to be far more akin to the meaning of system used in international relations; the concept of society does not, except in the systems of thought constructed by some functionalists, require consensus around coherent value systems. The existence of such systems is an empirical question, among many others, which arise in analysing societies.

From this discussion we can see that the distinction between system and society is suspect. Even if it were not – if we could accept the identification of society with consensus – there is still the question of the substantive (and terminological) relationship between international society and human society or societies in a wider sense. The terminological issue is not the most important, but it bears thinking about, since it is potentially confusing to talk of a society of states when most societies are understood to be composed of individual human beings. The substantive issue is more important: is international society a sub-society, or perhaps sub-culture, of human society in some wider sense? Or is it self-sufficient, with no theoretically articulable relationship to the larger pattern of human relations?

Reading Bull, we are left with the feeling that the relationship by analogy may be as important as any substantive relationship. World society is acknowledged as a reference point and together with world politics is accorded priority over the international. World society is, however, seen as something which at best is just starting to come into existence; it does not exist in a way comparable to international society. We see, therefore, that the priority of world society is purely nominal since in any sense which counts, the society of states is quite obviously stronger, indeed has greater reality. This conception of world society betrays, however, the same strong meaning of society which we noted above: world society does not exist, for Bull, because it lacks the coherent, shared values and framework of understanding which, to a degree at least, international society possesses.

What if world society, or in today's parlance, global society, does exist? In the weaker sense of a global system of social relations in which all human beings are, to some extent, connected and which covers the entire globe, we do indeed have such a world society. Indeed, whereas in the past it might have made sense to talk of discrete human societies, today the word can only consistently be applied to human society on a world scale. Other usages, whether referring to national, ethnic or tribal societies (British, Kurdish, Zulu) are increasingly arbitrary abstractions from the global flux of social relations.[20] World society exists through the social relations involved in global commodity production and exchange, through global culture and mass media, and through the increasing development of world politics.

The international system of states may appear to be the most important, or at least the most developed, system which orders global society. However, it is not the only set of institutions to be increasingly organised on a global scale, for economic and cultural institutional networks also have global reach, and we can also talk about these as systems within global society. It may even be the case that we can begin to talk about global society in terms of the development of common values and beliefs, and a common political culture, in which ideas of democracy and national status, for example, are widely diffused.

How are the concepts of global society and international society to be related? First of all, if the one is defined in terms of a weak (social relationships), and the other in terms of a strong (common values, consensus) meaning of society, the relationship is logically complex. Second, there is a case for distinguishing between a society of human individuals and one of states. Third, it is highly desirable that our conceptualisation should assist in defining the transformation of relationships between the international and the global. At the very least, there is a case for a terminological adjustment, but this would seem merely to be an entailment of a substantive theoretical reformulation.

We should distinguish between a society, its culture and institutions. Social relationships on a world scale constitute a society (in the weak sense). Within this global society there is a global economic system, not only with world markets, but also with globally coordinated production. There are increasingly the elements of a global culture, including a political culture, but there are also very many segmentations corresponding to state, national, ethnic, religious, political, class, cultural and lifestyle divisions. Within this global society, too, there are numerous global institutions, among which the state system (international system) is pre-eminent but not exclusively dominant, as well as many more locally based institutions.

From the point of view of global society, the development of what is called international society is the development of the institutions and the institutional culture of the state system in the direction of greater coherence and consensus. Redefining international society in this way we look at it as a development specific to the state system, but one which reflects this system's role in global society and is the product not only of developments within the system but also of the system's role in global society and its interaction with the structures, culture and other institutions of that society.

Viewed in this theoretical light, the development of what is called international society can no longer be seen in a purely contingent relationship to the development of global society. Certainly there is no automatic, mechanical connection between globalisation (in the sense of the extension and increasing integration of global society) and the integration of the state system seen in terms of international society. The latter has its own dynamics which do indeed need to be investigated empirically, both in themselves and in terms of their many and complex relationships to other manifestations of globalisation. Developments in the state system must, however, be studied in the context of the entire picture of the development of world society which has theoretical priority.

Adopting this standpoint, we need an understanding of the way in which the processes of economic expansion and cultural diffusion have increasingly created an integrated world society of which a more tightly integrated state system is an inevitable part. The problem is that global economic integration has been studied apart from the development of the state system, and global cultural integration has hardly been studied at all in general terms. These three main sets of processes are, however, what have together (over centuries and especially the last few decades) created the basis of a world society.

This perspective is important to current international relations debates because it explains why the international system is increasingly not self-sufficient; why sub- and supra-national actors are increasingly important in international politics; why, indeed, we are looking at post-international politics. It explains why we should stop seeing non-state actors as intruders into the system and society of states and see them instead as actors within global society of which the state system is an institutional component, and whose intrusion is therefore entirely normal and inevitable. It explains why the moral priority which Bull rightly accorded, in principle, to world society and politics over international society is not of purely utopian significance, as he seemed to believe, but of the utmost practical import in dealing with the issues of the day.

FROM THE IDEOLOGY OF STATES TO GLOBAL RESPONSIBILITY

The Cold War situation, in which the international state system contained the emergence of global society, is coming to an end. Groups, movements and institutions within global society are making themselves felt within the international state system which politically mediates global social relations. It is only right and proper that they should do so, even if it threatens the assumptions of the state system and the norms of international society such as sovereignty and non-intervention. This is not to say that these norms are wholly redundant, but it is to insist that they must be qualified by general accountability to the needs and wishes of the members of global society.

We should welcome this process, however embryonic it may be and however many strains it introduces into the state system, which will then spill over into the lives of people within global society. What is involved, however modestly and contradictorily, is the beginning of the development of what we may call global civil society, in which members of global society are starting to try to make the state system responsible – in the way in which national civil societies have, in the past, generated pressures to ensure the accountability of national states.

At the core of the development of global civil society is the concept of 'global responsibility'. Again embryonically, this idea can be seen at work in a variety of developments: the attempts by global ecological movements to make the state system respond to demands for global environmental management; the attempts by pressure groups to ensure that human rights and democracy are judged by a global standard; and the demands, fuelled by media coverage, to make respect for human needs and human rights effective principles in international conflicts. The pressure on Western governments to intervene to protect the Kurds – to accept responsibility for the indirect victims of their war against Iraq – and to intervene for purely humanitarian reasons in Bosnia-Hercegovina are recent manifestations of this principle of global responsibility.

Each of these recent interventions has implicitly or explicitly challenged the principles of sovereignty and non-intervention which have been seen as core assumptions of international society. The principles have, of course, been waived or varied in response to similar pressures in the past, and there is nothing to suggest that states are less willing to subordinate them largely, yet alone entirely, to principles of global responsibility. Rather there has been a real struggle between the instincts of statesmen to maintain the principles of sovereignty and non-intervention, and the pressure from global civil society to transcend them.

The instincts of President George Bush and Prime Minister John Major were to abstain, in practical terms, from the civil conflicts in Iraq after the Gulf War, even after they had morally and politically incited rebellion against Saddam Hussein. The Shi'a of southern Iraq were effectively abandoned to their fate in March 1991, with US troops a matter of miles from Basra, the main centre of rebellion. The Kurds were likewise abandoned until international political-media pressure suddenly built up in mid-April. Even after intervention, the Allies and the UN maintained the fiction of Iraqi sovereignty in seeking Iraqi agreement to the operation of UN relief agencies (the fiction cost them dearly in official currency rates and other Iraqi rake-offs). Nevertheless, in military terms the cease-fire agreement itself breached Iraqi sovereignty by providing for intensive UN surveillance of Iraqi military preparations.

In this episode, it was quite clear that Western leaders were operating with an ideology of international society, in which the defeated Iraqi state, although exposed as morally and politically bankrupt, was still accorded the rights and prerogatives of a sovereign state. While the allies were prepared to breach these in their own state interests (the control of weapons of mass destruction) they still upheld the concept of non-intervention where it was merely an issue of a threat to Iraq's own citizens. Only under severe political pressure from an implicit stance of global responsibility did they concede intervention.

In the Yugoslav case, the ideology of international society operated against any idea of intervention when it first became apparent – in the repression of Kosovo in the later 1980s – that an aggressive nationalist regime had come to power in Serbia which was precipitating the breakup of Yugoslavia. The conception that these were the domestic problems of a sovereign state prevailed, as Western states and international bodies continued to recognise Yugoslavia long after its demise had become inevitable, and without seriously attempting to intervene to regulate the breakup in terms of principles like respect for existing borders and the rights of minorities. When the bankruptcy of this policy was finally apparent, the EC transferred its recognition to the new states of Slovenia and Croatia again without attempting to regulate the conditions for Croatian independence in a way which would have created an acceptable recognition of Serbian minority rights. Its actions only stimulated the war in Croatia, which it then ineffectually attempted to monitor, and paved the way for the war in Bosnia-Hercegovina.

In the final irony, although recognising the new Bosnian state, the West made no attempt to help secure its reality on the ground, but largely abandoned it to its fate. Only when the media made it clear that this potentially included the slow starvation of half a million people in Sarajevo, the 'ethnic cleansing' of over a million Muslims and Croats, massacres and concentration camps, did the pressure of global civil society push the West to define – at the London Conference of August 1992 – the principles with which it should have tried to regulate the situation, politically, from 1989 or 1990 onwards, so as to prevent war. Under this pressure, too, West European military intervention is increasing under UN auspices but without any clear political goals.

The international society ideology of Western states has been cruelly exposed in these crises. *Ad hoc* forces from within the emerging global civil society have proposed different principles of intervention. What is surely required now is to systematise the demands of global responsibility in a new conception of the roles, rights and duties of citizens, society, states, the system of states, and international institutions. Much of the intellectual infrastructure for such a conception is already available in the principles already adopted by international organisations and theoretically subscribed to by states, as well as in the positions adopted by groupings in civil society.

The crucial issue, then, is to face up to the necessity that enforcing these principles would systematically breach the principles of sovereignty and non-intervention. A global society perspective requires recognition in the institutions and culture of the state system of the demands of society for accountability. This must include the increasingly systematic intervention of international society and international institutions in individual states which fail to meet acceptable standards.

This process, moreover, is not merely a matter of disciplining an Iraq or a Serbia, but also involves issues such as the role of the United States, Japan and the European Community states in the distribution of global wealth and the use of energy resources; it could also involve calling the United States to account for unilateral military interventions like those in Grenada and Panama. In this sense, the issues raised are large and the interests threatened are to some extent those of all states. This means, of course, that we are unlikely to see a fundamental and explicit shift in the direction advocated here. The issues are likely to remain foci of contestation over a very long period of time.

The global society perspective, therefore, has an ideological significance which is ultimately opposed to that of international society. No decisive result can be expected, at a political and ideological level, in the conflict between these two positions, for the simple reason that, while the pressures for global responsibility are growing, the strength of the international system and of the Great Powers within it are still formidable.[21] While the global society perspective can no longer be dismissed, as Bull dismissed Falk's earlier raising of global environmental perspectives, as naive or utopian, it is unlikely to become central to world politics in the short or medium term.[22]

What can be done is for international theorists and theorists of global society to clarify the relations between different systems of concepts, with the aim of producing consistent ideas which clarify the new realities of the post-Cold War era. It is to this task that this chapter has addressed itself, in the hopes of pointing out the ideological character and theoretical, historical and political limitations of the international society perspective.

NOTES

1. I have made such an attempt in *Marxism and Social Science: The Roots of Social Knowledge* (London: Pluto Press, 1975); for an auto-critique, see the introduction to the edited work, *Marxist Sociology Revisited* (London: Macmillan, 1985).
2. The term international society and similar theoretical terms are used throughout this chapter without quotation marks. This is not because the author believes that they exist, or that they are appropriate theoretical concepts with which to describe or explain reality, but simply because to use quotation marks would make the text extremely messy. The chapter is about the appropriateness of international society and similar concepts, and the author's views on which of these concepts should be employed will be made clear in due course.
3. Hedley Bull, *The Anarchical Society: A Study of Order in World Politics* (London: Macmillan, 1977), pp. 25–7. Bull's modern classic is referred to here as a representative work.
4. Nicholas J. Wheeler, 'Pluralist or Solidarist Conceptions of International Society: Bull and Vincent on Humanitarian Intervention', *Millennium* (Vol. 21, No. 3, Winter 1992), pp. 463–87. The reader is referred to this article for a fuller exposition of Bull's version of 'international society' theory. I

have benefited considerably from Wheeler's discussion although, as will be seen, there are fundamental differences between our approaches.

5. Bull, *Anarchical Society*, p. 43.
6. Martin Wight, *Systems of States* (Leicester: Leicester University Press, 1977).
7. 'The world society or community whose common good they [theorists of world justice] purport to define does not exist except as an idea or myth which may one day become powerful, but has not done so yet.' Bull, *Anarchical Society*, p. 85.
8. I have discussed these processes in my *Dialectics of War: An Essay on the Social Theory of War and Peace* (London: Pluto, 1988).
9. Anthony Giddens, *The Nation-State and Violence* (Cambridge: Polity, 1985); and Michael Mann, *States, War and Capitalism* (Oxford: Blackwell, 1988).
10. I have discussed this more fully in 'State Theory and the Post-Cold War World', in Michael Banks and Martin Shaw (eds) *State and Society in International Relations* (Hemel Hempstead: Harvester-Wheatsheaf, 1991), pp. 1–19.
11. James Mayall, *Nationalism and International Society* (Cambridge: Cambridge University Press, 1990).
12. James N. Rosenau, *Turbulence in World Politics* (Hemel Hempstead: Harvester-Wheatsheaf, 1990).
13. Barry Buzan, 'New Patterns of Global Security in the Twenty-first Century', *International Affairs* (Vol. 67, No. 3, July 1991), pp. 436–7. Buzan limits this community to the major capitalist powers, but the extensions I discuss seem reasonable developments of his argument.
14. The strengthening of international society is cautiously claimed by Buzan, ibid., pp. 437–9, while reiterating that 'The foundation of modern international society is the mutual recognition by states of each other's claim to sovereignty'. This is, however, precisely what is brought into question by recent developments.
15. The breaches of the principles of sovereignty and non-intervention in the Kurdish case are explained away by Mayall in terms of an international obligation arising 'because the coalition had inflicted such damage on Iraq as to reduce the country to chaos, making rebellion all but inevitable.' He argues that, therefore 'it would be imprudent in practice, and wrong in theory, to generalise from the international obligations towards the Kurds in favour of an international enforcement mechanism for human rights wherever they are abused...the obligation towards the Kurds does not arise from a general principle of human solidarity'. See James Mayall, 'Non-intervention, Self-determination and the "New World Order"', *International Affairs* (Vol. 67, No. 3, July 1991), pp. 427–8. This argument does not, however, deal with the Bosnian case, in which 'a general principle of human solidarity' has indeed been invoked.
16. Bull, *Anarchical Society*, p. 41.

17. See, for example, Ken Booth, 'Security and Emancipation', *Review of International Studies* (Vol. 17, No. 4, October 1991), p. 317, although his alternative is an unsatisfactory individualism. I have discussed the issue in more detail in '"There Is No Such Thing as Society": Beyond Individualism and Statism in International Security Studies', *Review of International Studies* (Vol. 19, No. 2, April 1993), pp. 159–75.
18. Bull, *Anarchical Society*, pp. 59–65.
19. Indeed, Bull dissociates himself from functionalism, ibid., pp. 75–6.
20. A telling discussion of this from an International Relations point of view, which goes from the question 'Is Britain Still Britain?' to 'Can There Still be a "British" Foreign Policy?' is provided by William Wallace, 'British Foreign Policy After the Cold War', *International Affairs* (Vol. 68, No. 1, July 1992), especially pp. 432–42.
21. It is still true, as Bull wrote, that 'the framework of international order is quite inhospitable to projects for the realisation of cosmopolitan or world justice', and almost as inhospitable to those for human justice. See Bull, *Anarchical Society*, pp. 87–8. It is also true, however, that the issues which these terms represent have become stronger and more pressing in the years since Bull's book was published, and notably since the end of the Cold War.
22. Ibid., pp. 302–5; most of his criticisms of Falk hit home, but there is no need for a global-society perspective to entail most of the points which are undermined.

4 A 'City Which Sustains All Things'? Communitarianism and International Society

N.J. Rengger

In the writings of scholars such as Hedley Bull, Martin Wight and Adam Watson, one conception stands out: international society. Unlike many other theorists of international relations, and unlike many political theorists and philosophers who have also written about international topics, these writers make this notion the centrepiece of their accounts. In their writings, international society has a totemic, sometimes all-encompassing importance. It is, for them, the source of values in the international system, values which allow the system to operate as it does. The Romans used to say about the eternal city that it was the 'city which sustains all things'.[1] Such, for writers including Bull, Wight and Watson, is the role of international society for international politics. This chapter, however, argues that their account depends on assumptions that are familiar to some communitarian political theory. Moreover, in the form in which it is presented by these writers at least, the theory of international society is incoherent. This has serious implications for notions of legitimacy and international order, in that these two concepts in particular are held to be dependent upon international society. Finally, I shall discuss what I take to be the implications of this reading of international society for political theory and world politics.

COMMUNITARIANISM IN POLITICAL THEORY

Before turning to the tradition of International Society, it is useful to consider communitarianism in general. Chris Brown has recently suggested that, as far as international relations is concerned, the history of the last two centuries can be written in terms of the debate between cosmopolitanism and communitarianism.[2] While in many senses I would agree with this, in recent political theory, communitarianism is associated with a rejection of a certain kind of liberalism represented by writers such as John Rawls, Robert Nozick and Ronald Dworkin.[3]

The list of prominent communitarians differs slightly from author to author, but a representative selection would include Charles Taylor, Michael Sandel, Alisdair Maclntyre and, usually, Michael Walzer.[4] What, then, are the basic sorts of arguments that communitarians favour? In essence, they have argued that the form of liberalism espoused by writers such as Rawls and Dworkin is insensitive to and, more seriously, hugely underrates the importance of our membership in a community and a culture for social theory. Will Kymlicka has correctly observed that these claims can take at least three forms. First, the claim that liberals exaggerate our capacity to distance or abstract ourselves from our social relationships and hence exaggerate our capacity for, and the value of, individual choice. Second, the claim, present in the work of Charles Taylor, that even if liberals have the right account of individuals' capacity for choice, they ignore the fact that this capacity can only be developed and exercised in a certain kind of social and cultural context. Third, the claim present in a number of communitarian, feminist and Marxist writings to the effect that the liberal emphasis on justice and rights presupposes and perpetuates, certain kinds of conflictual or instrumental relationships that would not exist in a true community.[5]

For some communitarians, however, these assumptions give rise to the view that, in important senses, community creates value. It may, and indeed should, also instantiate values and erect parameters for the criticisms of values, but no values can exist independently of communal identification. In a recent book, Richard Bellamy has suggested that communitarian liberals (such as Walzer, Joseph Raz and, perhaps, though he does not discuss him till later, Richard Rorty) adopt this position and that some other communitarians (for example, MacIntyre) adopt a very different view.[6] I shall concentrate on the communitarian liberal position as this is the form of communitarian argument that we find in the Wight/Bull/Watson understanding of international society.

Walzer expresses his version of this view in the preface to *Spheres of Justice*:

> One way to begin the Philosophical enterprise – perhaps the original way – is to walk out of the cave, leave the city, climb the mountain, fashion for oneself (what can never be fashioned for ordinary men and women) an objective and universal standpoint. Then one describes the terrain of everyday life from far away, so that it loses its particular contours and takes on a general shape. But I mean to stand in the cave, in the city, on the ground. Another way of doing philosophy is to interpret to one's fellow citizens the world of meanings that we share.

> Justice or equality can conceivably be worked out as philosophical artifacts, but a just or egalitarian society cannot be. If such a society isn't already here – hidden, as it were, in our concepts and categories – we will never know it concretely or realise it in fact.[7]

For this type of communitarian, then, it is the necessary embedding of these notions through and in the actual existence of communities, that creates the values to which communities adhere and that constructs the complex web of duties, rights and obligations that makes up a human society. It is this view, in form though not especially in substance, that characterises the writing on international society to which I shall now turn.

INTERNATIONAL SOCIETY AND INTERNATIONAL RELATIONS

As discussed above, the understanding of international society with which this chapter is concerned is a term particularly associated with one group of writers in International Relations – the so-called English or Classical school – and perhaps above all with one individual, Hedley Bull.[8] Although many other writers have also developed a notion of international society in their work, it is the understanding of international society associated with Bull, Wight and Watson that has had most influence.[9] Stanley Hoffmann has suggested that it is with the notion of international society that Bull, in particular, came into his own: 'it is society rather than system which he, virtually alone among contemporary theorists of international affairs, stresses and studies. System means contact between states and the impact of one state on another; society means (in Bull's words) common interests and values, common rules and institutions.'[10]

In this Bull was following the lead established by Martin Wight.[11] For Wight, the idea of international society, found in the work of past political thinkers as varied as Suarez, de Tocqueville, de Visscher and Burke, is best defined as 'the habitual intercourse of independent communities, beginning in the Christendom of Western Europe and gradually extending throughout the world'.[12] The nature of this society, Wight goes on to argue, is:

> manifest in the diplomatic system; in the conscious maintenance of the balance of power to preserve the independence of the member communities; in the regular operations of international law...; in economic, social and technical interdependence and the functional international institutions established...to regulate it. All these presuppose an international social consciousness, a world wide community sentiment.[13]

In Bull and Watson's edited collection, *The Expansion of International Society*, which can almost be read as an extended elaboration of Wight's argument, Bull identifies the First World War as the time by which 'international society', previously primarily self-consciously Eurocentric, had become a universal international society, and the period following the Second World War as that in which attempts were made 'to transform a universal society of states into one of peoples'.[14] Wight, however, implies that international society, as he understood it, accepted that states were not its exclusive members and suggests that it is only in the eighteenth century, with Wolff and Vattel, that there was seen to be a problem with the ascription of international rights to actors with, as it were, non-state personalities. Moreover, this transition was not, Wight believes, entirely eclipsed by the rise of the notion of state personality, expressed in more recent times by, among others, international lawyers such as James Brierly.[15]

In *The Anarchical Society*, Bull builds on Wight's argument, but departs from it in subtle but important ways. For Bull, the idea of international society is conceived by the natural law tradition of the sixteenth to the eighteenth century, most prominently, Victoria, Suarez, Gentili, Grotius, and Pufendorf.[16] This period of international society, according to Bull, has five principal characteristics: Christian values; the aforementioned ambiguity as to the membership of international society; the primacy of natural, as opposed to positive, international law; the assumption of universal society (the *respublica Christiana*); and finally, the lack of a set of institutions deriving from the cooperation of states. Bull's argument goes on to suggest, however, that the notion of the idea of international society develops through two further major stages: 'European international society' and 'world international society'. Bull's conclusion, echoing Wight's assertion of the tension implicit in his most famous essay, 'Western Values in International Relations', is that the element of international society is only one element in world politics, but that '[t]he idea of international society has a basis in reality that is sometimes precarious but has at no stage disappeared.'[17] Bull concludes by attacking notions of 'international anarchy' that ignore the persistence of the idea of international society, as relying too much on an overstated domestic analogy that, in its turn, ignores the elements of uniqueness in the predicament of states and state systems. This uniqueness, according to Bull, was recognised by certain theorists of international society in the eighteenth century and is implicit in the gradual abandonment of the idea of the law of nature in favour of 'law of nations' and ultimately of the adoption of the term international law – initially by Jeremy Bentham.[18] Bull reinforces this claim by reiterating

Wight's point that it was also in the eighteenth century that the key statement that states are the true and proper members of international society is made.[19]

Bull is, moreover, insistent that the notion of society in world politics is intimately connected with ideas of order and legitimacy in world politics. *The Anarchical Society* is, of course, subtitled 'A Study of Order in World Politics'. By order, Bull is clear that he means a pattern or regularity of social life such that it promotes certain goals and values. This will have three component parts; first, the fact that all societies seek to ensure that life will be in some measure secure against violence; second, that all societies will seek to ensure that all agreements, once made, will be kept; and third, that all societies will seek to ensure relative stability of possession. These Bull refers to as the elementary and primary goals of societies. As far as world politics is concerned, then, Bull suggests a division of the notion of order into international order, which he describes as a pattern of activity conducive to the maintenance of the elementary and primary goals of the society of states, and world order, described as a pattern of activity conducive to the maintenance of the elementary and primary goals of human social life as such. The latter, he thinks, is also in important respects prior to the former. He puts it this way, 'World order...is not only wider than international order or order among states, but also more fundamental and primordial than it, and morally prior to it.'[20] Thus, for Bull, not only is international society engaged in a transition from a society of states to one of peoples, but, in addition, it is engaged in an attempt at transition from international order to world order.

It is, of course, the existence and character of international society that confers legitimacy on particular acts in international affairs and illegitimacy on others. The immunity of diplomats, the normative force of international law, and ultimately the coercive sanction of the internal community as a whole is manifested in and through, and only possible because of, the existence of international society. Those who largely agree with Bull and Wight, at least about the centrality of international society, all express relatively similar assumptions.[21] Throughout the International Society literature two basic assumptions are made. First, that international society is a fact, however tenuous and fleeting, of international relations; and second, that this fact creates obligations on the part of the members of the society concerned. It is these two assumptions that has made the alleged fragmentation of contemporary international society so dangerous for Bull. It threatened to undermine all the good that international society, through the promotion of international order, can do.

Inevitably, therefore, the notion of society deployed here is dependent on seeing society and culture as locked in a parasitic embrace. The values and shared understandings that mark out international society must be culturally generated and sustained which, of course, implies that international and/or world order is equally dependent on such cultural generation and maintenance. Thus, the chief problem for theorists who wish to assert that international society is the crucial 'glue' that holds the international system together, is the alleged fragmentation of the western norms that created the society in the first place and, in any case, their questioning or rejection by many in contemporary world politics.[22] Bull himself believed that this fragmentation, although certainly threatened, had not yet fully occurred, and he was relatively optimistic about the prospects for international society.[23] However, as Hoffmann has remarked, this view gave rise to an unresolved tension:

> between Bull's awareness of the special importance of the great powers because of their evident stake in preserving international society...and his awareness of their inadequacy in a global international system in which they cannot fulfil their traditional functions alone anymore – for two reasons: because of the greater capacity of smaller powers to resist and because of the greater potency of ideologies of resistance and of international inequality.[24]

I shall come back to these tensions in a moment but, for now, it is worth repeating that the theory of international society as put forward by Bull and other 'classical' writers is both an empirical fact about how international relations works and a normative claim about what follows in international relations. This is unusual, for other writers who use the term tend to use it in one sense or the other. For Evan Luard, for example, it is an explanatory concept in what amounts to an historical sociology of international relations,[25] whereas for Philip Allott, international society is almost entirely a normative term because, for him, it does not yet exist but must be brought into being.[26] This dual sense that international society has in Bull's writings is the source of some of the problems with the notion; especially when the communitarian aspects of international society are borne in mind. It is to these, then, that the chapter now turns.

COMMUNITARIANISM AND INTERNATIONAL SOCIETY

Before looking at the implications of this analysis for international relations, it would be useful to look at the links between communitarianism and international society. On the surface there does not seem to be much that links them. Communitarianism, in its contemporary guise at least, is about self-contained communities. International society is about a society of such communities. Nonetheless, there are two principle areas where the classical account of international society overlaps with contemporary communitarianism. First, international society becomes something that is contrived: 'artificial' in the Humean sense.[27] It is recognised by states and arises out of their situation in an anarchic world where there are elements of cooperation as much as conflict. As Bull writes, 'The element of international society has always been present in the modern international system because at no stage can it be said that the conception of the common interests of states, of common rules accepted and common rules worked by them, has ceased to exert an influence.'[28] As such, if international society is a genuine society, it is simply because its membership is composed of fictive persons - states, rather than biological ones. Bull effectively gives what Martin Wight termed the rationalist answer to the question 'what is international society?' 'It is a society but different from the state.'[29]

Many communitarians have stressed that their understanding of community is not simply coterminous with the state. Charles Taylor, for example, elaborates a view of the 'modern' identity which implies a certain sense of community which is clearly communitarian but, equally clearly, non-statist.[30] Even Michael Walzer, perhaps the communitarian most obviously committed to what one of his critics has called 'the romance of the nation state',[31] has admitted that the rights people have 'follow from shared conceptions of social goods (that are) local and particular in character'.[32] Such conceptions need not be national or statist, therefore, they might grow out of shared conceptions of particular communities at particular times.

Such, indeed, is how the Wight/Bull International Society tradition portrays the idea of international Society. The assumption that cultural homogeneity is necessary for a 'strong' international society implies that there must be a link of the sort that Walzer and Taylor are talking about - even though Walzer certainly talks of communities as states most of the time. In other words, there is a similarity in the form of the international society and communitarian argument in that each assumes a degree of cultural homogeneity which generates certain shared concerns, interests and values which, in their turn, create, encourage and maintain a set of obligations. 'Within international society', Bull argued, 'order is the *consequence...of a sense of common interests in the elementary goals of social* life.'[33] It is this 'sense of common interests' that creates international society which, in turn, creates the possibility of international order.

Thus, it seems clear that the forms that international society arguments take in the classical school are communitarian in the sense termed by Bellamy as 'Communitarian liberal'. Neither Bull nor Wight nor any of their colleagues argue that there is a form of the good to which all societies - including the society of states - should bend their will; the fact of the society is the source of the obligations that spring from it. This creation is what allows us to talk of an international community or international society and which, therefore, allows us to explain and prescribe in its name. Such an argument clearly follows at least the structure of the sort of argument that communitarian liberals deploy in their critique of 'atomistic' liberals.[34]

COMMUNITARIANISM, INTERNATIONAL SOCIETY AND WORLD POLITICS

In so far as international society is a form of communitarianism, what are the implications of this? I shall argue that the principal arguments derived from the premises of international society as sketched above are not sustainable if those premises are communitarian in the sense suggested.

As already pointed out, international society has both an explanatory and an ethical focus. These have an obvious connection in that, as far as its account of the nature of the international system is concerned, the tradition of International Society is perfectly right to stress those aspects of the history of world politics that have often been dropped, ignored or marginalised by more mechanistic accounts. However, there are two points to be made here. The first, as implied earlier, is that the historical story told by theorists of international society is itself open to serious revision. To give just one example, understandings of the work of Grotius which emphasise that Grotius is following on from the 'tradition' of Vitoria,[35] under-rate the extent to which Grotius is distancing himself from the positions of Vitoria by echoing the work of writers opposed to the latter in important respects, such as Suarez, Sepulvada and Luis De Molina.[36] The significance of this is that it implies that (a) understandings of international society do not make sense outside wider ethical and political frameworks including self-conscious theories of the state – one of the sources of the differences between Grotius and Vitoria; and (b) that, as a result, the so-called 'tradition' of International Society is in fact a scissors-and-paste construct taken from a wide variety of past traditions. As Roberts and Kingsbury have noted and other communitarians (such as Alisdair

MacIntyre) make patently clear, the notion of an intellectual tradition is deeply problematic and the use to which Wight and Bull, for example, put it is highly stipulative.[37]

A second, and more obviously theoretical problem, however, is the character of the 'rules' and 'norms' that are held to be the basis of the 'common values' which are manifest in international society. In this, the theorists of international society are close to some realists (for example, Reinhold Niebuhr, Walter Lippman, Hans Morgenthau and George Kennan),[38] some critical theorists (Robert Cox and Andrew Linklater)[39] and some recent normative theorists (Terry Nardin)[40] in holding a 'reflective' view of international politics. I use the term 'reflective' in the same manner as Robert O. Keohane in his article, 'International Institutions: Two Approaches', in which he suggests that there are two sets of approaches to the study of international institutions in particular and international politics in general.[41] Keohane terms the first 'rationalistic', which he argues covers a wide variety of different approaches that accept what Herbert Simon called a 'substantive' conception of rationality - that is, this view characterises 'behaviour that can be judged objectively to be optimally adapted to the situation'.[42] Thus neo-realist theories of international politics would be avowedly rationalistic. Keohane also believes his own work is rationalistic. The second group consists of those writers who have emphasised that:

> individuals, local organizations and even states develop within the context of more encompassing institutions...it is not sufficient in this view to treat the preferences of individuals as given exogenously: they are affected by institutional arrangements, by prevailing norms, and by historically contingent discourse among people seeking to pursue their purposes and solve their self-defined problems.[43]

To those who argue this, Keohane gives the name 'reflective' – 'since all of them emphasise the importance of human reflection for the nature of institutions and ultimately for the character of world politics'.[44]

It is clear that the International Society tradition would fit into this second category. However, advocates of international society would adopt a rather different emphasis to those whom Keohane cites in his article: Richard Ashley, Hayward Alker, John Ruggie, Friedrich Kratochwil and Robert Cox. These writers, as Keohane says, are 'imbued with a sociological perspective on institutions [and] emphasise that institutions are often not created consciously by human beings but rather emerge slowly through a less deliberative process'.[45] The classical school, conversely, stresses that it is precisely human artifice and invention that has created international society, though it has often arisen, of course, from circumstances that are not of humans' own intentional making. It is worth mentioning also that this characterisation very neatly fits Taylor's description of a 'holistic' ontology, which he applies to communitarians to distinguish them from 'atomistic' liberals, thus reinforcing the communitarian overtones of ideas about international society.

A question arises, however, over the character of the artifice and the forms of cooperation to which it gives rise. For 'international society' to be a 'fact', it must include norms, rules and procedures that are not simply rules of thumb but which are able to create illocutionary and normative force. This is where the empirical/explanatory and the normative arguments depend on one another. People must believe in these 'common values' for them to have any explanatory purchase and it is because they believe them that they create obligation. Lastly, it is because they create obligation that international society can help to explain international order which is not just equilibrium or stability. This explanatory capacity is an important factor that separates the tradition of international society from various forms of realism.

This emphasises a significant point. International society is in important respects a quasi-contractarian type of argument despite its tacit Humean assumptions: because we have created certain institutions and we must rely on them for our continued peaceable existence, we should accept the obligations that arise out of them.[46] However, it is communitarian contractarianism and, therefore, it is in this context that the true significance of the communitarian basis of international society becomes apparent. Unlike many other reflective writers on world politics, for example, some critical theorists, the theory of international society is voluntarist, not only in the obvious sense that if people do not accept an ethical view it is unlikely to receive much attention or act as a justifying reason for action, but also in the strong sense, in that it is our creation and acceptance of the norms of international society that alone creates the obligation to follow them. Thus, the appeals that Bull and others make on behalf of international society are a curious blend of the ethical and the self-interested; they are thus characterised by what we might call, following Humean language, 'weak' altruists.

There are two problems with this. The first is to decide if such arguments can provide us with a way of adjudicating debates within a shared system of values (i.e. how can disputes within international society be resolved?). The second is to ask whether such arguments can provide us with reasons for action that permit us to sacrifice self-interest to duty. For, if we are not to end up adopting effectively realist assumptions, whatever we add by way of pious language, then international society must be able to create at least some obligations that are binding on us whatever our self-interest.

The most recent and sophisticated communitarian defence to the first objection is provided by Walzer who suggests that dispute within a community is usually settled by whoever can give the most 'authentic' interpretation of the community.[47] However, as Brian Barry has pointed out:

> Surely the issue is not who can claim most of the tradition but who can claim the best of it...but if once we allow a social critic to say that, although he is not offering the most authentic reconstruction of the whole cultural tradition, he is picking out the bits worth preserving, we cannot avoid asking: How does the critic decide which are the good bits?[48]

In the case of international society, the problem is all the more pressing. Bull, for example, expects us to ask questions of the sort 'what are the patterns of activity supportive of the society of states?' Can we answer this, however, unless there is, at least potentially, some standard outside the existing 'patterns of activity' which could allow us to say that A rather than B under circumstances X are more appropriate. As a form of ethical judgement it also slides imperceptibly into a rather curious act of utilitarianism with a sliding scale of values; in principle nothing is forbidden; it depends on whatever the 'consensus of shared values' happens to permit at any given time. Witness, for example, the ever-increasing slippage in the laws of war from the early modern period to our own.[49]

Given the above, it seems that the nature of rule following within the international system cannot be explained by the existence of international society as understood by Bull or Wight; nor can the notion prescribe ethical action in the required sense, as the consensus that forms international society and provides the framework for ethical decision is always a moving target. While it might be the case that states will cooperate for self-interested reasons, such actions do not need the Bullian notion of international society to explain them, as writers such as Robert Axelrod, Robert Keohane, Kenneth Oye and Robert Jervis have shown.[50] The only way of asserting otherwise is if the existence of international society could provide a way of explaining international politics, and especially the normative component of international politics, that gives us additional reasons for supposing, for example, that a state's obligations should compel it to act even if it is not in its self-interest to do so. Yet one cannot provide that on the sort of communitarian logic that structures such accounts of international society, as they rely on ethical norms as the creation of a particular consensus on ethical values: if a state does not share in them, while it might be forced to comply, it is under no ethical obligation to do so, except a prudential one. Of course, it is precisely this problem that makes it easy to see why Bull, for example, oscillated so much between a semi-realist position, especially in his early work, and the quasi-cosmopolitanism of the *Hagey Lectures*.[51] Yet this means that, while it provides more than just a useful corrective to many of the rationalistic interpretations of the international system currently on offer, the tradition of international society, as outlined and defended by the classical school, is ultimately incoherent.

AFTER 'INTERNATIONAL SOCIETY'?

What, then, is left if we assume that the notion of international society, in its currently most influential form, is not an effective option? In what follows, I want to look at three possible avenues of approach, all of the reflective type mentioned above. I shall assume that the reflective path has at least as much to offer as the rationalist one when it comes to understanding the nature of world politics. Of course, I do not want to suggest that either possesses a monopoly on truth, but since the rationalist approach in general has been much more thoroughly explored, I want to look at what options might be open to those inclined to a more reflective approach and suggest what the implications of my argument so far might be for such options.

The first option would be to move beyond the relatively straightforward communitarianism manifested by the classical school and, indeed, many other normatively inclined theories of world politics, into postmodern or poststructural interpretations of our contemporary circumstances. This indeed is a step that a growing number of reflective theorists are making – for example, Hayward Alker, Richard Ashley, David Campbell, James Der Derian, Jim George and Rob Walker.[52] The advantages of these approaches – there are a wide variety of them[53] – have been well articulated by Walker and Der Derian in two recent books which stress features of contemporary world politics marginalised by normal discussion; to wit the sense of spatio-temporal fragmentation that characterises world politics.[54]

A second and related option is to continue and deepen the investigation of the nature of the rules and norms that govern world politics and, as a result, reformulate the understanding of international society and what helps to constitute it. Such an option would very often incorporate much of the traditional view of international society, but its diagnosis and prognosis of the nature of world politics in general and international society in particular would be very different. Moreover, it would require much empirical and historical work. Normative projects of this kind are visible in the writings of, among others, Terry Nardin, Friedrich Kratochwil, Nicholas Onuf and, in some respects, the work of Allott referred to earlier.[55] More empirical work in this area, though it also has normative and (especially in the latter case) theoretical reference, includes work as varied as that of Robert H. Jackson, James Mayall and Justin Rosenberg.[56]

Both sets of projects have much to recommend them. However, there is a third way forward for reflective theorists. This is to attempt to formulate an understanding of world politics that can provide us with a reason for assuming 'strong altruism' in world politics and that articulates what Brown has called both moral and institutional cosmopolitanism.[57] There are, of course, a number of ways in which such a project can be attempted. One such, for example, is Onora O'Neill's articulation of a Kantian cosmopolitan view of international justice and ethics.[58] O'Neill's view is, in this, sense related to the work of those, like Charles Beitz and Linklater, who have also advocated a cosmopolitan approach to international relations.[59] However, the difference is the extent to which it attempts to integrate the moral and institutional demands of the cosmopolitan approach and is rooted on a substantial rearticulation of the basis of Kantian Practical reason.[60] The strength of this view is that it recognises the necessity of linking the normative and explanatory parts of the enterprise in a particular way, such that it makes our understanding of the character of the moral life central for both explanation and prescription. Such a project involves more than a rethinking of modes of certain forms of reasoning in the modern world; it would amount to a complete reconceptualisation of the nature of the modern world and how we should see it both empirically and ethically.

This approach would integrate aspects of the other two types of reflectivism in that it would necessarily involve the problematisation of 'modernity' understood as that complex web of associations, processes and practices that comprise the modern world. However, it would assert much more strongly than either the centrality of ethical (and even perhaps aesthetic) modes of reasoning and judgement in our understanding of that phenomenon. In other words, in seeing such modes of judgement as central to our explanation of – as well as to our normative thinking about – modernity.

Within this reconceptualisation there would, of necessity, be a place for notions of international society. In our current circumstances, the identification of a non-communitarian liberal way of conceiving the notion of international society is central to the articulation of a sense of practical reasoning in contemporary world politics – of both an ethical and a prudential sort[61] – that can give us ways of discussing, for example, order and legitimacy in world politics that are neither drained of normative content nor simply masks for otherwise exogenous preferences or interests.[62] Such an account, however, would situate understandings of international society in a much wider historical and normative frame of reference than does the work of writers in the 'international society tradition'. As O'Neill recognises, it would also enable us to integrate aspects of the communitarian approach, especially those that are not so strongly committed to the communitarian liberal ideas defined above.[63] I would suggest, however, that such an activity might take us beyond the acceptable limits of Kantian practical reasoning and that we might need to rearticulate aspects of the real classical tradition, of Plato, Aristotle and the Stoics if we are to retrieve our otherwise failing sense of the political.[64]

Be that as it may, such a way of seeing the nature and character of world politics would put paid to the pride of place notions of international society have in the works of Wight, Bull, Watson and their colleagues. There will, of course, be a need for a conceptualisation of the links that bind our political communities together and we should reflect on the character and force of the obligations they engender. However, the best way of reconceiving the nature of international society is to recognise that, in such a view, it will no longer be a unique and specific set of obligations either of 'states' or 'peoples' it will be one, among many, of the complex matrix of understandings and obligations that shape our sense of self and other, of individual, community and world. No longer will it be, in any sense, the 'city that sustains all things'.

NOTES

This chapter was written while I was a visiting fellow at the Centre for International Studies at the LSE. I am very grateful to James Mayall and the staff of the Centre for their hospitality and for the collegiality and scholarly companionship of my other fellows. I am also very grateful for discussions with a number of people in the Government and International Relations Departments at the LSE, especially Brian Barry, Mark Hoffman, Brendan O'Leary and Justin Rosenberg. A slightly different version of this paper was given both at the ECPR joint sessions of workshops 1992 held at Limerick, Republic of Ireland and at the Essex Human Rights centre conference on 'Legitimacy and Territoriality'. I am grateful to all participants for their comments, but was helped especially by James Mayall (again), Robert Jackson,

Barry Buzan, Barbara Allen Roberson and Adam Watson at Limerick and Onora O'Neill and Debbie Fitzmaurice at Essex.

1. The phrase is from Lactantius, 'Divinae Institutiones', *Corpus Scriptorum Ecclesiasticorum Latinorum.*
2. Chris Brown, *International Relations Theory: New Normative Approaches* (Hemel Hempstead: Harvester, 1992).
3. See John Rawls, *A Theory of Justice* (Oxford: Oxford University Press, 1971); Robert Nozick, *Anarchy, State and Utopia* (New York, NY: Basic Books, 1974); and Ronald Dworkin, *Taking Rights Seriously* (London: Duckworth, 1977).
4. See Charles Taylor, *Sources of the Self* (Cambridge: Cambridge University Press, 1989); Michael Sandel, *Liberalism and The Limits of Justice* (Cambridge: Cambridge University Press, 1986); Alisdair MacIntyre, *After Virtue* (London: Duckworth, 1981 [second edition, 1987]); MacIntyre, *Whose Justice? Which Rationality?* (London: Duckworth, 1988); MacIntyre, *Three Rival Versions of Moral Inquiry* (London: Duckworth, 1990); Michael Walzer, *Just and Unjust Wars* (London: Pelican, 1977); and Walzer, *Spheres of Justice* (Cambridge: Cambridge University Press, 1983).
5. Will Kymlicka, *Liberalism, Community and Culture* (Oxford: The Clarendon Press, 1991), pp. 1–2.
6. See Richard Bellamy, *Liberalism and Modern Society* (Cambridge: Polity, 1992), chap. 5.
7. Walzer, *Spheres of Justice*, p. xiv. Walzer does sometimes talk of some allegedly universal standards of ethical judgement, but does not give any real reason for believing in them, and the structure of his argument is thoroughly communitarian.
8. I am very uncertain about terminology here as there are good reasons for rejecting all such labels. For convenience, references to the classical school refer to the writings primarily of Martin Wight, Hedley Bull, Adam Watson and Herbert Butterfield and, to an extent, to the writings of some other members of the British Committee for International Theory, that they successively chaired. However, that there were many differences between these writers as well as similarities is quite apparent. On the understanding of International Society, however, they largely agreed. For discussions of the 'English School', see Roy E. Jones, 'The English School of International Relations: A Case for Closure', *Review of International Studies* (Vol. 7, No. 1, 1981), pp. 1–12; and N.J. Rengger 'Serpents and Doves in Classical International Theory', *Millennium: Journal of International Studies* (Vol. 17, No. 2, Summer 1988), pp. 215–25.
9. It is well known that Bull's writings have been much less influential in the United States where he has been regarded with a variety of emotions ranging from wary respect to complete hostility and lack of comprehension. In part, this is doubtless because of Bull's well-known and virulent critiques of the

scientific method, as well as his undoubtedly abrasive and combative manner. It is also worth bearing in mind that those American scholars who were closest to Bull (Stanley Hoffmann, for example) were themselves not usually devotees of the 'scientific' approach to world politics that was, and remains, dominant in American treatments of these subjects. Nonetheless, in some recent work, American scholars, even of a positivist inclination, have begun to suggest that Bull's emphasis on international society might be fruitful. This is especially true of some of those associated with an 'institutionalist' or regime centred approach. See, for example, Robert Keohane, 'International Institutions: Two Approaches', in Robert O. Keohane, *International Institutions and State Power* (Boulder, CO: Westview Press, 1989), pp. 158-82; and the essays by Donald J. Puchala, Raymond F. Hopkins, and Oran Young in Stephen D. Krasner (ed.), *International Regimes* (Ithaca, NY: Cornell University Press, 1982). For a fuller discussion of this linkage, see Tony Evans and Peter Wilson, 'Regime Theory and the English School of International Relations: A Comparison' in *Millennium: Journal of International Studies* (Vol. 21. No. 3), pp. 329–51. See also, Hedley Bull, *The Anarchical Society: A Study of Order in World Politics* (London: Macmillan, 1977) and, for examples of his critiques of the scientific method, Bull, 'International Theory: The Case for a Classical Approach', *World Politics* (Vol. XVIII, April 1966) pp. 361–77; and Bull, 'New Directions in the Theory of International Relations', *International Studies* (Vol. 14, No. 2, 1975), pp. 158–79.

10. Stanley Hoffmann, 'International Society', in J.D.B. Miller and R.J. Vincent (eds), *Order and Violence: Hedley Bull and International Relations* (Oxford: The Clarendon Press, 1990), p. 22.
11. Aspects of this section are drawn from my analysis in, 'Culture, Society and Order in World Politics', in John Baylis and N.J. Rengger (eds), *Dilemmas of World Politics* (Oxford: Clarendon Press, 1992), pp. 86–8.
12. Martin Wight, 'Western Values in International Relations', in Herbert Butterfield and Martin Wight (eds), *Diplomatic Investigations* (London: Allen and Unwin, 1966), pp. 86–98.
13. Ibid., pp. 96–7.
14. Hedley Bull, 'The Emergence of a Universal International Society' ch. 7 in Hedley Bull and Adam Watson (eds), *The Expansion of International Society* (Oxford: Clarendon Press, 1986), pp. 117–126, quote pp. 125–6.
15. See, for example, James L. Brierly, *The Law of Nations*, 2nd edn (Oxford: Oxford University Press, 1936).
16. This development is covered brilliantly by Richard Tuck in his *Natural Rights Theories* (Cambridge: Cambridge University Press, 1979). Although he does not discuss Gentili, his account is very different and, in my opinion at least, much more satisfactory than Bull's. See, for a full appreciation of the development of modern natural law and the errors in Bull's version of it: Francisco De Vitoria, *Commentarios a la Secunda Secundae de Santo*

Tomas (ed.) by V.B. de Heredia, (Salamanca, 1934); Domingo De Soto, *De Iustitia et Iure* (Salamanca, 1553); Franciso Suarez, *De Legibus ac Deo Legislatore* (Coimbra, 1612); Alberico Gentili, *De Jure Belli Libri Tres* [1598] (London: James Brown Scott, 1964); Hugo Grotius, *De Iure Praedae* (The Hague, 1607); Grotius, *De Jure Belli ac Pacis* (Paris, 1625); and Samuel Pufendorf, *De Iure Naturae et Gentium* (1672). Part of the problem with the reading of these writers given by Wight, Bull and others is that they pay insufficient attention to the context of the evolution of these ideas. For example, in *The Anarchical Society,* Bull references Kelsey's 1925 translation of Grotius's *De Jure Belli ac Pacis* (Oxford: The Clarendon Press). As Tuck points out, however, (*Natural Rights Theories*, p. 73, n. 31), many of the most easily available translations are based on the heavily revised printing of *De Jure* published in 1631. This can distort the perception of both Grotius's intentions and the internal structure of his thought. While this is only a minor point in the current context, it leads, I think, to some very significant distortions in Bull's view of the historical origin and provenance of the notion of international society. I have discussed these points more fully in 'Discovering Traditions? Grotius, International Society and International Relations', in *The Oxford International Review* (Vol. 3, No. 1, Winter 1991), pp. 47–50.

17. See Wight, 'Western Values'; and Bull, *Anarchical Society*, p. 4.
18. See Jeremy Bentham, *The Principles of Morals and Legislation* (New York, NY: Hafner, 1948) p. 326.
19. Bull's assertion of this point is backed up with a reference to Vattel's *Droit Des Gens* but again, I think that the intellectual history of the eighteenth century is much murkier than Bull would have it. The notion of 'state personality' is already present in the writings of Pufendorf, but in both Pufendorf and Vattel it should not, I think, be taken to assume the existence of no other rights. As Tony Carty points out in *The Decay of International Law* (Manchester: Manchester University Press, 1986), p. 90, Vattel is asserting a legal category for the interpretation of state conduct when he asserts the principle of non-intervention and assumes states as entities – there is little else in his notion. Moreover, many other eighteenth-century theorists writing on international topics, for example David Hume, adopted very different perspectives. See David Hume, *Essays: Moral, Political and Literary*, Eugene F. Miller (ed.), (Indianapolis, IN: Liberty Classics, 1985), especially his writings on the balance of power (pp. 332–41) and the balance of trade (pp. 308–326).
20. Bull, *Anarchical Society*, p. 315.
21. See, for example, Robbie Purnell, *The Society of States* (London: Allen and Unwin, 1972); Murray Forsyth, H.M.A. Keens-Soper and Peter Savigear (eds), *The Theory of International Relations* (London: Allen and Unwin, 1970); and the group of writers involved in the project which has led (thus far) to three edited collections: Michael Donelan (ed.), *The Reason of States*

(London: Allen and Unwin, 1978); James Mayall (ed.), *The Community of States* (London: Allen and Unwin, 1982); and Cornelia Navari (ed.), *The Condition of States* (Milton Keynes: Open University Press, 1991). Perhaps the two best recent statements are James Mayall, *Nationalism and International Society* (Cambridge: Cambridge University Press, 1990); and Robert H. Jackson, *Quasi-States: Sovereignty, International Relations and The Third World* (Cambridge: Cambridge University Press, 1990). I should stress that I do not suggest that these writers are at all slavish followers of Bull and Wight, only that they take the Bull/Wight notion of international society as their starting-point.

22. For a discussion of this, though I have some doubts about this argument now, see N.J. Rengger, 'Incommensurability, International Theory and the Fragmentation of Western Political Culture', in John Gibbins (ed.), *Contemporary Political Culture* (London: Sage, 1989), pp. 237–50.
23. See the 'Conclusion' to Bull and Watson (eds), *Expansion*, pp. 425–35.
24. Hoffmann, 'International Society', p. 31.
25. See, for example, Evan Luard, *Types of International Society* (New York, NY: The Free Press, 1976). A similar sense is observable in Marcel Merle, *Sociologie Des Relations Internationales* [4th edn] (Paris: Dalloz, 1988), although Merle does not use the term.
26. See Philip Allott, *Eunomia: New Order For A New World* (Oxford: Oxford University Press, 1990).
27. Hume famously refers to justice as an artificial virtue in both the *Treatise of Human Nature* and the second *Enquiry, (Enquiry Concerning the Principles of Morals)*. In the *Treatise* he gives his best elaboration of the notion when he remarks that 'there are some virtues that produce pleasure and approbation by means of an artifice or contrivance which arise from the circumstances and necessities of mankind', David Hume, *Treatise of Human Nature*, edited by L.A. Selby Bigge, revised by P.H. Nidditch (Oxford: The Clarendon Press, 1978), p. 477. It is worth pointing out that Hume added that 'though the rules of justice be artificial they be not arbitrary' (Book III, Part 2, Section 1, p. 484). This is effectively how Bull, especially, sees international society; arising from the circumstances and necessities of mankind and in that sense artificial, a human contrivance, but not an arbitrary one that can be changed at will.
28. Bull, *The Anarchical Society*, p. 42.
29. See Martin Wight, *International Theory: The Three Traditions*, Brian Porter and Gabrielle Wight (eds), (Leicester: Leicester University Press, for the Royal Institute for International Affairs, 1992), p. 48.
30. See Taylor, *Sources*, especially parts 1 and 3.
31. See David Luban, 'Just War and Human Rights', in Charles Beitz *et al.*, *International Ethics* (Princeton, NJ: Princeton University Press, 1981), pp. 195–216.
32. Walzer, *Spheres of Justice*, p. xv.

33. Bull, *Anarchical Society*, p. 65. Emphasis added.
34. For a distinction between liberals and communitarians that relies on the distinction between (respectively) atomistic and holistic ontologies, see Charles Taylor, 'Cross Purposes: The Liberal-Communitarian Debate' in Nancy Rosenblum (ed.), *Liberalism and the Moral Life* (Cambridge, MA: Harvard University Press, 1989), pp. 159–82.
35. This, of course, is Bull's argument which has recently been repeated and amplified by Adam Roberts and Ben Kingsbury in their excellent, 'Introduction: Grotian Thought in International Relations' to Hedley Bull, Adam Roberts and Ben Kingsbury (eds), *Hugo Grotius and International Relations* (Oxford: The Clarendon Press, 1990), pp. 1–64.
36. For a detailed discussion, see Rengger, 'Discovering Traditions', pp. 48–9; and Tuck, *Natural Rights Theories*, chs 4, 7 and 8.
37. See Roberts and Kingsbury, 'Introduction'; Alisdair MacIntyre, *After Virtue* (London: Duckworth, 1981, 2nd edn 1987); MacIntyre, *Whose Justice? Which Rationality?* (London: Duckworth, 1988); and *Three Rival Versions of Moral Enquiry* (London: Duckworth 1990).
38. For a good discussion of these writers which indicates why I think they are very close to many International-Society-type arguments, see Joel Rosenthal, *Righteous Realists: Responsible Power and American Culture in the Nuclear Age* (Baton Rouge, LA: University of Louisiana Press, 1991).
39. See Robert Cox, *Production, Power and World Order* (Oxford: Oxford University Press, 1990); Andrew Linklater, *Men and Citizens in International Theory* [2nd edn] (London: Macmillan, 1990); and Linklater, *Beyond Realism and Marxism: Critical Theory and International Relations* (London: Macmillan, 1989).
40. Terry Nardin, *Law, Morality and the Relations of States* (Princeton, NJ: Princeton University Press, 1983).
41. See Robert O. Keohane, 'International Institutions: Two Approaches', chap. 7, in his, *International Institutions and State Power* (Boulder, CO: Westview, 1989), pp. 158–179.
42. Keohane, ibid., p. 160, citing Herbert Simon, 'Human Nature in Politics: The Dialogue of Psychology with Political Science', *American Political Science Review* (Vol. 79, No. 2, 1985), pp. 293–304.
43. Ibid., p. 161.
44. Ibid., p. 161.
45. Ibid., p. 170.
46. For a very different, but related and explicitly contractarian, argument, see John Charvet, 'Contractarianism in International Political Theory' (unpublished paper, 1992).
47. See Michael Walzer, *Interpretation and Social Criticism* (Cambridge, MA: Harvard University Press, 1987) and *The Company of Critics: Social Criticism and Political Commitment in The Twentieth Century* (New York, NY: Basic Books, 1988).

48. Brian Barry, 'Social Criticism and Political Philosophy', ch. 1, in Barry, *Liberty and Justice: Essays in Political Theory 2* (Oxford: The Clarendon Press, 1991), pp. 9–22, quote pp. 18–19.
49. A good discussion is James Turner Johnson, *Ideology, Reason and the Limitation of War* (Princeton, NJ: Princeton University Press, 1975); and *Just War Tradition and The Restraint of War* (Princeton, NJ: Princeton University Press, 1981).
50. See, for example, Robert Axelrod, *The Evolution of Co-operation* (New York, NY: Basic Books, 1984); and Kenneth A. Oye (ed.), *Co-operation Under Anarchy* (Princeton, NJ: Princeton University Press, 1985).
51. Compare, for example, Hedley Bull, *The Control of the Arms Race* (London: Weidenfeld and Nicholson, for the International Institute for Strategic Studies, 1961); and Bull, *Justice in International Relations: The Hagey Lectures* (Waterloo, Ont.: University of Waterloo, October 1984).
52. See, for example, the special issue of *International Studies Quarterly* (Vol. 34, No. 3, September 1990), Richard K. Ashley and Rob Walker (eds); R.B.J. Walker, *Inside/Outside: International Relations as Political Theory* (Cambridge: Cambridge University Press, 1992); James Der Derian and Michael Shapiro (eds), *International/Intertextual Relations: Postmodern Readings of World Politics* (Lexington, MA: Lexington Books, 1989); and James Der Derian, *On Diplomacy: A Genealogy of Western Estrangement* (Oxford: Basil Blackwell, 1987).
53. See N.J. Rengger, 'No Time like the Present? Postmodernism and Political Theory', *Political Studies* (Vol. XL, No. 3, September 1992), pp. 561–70.
54. Walker, *Inside/Outside*; and Der Derian *Anti-Diplomacy*.
55. Terry Nardin, *Law, Morality and The Relations of States* (Princeton, NJ: Princeton University Press, 1983); Friedrich Kratochwil, *Rules, Norms and Decisions: On the Conditions of Legal Reasoning in International Relations and Domestic Affairs* (Cambridge: Cambridge University Press, 1989); and Nicholas Onuf, *World Of Our Making* (Columbia, SC: University of South Carolina Press, 1989).
56. Jackson, *Quasi-States*; Mayall, *Nationalism and International Society*; and Justin Rosenberg 'What's the Matter with Realism?', *The Review of International Studies* (Vol. 16, No. 4, October 1990), pp. 285–304; and 'Secret Origins of the State: The Structural Basis of Raison d'état', *The Review of International Studies* (Vol. 18, No. 2, April 1992), pp. 131–60.
57. Brown, personal discussion with author. See also his *International Relations Theory*.
58. See Onora O'Neill, 'Transnational Justice', chap. 7, in David Held (ed.), *Political Theory Today* (Oxford: Polity, 1991), pp. 276–304; *Constructions of Reason* (Cambridge: Cambridge University Press, 1989); and *Faces of Hunger* (London, 1986). Another account of world politics sharing aspects of this project is, I think, Ken Booth's advocacy of a 'utopian realism'. See

his 'Security in Anarchy: Utopian Realism in Security and Practice', *International Affairs* (Vol. 67, No. 3, July 1991), pp. 527–46.

59. Charles Beitz, *Political Theory and International Relations* (Princeton, NJ: Princeton University Press, 1979); Linklater, *Men and Citizens.*
60. See O'Neill, *Constructions of Reason.*
61. For a first attempt at the implications of this in the context of international order, see N.J. Rengger, 'No Longer "A Tournament of Distinctive Knights": Systemic Transition and the Priority of International Order', ch. 7, in Robin Brown and Mike Bowker (eds), *From Cold War to Collapse: Theory and World Politics in the 1980s* (Cambridge: Cambridge University Press, 1993), pp. 143–74.
62. O'Neill agrees with this point. See her comment in 'Transnational Justice' that embedding a truly cosmopolitan conception of justice would need very considerable institutional reform in world politics as much as theoretical and normative work. O'Neill, 'Transnational Justice'.
63. See her forthcoming book *Justice and the Virtues.*
64. See N.J. Rengger, 'Political Philosophy and World Politics', paper to the BISA Conference, Swansea, 1992, where I have made a start at elaborating the specifics of this approach.

5 Hedley Bull and the Idea of Diplomatic Culture[1]

James Der Derian

> A text is not a line of words releasing a single 'theological' meaning (the 'message' of the Author-God) but a multi-dimensional space in which a variety of writings, none of them original, blend and clash.
>
> Roland Barthes, *The Death of the Author*[2]

Why one idea of an author resonates and travels in international theory while another falls silent (or upon deaf ears) and stays provincial is a difficult and, in this case, a somewhat morbid question, both in the personal sense and in the social sense that Gramsci identified as symptomatic of a society or theory dying before a new one could be born. The author in question is Hedley Bull; the other idea is diplomatic culture.

This essay examines the importance of diplomatic culture in Bull's understanding of international society, but takes a critical step further to ask whether it is time to revive and expand our understanding of diplomatic culture as forces of fragmentation appear ascendant in world politics. The task is not an easy one. Apart from the conceptual and definitional difficulties attending an analysis of any type of culture, contemporary neglect of the idea of diplomatic culture can be attributed in part to the general stasis of the classical or 'English' school of International Relations theory at a time when diplomacy has undergone rapid transformation.[3] However, other factors must also be taken into account, not least the reluctance of the prevailing positivist approaches of North American International Relations to take culture seriously. Both these reasons will be investigated in this essay, not only in the context of Hedley Bull's own writings on the subject but also in light of the introduction of critical theory into debates in the discipline. Besides being one small way to learn from and to honour a thinker who filled large gaps in our knowledge of international relations, such an investigation might just enhance the prospects for a cosmopolitan diplomatic culture as well as a more open international theory.

In terms less familiar for the field, the purpose of this chapter is theoretically to deconstruct, genealogically reconstruct, and dialogically imagine Bull's idea of diplomatic culture.[4] This means that this essay will mimic the dialogic of diplomacy, speaking not *of* but *to* an other. This particular, irreplaceable other, or in Roland Barthes' language, 'Author-God' might be dead, but his text is not. Not only to compensate for an uncomfortable asymmetry, not merely to overcome the disquieting silence evoked by the proximal death of an author-mentor, but out of recognition of the consequentiality as opposed to the intentionality of Hedley Bull, the critic must in response *reopen* the text to new interpretations, different periods, and most importantly, other texts. As expressed by Mikhail Bakhtin and after him Barthes, what gives meaning to, what makes *possible* the text is this very intertextuality. The task then is to situate Bull's seminal idea of diplomatic culture, not just at the important historical points of influence with others within his own cohort of classical thinkers, but also at some of the intellectual crossroads like continental philosophy which he looked down, often with an eyebrow raised in scepticism, but never travelled. Such a strategy of reading does not measure Bull's contributions to international theory by his stature at death, which was by all accounts considerable, but by the philosophical openness of his texts which continue to give them a rich interpretive life after his death.

There are several ways not to approach the idea of diplomatic culture. The definitional route to understanding any cultural concept is so strewn with proprietary claims that one would hope for an authoritative sign, such as 'See Dictionary'. However, this would provide only a semantical detour rather than the required interpretive description. My own interpretation is that diplomatic culture is about understanding and bringing alien peoples into the dominant international discourse of the day, and that a diplomatic culture facilitates movement – of ideas, people, and sometimes even armies – across alien boundaries. As a student of diplomacy, I do not intend to test this view against Hedley Bull's concept of diplomatic culture through a systematic, ethnographic study of foreign cultures; nor do I intend to voyage heroically to distant lands, in the manner of noted anthropologists like Geertz, Mead or Evans-Pritchard, to observe and interpret the illusive meaning of, say, conversations and behaviour at a diplomatic reception.[5] Rather, I wish to present an argument for the important *meta-theoretical* role diplomatic culture plays in Hedley Bull's work on international society, in the sense of how we think and set the terms by which we judge international relations in general.

To make of diplomatic culture, as well as its study, something more than how one state in practice gets something from another state, or how the critic in thought gets something from a silent other, a critical inquiry or genealogy must be made into the heterologue, or in Bakhtin's term, the *polyphony* which surrounded Bull at the time he began to play with the idea of diplomatic culture. Clearly, Bull was not one to decry intellectual rigour or resist making judgements in his work. Indeed, in 'International Theory: The Case for a Classical Approach' he famously – as well as polemically – promoted both activities over the sterile methodologies of the behaviourists.[6]

Thirty years on, his advice still holds against those who would like International Relations to be only a continuation of behaviourism by other means, most notably, positivist, rational choice ones. In support of Bull, I would argue that the internal monologue of many of the positivists in the discipline, which in the name of parsimonious theory, aims at and valorises logical closure, excludes any inquiry into diplomatic culture which is constructed from an open, and often intentionally ambiguous dialogue. This inability of the positivists to recognise, let alone engage in, meta-theoretical conversations, in the sense of dialogical queries and responses between the thinker and the world-text of international relations, pre-empts understanding shifts in historical meanings as well as systemic change in the diplomatic culture. When Bull singles out the mimetic models of the scientific school as a 'great disservice to theory', we get a better sense of why the positivists can speak but cannot reply to reality:

> I know of no model that has assisted our understanding of international relations that could not just as well have been expressed as an empirical generalization. This, however, is not the reason why we should abstain from them. The freedom of the model-builder from the discipline of looking at the world is what makes him dangerous; he slips easily into a dogmatism that empirical generalization does not allow, attributing to the model a connection with reality it does not have, and as often as not distorting the model itself by importing additional assumptions about the world in the guise of logical axioms. The very intellectual completeness and logical tidiness of the model-building operation lends it an air of authority which is often quite misleading as to its standing as a statement about the real world.[7]

Have successive generations of positivism, from formal game theory to structuralist realism to neo-liberal institutionalism, nullified the potency of Bull's polemic? I think not: but it is not the purpose of this essay to recycle, or worse, refight old battles. It is, rather, to make the critical point that the new behaviourism, particularly its resurgence in rational choice and game theory, suffers not for its high level of abstraction and lack of realism, but for its abuse of simulation and surfeit of *hyperrealism*, in which models begin to precede and engender the reality which they purport to model. In other words, do we risk becoming so mesmerised by the technical brilliance, peerless morphology, and operational complexity of the latest model that the simulated figuration will totally displace the historicised reality? In turn, will it not be so much a matter that the classicists cannot measure the reality of international relations – a recurring complaint of past behaviouralists – as that they will not be able to measure up to the simulated hyperreality of the neo-behaviourialists?[8] These are all concerns anticipated by, I would argue, Bull's own investigation into the idea of diplomatic culture.

It is telling (though hardly definitive) that the first set of 'central questions' which Bull asks in making his argument for the classical approach involves the existence and role of culture in international relations:

> For example, does the collectivity of sovereign states constitute a political society or system, or does it not? If we can speak of a society of sovereign states, does it presuppose a common culture or civilization? And if it does, does such a common culture underlie the worldwide diplomatic framework in which we are attempting to operate now?[9]

In the absence of a critical meta-theory, a positivist approach to international relations cannot begin to answer such questions. But positivists may well prefer not to *ask* such questions, arguing that the whole idea of diplomatic culture is too vague, ambiguous or unverifiable to warrant serious intellectual attention. On this score the best response still comes from Raymond Aron, who cautions us that 'the ambiguity in "international relations" is not to be imputed to the inadequacy of our concepts: it is an integral part of reality itself'.[10] Equally, Bull would not want us to claim too much for his idea of diplomatic culture, to make it a unifying label for a phenomenon which is too complex and ambiguous to be reduced to a single concept and a single voice. Hence, my purpose is not to resurrect Bull's idea of diplomatic culture through an act of identification or sanctification, but to reincarnate the idea through an interpretive inquiry.

A THEORETICAL DECONSTRUCTION OF DIPLOMATIC CULTURE

Even a cursory review of Bull's major books, articles and book reviews, comprising a body of work which stretches over three decades, reveals a continuing concern with the broad notion of how a common culture underlies the diplomatic framework.[11] I believe that Bull's multiple use of culture can best be pictured as three concentric circles divided into intellectual and moral half-circles. The outer, all-encompassing circle is the 'world' or 'cosmopolitan' culture which underlies international society. It is this meaning of culture to which Bull refers when he states in *The Anarchical Society* that 'all historical international societies have had as one of their foundations a common culture'.[12] A line divides this culture, and bisects the interior circles of culture as well, into (i) 'a common *intellectual* culture – such as a common language, a common philosophical or epistemological outlook, a common literary or artistic tradition – the presence of which served to facilitate communication between the member states of the society'; and (ii) 'common *values* – such as a common religion or a common code – the presence of which served to reinforce the sense of common interests that united the states in question by a sense of common obligation.' Within this circle operates the 'international political culture', by which Bull means 'the intellectual and moral culture that determines the attitudes towards the states system of the societies that compose it'. Finally, at the centre of the three concentric circles, the core of international society can be found: 'the diplomatic culture – the common stock of ideas and values possessed by the official representatives of states.'[13]

In the chapter on diplomacy in *The Anarchical Society*, Bull emphasises the critical *symbolic* role diplomacy and its culture play in bringing cohesiveness to international society. He writes that 'the diplomatic profession itself is a custodian of the idea of international society'; and he marvels at the integrating power of the diplomatic culture at a time when its aristocratic and elitist underpinnings have come under intense attack:

> The remarkable willingness of states of all regions, cultures, persuasions and states of development to embrace often strange and archaic diplomatic procedures that arose in Europe in another age is today one of the few visible indications of universal acceptance of the idea of international society.[14]

It should be apparent that diplomatic culture is a key concept in Bull's formulation of an international society. How did this conceptual relationship develop? As I have said, the purpose of this investigation, as with any deconstruction or genealogy, is not to discover immaculate beginnings or attach causal laws to an idea. It is, rather, to search for the clash of ideas and texts, when one interpretation is constituted through dialogue or confrontation with an alien interpretation. Judging from a review of Bull's papers, I would say one such encounter took place at the Australia National University in 1975, when Bull organised a term-long seminar on the idea of world-society. Participants included J.D.B. Miller, Vendulka Kulbalkova, Murray Forsyth, Ralph Pettman and R.J. Vincent.

In his introductory paper, 'World Society: Some Definitions and Questions', Bull took great pains (and judging from the acerbity of the text, inflicted some too) to distance his idea of a common culture from that of the world society writers.[15] After invoking his now-familiar definition of international society ('an international system that is marked not only by...contact and interaction, but also by a sense of common interests and perhaps common values'), he goes on to distinguish it from three meanings of 'world society'. First he cites the identification of world society with 'human society': this sense, says Bull, is 'uncontroversial and also, of course, quite uninteresting'. The second meaning refers to 'a worldwide pattern of social interaction or interdependence, including the 'international system' or 'states system', but also embracing 'actors other than states': Bull finds this sense 'also uncontroversial, but many writers find it sufficiently interesting to publish books about it'. The third sense, however, warrants discussion: 'a worldwide pattern of social interaction or interdependence that is characterised also by a sense of common interests or values, and by common rules and institutions giving expression to these common interests or values: a society worldwide in scope that is *integrated*'. There appears to be some agreement over the desirability of such a society; the debate Bull wishes to address is whether 'world society in this sense is at least in process of becoming'.[16]

To investigate these claims, the works of well-known participants in the debate were set up, some might say, to be critically queried on some of their claims.[17] What is interdependence, and is it the basis of a world society? Is economic interdependence playing the most significant part in the emergence of transnational relations? Or, is it more credible to say that a technological unification of the globe is the most likely source of a world society? How do strategic interdependence and 'world law' fit into this scheme? Bull treats these questions – which in due course were to be taken up by members of the seminar – very seriously (that is to say, with respectful scepticism rather than dismissive wit) but he casts them as questions posed by *others* and only of peripheral importance to what is really happening in international relations. However, on the question of *cultural* interdependence, Bull stops citing other views ('world society is said to be especially the product of economic interdependence', 'it is often claimed that international law is giving place to world law', etc.) and presents his own:

> *World culture* is something that presumably underlies the world society, just as the 'diplomatic culture' and the wider 'international political culture' underlay the society of states. It is important to distinguish world culture in the sense of (i) a common intellectual culture or stock of ideas that facilitates communication (common language, common epistemology, and understanding of the world, common technology) and (ii) common values. In what sense is there a world culture, and how does it relate to world society?[18]

R.J. Vincent took it upon himself to attempt an answer to Bull's question. It would seem from the introduction to his paper, 'World Society and World Culture', that it was not an easy task; as Vincent put it 'to be asked, or worse, to volunteer to present a paper on world culture to a seminar that does not believe in world society is to know what it is like to be an initiate at some tribal rite'.[19] The bulk of the paper presents an argument for an emergent world culture and an account of the obstacles it faces. But of interest to this inquiry is how Vincent is forced to do what had not yet been done: first, to provide a self-consciousness about definitions of culture in the context of world politics; and second, to suggest a variety of possible approaches for understanding how culture functions in this context. Many of his definitions build on the foundation laid by Bull:

> Culture in the context of world society, a world culture might be distinguished from the more familiar international relations' animals of diplomatic culture and international culture. Diplomatic culture is the culture derived from the aristocratic cosmopolitanism of dynastic Europe which provides custom, precedent and manners for the rather precious society of diplomatists. These diplomatic niceties are social manifestations of a more substantial culture underlying the society of states – the international culture whose values find formal expression in the treatises of international law, and whose character is revealed in quasi-legal principles like the balance of power.[20]

It is in his dialogue with Bull's ideas on culture that we are made aware of elements of international and diplomatic culture which were previously implicit or simply not thought about. I would argue that this dialogue, in particular when Vincent poses the differences between Bull's idea of international culture and his own view of world culture, greatly increases the heuristic value of international – and by extension, diplomatic – culture for world politics. Drawing from Adda B. Bozeman's account of ancient states-systems, Vincent marks the boundaries of the two cultures:

> My starting-point for thinking about world culture is where international culture stops. International culture is a minimalist culture of procedure rather than substance, of agreed ways of disagreeing, of *cuius regio eius religio.* Its cardinal principles of sovereignty and non-intervention unite international society around the doctrine that independence is the value which above-all requires respect. They seek to *exclude* states from each other's areas of competence. By world culture, I intend something more *inclusive*, which unites across international frontiers rather than relying on a principle of division, and which can be said to have in it substance as well as mere rules of procedure.[21]

This is an insightful statement, but one which contains a slightly disingenuous element. If diplomatic culture is an elitist manifestation of international culture, and if it is assimilated and transmitted by the official representatives of states, both of which are claims made by Bull and acknowledged by Vincent, then Vincent's 'starting-point for thinking about world culture' stops just about where the most significant international activities take place, that is, between states. In other words, in his effort to find an inclusivist concept of culture, Vincent radically delimits its usefulness for the study of international relations. On the other hand, the different heuristic values attached to the different notions of culture probably reflect conflicting premises: an aspirational notion of world culture makes sense if one sees an increasing interdependence on political, economic, legal and strategic levels eroding the boundaries of states.

In the interests of a dialogical reading, I would dissent from this view – and recite my opening premise – by claiming that the concept of diplomatic culture is most useful when one accepts that it is not interdependence but rather alienation which demarcates relations between the dominant institutions of international relations, with states at the top of the list of estranged international actors, but with other transnational institutions, which are commonly construed as leading the way to an interdependent world, included as well. For the moment, I will make rather than prove this assertion in order that I might investigate the implications of the premise that it is difference, deviance, and otherness which constitute and reveal the need for a diplomatic culture.[22]

The relating of alienation, in the general sense of something made foreign or separate, to diplomatic culture is evident if not explicit in the writings of others with whom Hedley Bull engaged in dialogue. In *Power Politics*, Martin Wight remarks that 'Alien societies had different principles of existence from Europe' which created the 'possibility of conflict' as well as the need for Western cooperation.[23] Furthermore, in *System of States*, he goes to great lengths to show how estrangement between Western Christendom and the Turks served as an impetus to the conferences and intercourse among the European powers which prefigured the establishment of a diplomatic system.[24] Similar themes are also present in Adam Watson's work on diplomacy when he asserts that 'initially diplomacy appears as a sporadic communication between very separate states', and that some 'states remained alien to the cultural and historical assumptions which engendered the rules and conventions of European diplomacy.'[25]

It is my contention that the existence of a diplomatic culture only becomes self-evident, and subject to inquiry, when the values and ideas of one society are estranged from another. This thesis is supported by investigation into several of the functions of diplomatic culture. First, it helps define and validate social and political boundaries between alien groups, as well as groups of alien ideas. From the beginnings of diplomatic culture we can discern the construction of three interpenetrating boundaries of alienation: there is the vertical estrangement between 'high' (civilised and Western) and 'low' (barbarian and non-Western) cultures; the horizontal estrangement between political actors; and the universalist estrangement between the society and self.

Second, diplomatic culture abets the canonisation and imposition of peripheral alien cultures. Early examples would be Charlemagne's institutionalisation of Roman cultural practices, and the adaptation and integration of Byzantine customs and ceremonies into Western diplomacy. The emphasis of cultural over juridical elements, such as diplomatic immunities and privileges, may seem inappropriate to the modern purveyor of diplomacy; but I would argue that the cultural practices were even more important during the emergence of a diplomatic system because they sanctioned the first *movements* across social and political boundaries.

This represents a third and highly significant function of diplomatic culture: the mediation through ritual and protocol of the alienation which accompanies the crossing of state and status frontiers. These functions give us reason to redefine and reinterpret diplomatic culture as the *symbolic* mediation of estrangement.[26]

GENEALOGICALLY REMEMBERING DIPLOMATIC CULTURE

A brief historical account of diplomacy might help to clarify some of these abstract theoretical claims. I prefer to use a genealogical approach because it provides us with a method to trace the history of a contested idea without boiling it down to an ahistorical essence.[27]

From when the earliest diplomats-*cum*-messengers lost their mythical wings (be it from foot or shoulder) to their cloaking with the robes of the sovereign state, knowledge of diplomacy has been the stuff of biography and anecdote rather than theoretical inquiry. The classical period of diplomacy, when officially-accredited agents of sovereign authorities managed the international system through negotiation backed by power, has yielded more reflective writings. In this period diplomacy expanded in thought and in practice, and with the manipulations of great-power politics the expansion took place in a quasi-orderly if sometimes bloody fashion to the Americas, Africa and Asia. Ironically, as the domestic political power of the *anciens régimes* began to decline in the nineteenth century, its grip on diplomacy grew more tenacious, contributing to the (first) great disaster of the twentieth century.[28] I will leave it to the more casuistic to determine whether this represented an irony of dialectical history or the cunning of desperate men. What I wish to introduce is the idea of how, as the power of dynastic consanguinity congealed and then irrevocably attenuated, the ontology of diplomacy shifted from a natural, commonsensical to an alienated, meta-theoretical state, that is a cultural one.

The first signs of a shift, and the first rumblings of a diplomatic theory, can be detected when Abraham de Wicquefort, François de Callières, Antoine Pecquet and others argued that more than blue blood was necessary in the constitution of the 'ideal ambassador'.[29] In their works diplomacy is studied as a culture, in terms of a body of thought of how civilised behaviour was to be propagated among 'ideal ambassadors', and in terms of a body of individuals through which civilised behaviour was to be reproduced in the institutions of the international society.[30] However, as the aristocratic veneer of the diplomatic corps wore thin under the pressure of democratic movements, a dormant vernacular of diplomacy came to dominate the thinking about the culture. 'Tact and intelligence', rather than theory, is offered by Ernest Satow as a guide to diplomatic practice.[31] In his classic work *Diplomacy*, Harold Nicolson pronounces, somewhat complacently, that 'the main informative influence in diplomatic theory...is common sense'.[32] It would seem that diplomatic theory, at least in the sense of a classical, normative rumination about the practice and principles of diplomacy, effloresced in the eighteenth century and then sank out of sight and out of mind.

There are several reasons for this. After a formidable rearguard action and lengthy time-lag (when compared to the evolution of domestic institutions), the aristocratic diplomatic corps eventually gave way to a meritocracy (taking into account, of course, the right schools, gender and political affiliations). Pragmatic concerns of schooling initiates replaced the normative and reflective writings of the seminal diplomatic theorists, like de Wicquefort and de Callières. Second, it is difficult to theorise about common sense.[33] As a folkloric, cultural universal, it *absorbs* meaning, and pre-empts the kind of intellectual and systematic interpretation which the study of diplomacy requires. Finally, there is the obvious absence of a supra-sovereign authority, both in the system of diplomacy and in the system of reason which seeks to understand diplomacy. Common sense may be a primitive intellectual construct, but in the absence of an alternative international discourse, it was, as many would argue, the best interdiscursive tool available.

However, can historical generalisations and reflections about the commonsense 'essence' of diplomacy stand in for theory? Is there an alternative? Judging from the first sequel to Satow and Nicolson of any explanative worth, Adam Watson's *Diplomacy: The Dialogue Between States*, we can discern a promising turn toward reflective thinking supported by historical inquiry.[34] The anchoring of diplomatic practice to the idea of dialogue is obvious – and useful because of its obviousness. But it does not constitute a theory: it is a concept in search of a theory which can, as Hegel said, make the familiar unfamiliar in order that it may be cognitively understood. Whether we call it distancing, estrangement, defamiliarisation or more trendily, deconstruction, the theoretical task became, I believe, to challenge our habitual or 'natural' ways of looking at diplomacy.

Watson's idea of diplomacy as dialogue takes an admirable stab at it, but it cannot help but fall short, for as power disperses and diffuses in the contemporary states system, and as diplomatic utterances multiply and accelerate in the international communication web, we must ask whether the dialogue has become an unmanageable *heterologue*. Is modern common sense only masquerading as a neutral, universal discourse, acting as a rearguard action for a modernist diplomacy beset by fragmenting powers and alienated cultures?

Interconnected by common beliefs, norms and goals, the multipolar system of eighteenth- and nineteenth-century Europe could sustain a diplomatic dialogue among the great powers. It is, however, difficult to view diplomacy as a dialogue, let alone a heterologue, at a time when the great powers' invocation of common sense seems indistinguishable from *le droit de convenance*, and their post-Cold war diplomacy inseparable from *Realpolitik*. In short, how are we, as a preliminary to understanding the value of Hedley Bull's idea of diplomatic culture, to construe the structure of diplomacy today? As a monologue of the mighty one (once two), a dialogue of the middling many, or a babble of the impotent plenum?

DIALOGICALLY IMAGINING DIPLOMATIC CULTURE

It is quite possible that we cannot fully understand Bull's idea of diplomatic culture within the intellectual framework of the classicists. To assert that diplomatic culture is merely the façade of power politics, to believe that a truth about diplomatic culture can be negotiated, or to hope that diplomatic culture is a world culture in the making, all are mental activities which can adequately be described and perhaps even explained within the three classical traditions of international theory: the Machiavellian, Grotian and Kantian. It is, however, questionable whether the three classical traditions are up to the intellectual and prescriptive tasks of the late modern culture of a transformative international society in which the diplomatic culture currently functions and defines itself. Bull tentatively identifies the existence of such a culture, but acknowledges the shortness of its reach and the bias of its grasp:

> It is important to bear in mind, however, that if contemporary international society does have any cultural basis, this is not any genuinely global culture, but is rather the culture of so-called 'modernity'. And if we ask what is modernity in culture, it is not clear how we answer this except by saying that it is the culture of the dominant Western powers.[35]

More evasive than persuasive, the passage nonetheless does underscore Bull's awareness of the important role of culture – and its resistance to a global or final explanation. In the last section of *The Anarchical Society*, on the prospects for international society, he does elaborate on the relation of modernity to the diplomatic culture. It bears quoting at some length, for it is a key passage.

> We may say that in this world international society there is at least a diplomatic or elite culture, comprising the common intellectual culture of modernity: some common languages, principally English, a common scientific understanding of the world, certain common notions and techniques that derive from the universal espousal by governments in the modern world of economic development and their universal involvement in modern technology. However, this common intellectual culture exists only at the elite level; its roots are shallow in many societies, and the common diplomatic culture that does exist today is not powerfully reinforced by an international political culture favourable to the working of the states system.[36]

After having dismissed – and in some cases demolished – the extensive arguments for the decline, obsolescence, and reform of the states-system, which ranged from the wetter varieties of the interdependency theories to the 'radical salvationism' of Richard Falk, Bull leaves himself a final paragraph for his own views on the future of the international society. That culture should be the keystone to his final statements, makes up, I would argue, for its paucity in the rest of the text:

> The future of international society is likely to be determined, among other things, by the preservation and extension of a cosmopolitan culture, embracing both common ideas and common values, and rooted in societies in general as well as in their elites, that can provide the world international society of today with the culturally more homogeneous international societies of the past.[37]

Bull is not simply advocating a unilateral process of western homogenisation. That historical moment, in spite of the recent spate of neo-Hegelian triumphalism, has passed. Moreover, its resurrection is undesirable, because any so-called cosmopolitan culture could not help but reflect and constitute the dominant particularist interests of the West. In Bull's view, it is not simply the case that the expansion of international society inexorably leads to a universal global culture. It is a matter of cultural accommodation where necessary and incorporation where desirable of *alien*, non-Western elements which might 'provide a foundation for a universal international society'.[38] That is as far as he is willing to go.

Bull's rare excursion into the future of international society appears to reflect the view of three of the thinkers he held highest: Victoria, Grotius and Kant. But where does Bull leave us today: reasoning about the viability of diplomatic culture, believing in its utopian possibilities, or, in the style of the cynical realist, denigrating its future as merely a recycling of its past? As I said at the beginning of this essay, and as Bakhtin showed literally if not logically, there can be a penultimate but never a final word from the author; and I believe I heard it at a lecture Bull gave on Kant's *Perpetual Peace*. At the end of the lecture he quoted Kant:

> The process of creation, by which such a breed of corrupt beings has been put upon the earth, can apparently be justified by no theodicy or theory of Providence, if we assume that it never will be better, nor can be better, with the human race....We shall thus be inevitably driven to despair...if we do not admit that the pure politics of right and justice have objective reality and that they can be realised in fact.[39]

To punctuate Kant's point, Bull cautioned against the view that Kant was indulging in 'shallow optimism'. Rather it was an optimism 'grounded in despair', and Bull, out-loud, imagined that Kant, 'having looked into the abyss, and said looking down makes me giddy, said I can only go on climbing if I look up'.[40]

There is a powerful message here. Against the inevitably conflictive effects of self-help in international relations, Hedley Bull applied the power of a positive intellectual pessimism. He recognised the state as paramount, insecure, a monad; but he intellectually reconstructed the diplomatic culture as the historical bridge between states. More than ever, the message bears reinscription. Relations between states remain fraught because of the continued strains of unequal development, nationalist differences and religious conflict. However, in contrast to the monologues of unipolar regimes of truth and power, as embodied by the technoscientific power of a universalising 'West', there can be found in the linking of multiple queries and responses from opposing cultures a potential power to transform international relations, from a discourse of *either* order *or* justice, *either* war *or* peace, *either* one power *or* many powers, to *both/and* all of these things: in Bull's apt oxymoron for this condition of tragic hope, an anarchical society. States will continue daily to construct and confront their alien others. Yet, through the idea of a diplomatic culture, Bull dismantled many of the fixed oppositions and supposedly eternal enmities of world politics, and renovated an historical mediation of strangers that had fallen into neglect. In the process he revealed an ethical function at work, giving us a better sense of how the idea of diplomatic culture enhances the *becoming* of a truly international society.

NOTES

1. This paper was first presented at a panel on Hedley Bull at the annual meeting of the British International Studies Association in December 1986. Despite efforts at revision, and the well-intentioned suggestions of the editors, it remains stuck in a time and state of mind that fails to do Hedley Bull sufficient justice. I regret that, and absolve from any responsibility all those who offered their generous help. They include: Mary Bull, Carole Charlton, Jean Bethke Elstain, Adam Roberts, John Vincent and Adam Watson.
2. Roland Barthes, *Image-Music-Text* (New York, NY: Hill and Wang, 1977), p. 146.
3. For details of these transformations, see James Der Derian, *On Diplomacy: A Genealogy of Western Estrangement* (Oxford: Blackwell Press, 1987).

4. 'Deconstruct'; 'genealogy'; 'dialogic': rather than rely on secondary accounts, as is the tendency in International Relations theory, one can learn more from a primary encounter with these ideas: see, Jacques Derrida, *A Derrida Reader*, P. Kamuf (ed.), (New York, NY: Columbia University Press, 1991); Michel Foucault, *The Foucault Reader*, P. Rabinow (ed.), (Harmondsworth: Penguin, 1984); Mikhail Bakhtin, *The Dialogic Imagination: Four Essays by M.M. Bakhtin*, M. Holquist (ed.), trans by C. Emerson and M. Holquist (Austin, TX: University of Texas Press, 1981); and Roland Barthes, *Selected Writings*, S. Sontag (ed.), (London: Fontana, 1983).
5. This is not to imply that such a project would have no intellectual value. In fact, Bull once submitted a proposal along these lines to the Ford Foundation and asked if I might be interested in doing some of the field work. The funding for this part of the proposal did not, as far as I know, materialise. What I do know is that Bull had no intention of undertaking the kind of survey analysis popular with the scientific school. In a review of a manuscript on the views of diplomats based on interviews and questionnaires, Bull pulled no punches: 'The ms. is entirely without merit, and is not even a good example of this ludicrous and deplorable genre. Its language is cumbersome and pretentious, its underlying assumptions crudely behaviourist, and where it makes content [sic] with the world what it has to say is banal.... I do not know of any other works that provide a quantative analysis of diplomats' responses to questionnaires: the lack of such studies reflects the fact that most authors have more sense than to seek to write books about such triviality.' From Hedley Bull's papers, which remain uncatalogued, and are now kept at Nuffield College, Oxford.
6. Hedley Bull, 'International Theory: The Case for a Classical Approach', *World Politics* (Vol. XVIII, No. 3, April 1966), pp. 361–77.
7. Ibid., p. 371
8. For two highly evocative studies of simulation and hyperrealism, see Jean Baudrillard, *Simulations* (New York, NY: Semiotext(e), 1983); and Umberto Eco, *Travels in Hyperreality* (New York, NY: Harcourt Brace Jovanovich, 1986).
9. Bull, 'International Theory', p. 367.
10. Raymond Aron, *Peace and War: A Theory of International Relations* (London: Weidenfield and Nicholson, 1962), p. 7.
11. This can be substantiated by two large file folders on culture, which can be found in Bull's collected papers.
12. Hedley Bull, *The Anarchical Society: A Study of Order in World Politics* (New York, NY: Columbia University Press, 1977), p. 316.
13. Ibid.
14. Ibid., p. 183.

15. Hedley Bull, 'World Society: Some Definitions and Questions', paper presented on 30 June 1975 to the *Seminar on World Society* in the Department of International Relations, Research School of Pacific Studies, Australian National University. The paper is from Bull's collected papers at Nuffield College.
16. Ibid.
17. Joseph Nye and Robert O. Keohane (eds), *Transnational Relations and World Politics* (Cambridge, MA: Harvard University Press, 1973); George Modelski, *The Principles of World Politics* (New York, NY: The Free Press, 1972); John Burton, *World Society* (London: Cambridge University Press, 1972); and Harold and Margaret Sprout, *Towards a Politics of the Planet Earth* (New York, NY: Van Nostrand Reinhold Co, 1971), are placed alongside those of some international lawyers, C.W. Jenks, *The Common Law of Mankind*; P. Corbett, *From International Law To World Law*; and P. Jessup, *Transnational Law*.
18. Bull, 'World Society: Some Definitions'.
19. R.J. Vincent, 'World Society and World Culture', paper presented at the *Seminar on World Society*, 11 August 1975, ANU, in Hedley Bull's collected papers at Nuffield College.
20. Ibid.
21. Ibid.
22. For further consideration of the relationship of diplomatic culture to alienation, see chapter 3 'Diplomatic Culture', in my *On Diplomacy*, pp. 30–43.
23. See Martin Wight, *Power Politics* (Lonodn: Pelican, 1979), p. 302.
24. See Martin Wight, *Systems of States* (Leicester: Leicester University Press, 1977).
25. Adam Watson, *Diplomacy: The Dialogue Between States* (London: Eyre Methuen, 1982), p. 15.
26. For details of all these, see my, *On Diplomacy*.
27. See Michel Foucault, 'Nietzsche, Genealogy, History,' in M. Foucault, *Language, Counter-Memory, Practice* (Oxford: Blackwell, 1977), pp. 139-64.
28. See Arno J. Mayer, *The Persistence of the Old Regime: Europe to the Great War* (London: Croom Helm, 1981).
29. See Maurice Keens-Soper's short but excellent account of the early diplomatic theorists, 'François de Callières and Diplomatic Theory', *The Historical Journal* (Vol. XVI, No. 3, 1973), pp. 485–508.
30. Ibid.
31. Ernest Satow, *Satow's Guide to Diplomatic Practice*, Lord Gore-Booth (ed.), (London: Longman, 1979), p. 6.
32. Harold Nicolson, *Diplomacy* (London: Oxford University Press, 1969), pp. 20 and 24.

33. My efforts elsewhere will probably attest to this: see the chapter on 'Mytho-diplomacy' in *On Diplomacy*, pp. 44–67.
34. Watson, *Diplomacy*.
35. Bull, *Anarchical Society*, p. 32.
36. Ibid., p. 317.
37. Ibid.
38. Ibid.
39. Hedley Bull, Oxford University lecture notes to *Theory and Practice of International Relations 1648–1789*.
40. Ibid.

6 Reconstructing World Politics: The Emergence of Global Civil Society

Ronnie D. Lipschutz

Modern environments and experiences cut across all boundaries of geography and ethnicity, of class and nationality, of religion and ideology: in this sense, modernity can be said to unite all mankind. But it is a paradoxical modernity, a unity of disunity: it pours us into a maelstrom of perpetual disintegration and renewal, of struggle and contradiction, of ambiguity and anguish.

Marshall Berman[1]

To talk of civil society is to reserve the priorities of political economy. It is to assert that human beings and their desires can alter otherwise determinant structures. It is to open unexpected possibilities rather than to focus on the conditions that make defeat inevitable. It is to believe that not only change will happen, but that it probably has already happened – even without our knowing.

Alan Wolfe[2]

GLOBAL CIVIL SOCIETY AND THE WORLD TODAY

Amid the vociferous debates underway about the nature of state action, the structure of the international system, and the 'true' character of international relations,[3] there is an emerging recognition that the focus on 'structure' and 'process' as the central concerns of the discipline is too limiting; the neo-classical approaches tend to ignore or downplay other forces at work in world politics. Both the 'neo-realist' and 'neo-liberal' approaches remain state-centric, regarding states as dominant and able to minimise the influence or significance of other, non-state, actors. Comparisons of the medieval system with the modern state system, as a means of addressing disputes between neo-realists and institutionalists, are also in vogue.[4] These debates are somewhat sterile, for they centre on comparisons of static, idealised social and political arrangements, and fail to say very much about how the two systems coexisted during the period of transformation, or how participants could have been aware that a transformation was underway. By arguing that transformation can be detected only when direct, and successful, challenges to the territorial state take place, many of these writers disregard the nature of social transitions and the ways in which social arrangements sometimes succumb to simultaneous subversion from within and without.

By adhering to a state-centred approach, and placing such stringent conditions on the detection of transformation, these writers may be ignoring the emergence of a parallel arrangement of political interaction, one that does not take anarchy or self-help as central organising principles, but is focused on the self-conscious constructions of networks of knowledge and action, by decentered, local actors, that cross the reified boundaries of states as though they were not there. This arrangement, or 'global civil society', is not new. Indeed, it is difficult to determine its origins, but it may already have done much to modify and dampen the conflictual nature of what is, after all, a socially constructed anarchy.[5] Significant today, however, is the growing 'density' and visibility of global civil society and its impact on the socially constructed realm of international politics. A number of writers have raised the notion of global civil society, in one form or another. Hedley Bull speculated on a 'new mediaevalism';[6] James N. Rosenau has written about 'sovereignty-free actors';[7] and the terms 'international civil society' and 'global civil society',[8] are becoming increasingly familiar to members of the discipline.

Why is the notion of global civil society significant and worth closer investigation? There are, I think, two reasons. The first is that there is not one, but many heteronomous[9] transnational political networks being established by and among actors within civil society who themselves are, in a sense, 'imagined communities',[10] and who are challenging and changing, from below, the nation-state system. The second reason is that the growth of global civil society represents an ongoing project of civil society to reconstruct world politics. As this project proceeds, civil society is becoming global and therefore a political force to be reckoned with in a way that has not been the case since the medieval period. This is not to suggest, however, that the nation-state, as an actor, is finished – indeed, it is likely that the nation-state will be around, in one form or another, for some time to come. Yet, as Alan Wolfe suggests, change is happening, even if we are not fully aware of it, and we cannot ignore this change if we are to portray accurately contemporary international relations.[11]

The term 'civil society' is used mindful of its association with the 1989 and 1991 revolutions against Communism, but also as a means to escape from what Crawford Young has called the 'cast-iron grid [of the state system that] exercises a transcendent despotism over reality'.[12] Our current notions of civil society are informed by the recent experiences of Eastern Europe and the former Soviet Union, where the term was applied to those aspects of social and cultural life that had not been captured or colonised by the totalitarian state.[13] In what used to be called 'the West', the idea that one might even think about civil society in similar terms has always been a non-starter. Yet, in a sense, even societies in the West have been 'colonised' by their states, for two reasons: first, in the sense that the state has taken control of certain political realms, such as foreign policy. As a result, the notion that foreign policy could be conducted autonomously of a state's bureaucratic apparatus has had little credence, either in terms of effectiveness or legitimacy.[14] Indeed, the idea that the international state system is the place where politics across borders happens has tended to delegitimise even the conceptual possibilities of political action outside of a state framework.[15] Second, as a consequence of this statist monopoly, in liberal economies only the realm of consumption has been left to civil society: one's politics, in effect, become what one consumes.[16] However, as I will argue below, it is the very homogeneity and pervasiveness of this consumer culture – and its extension to institutionalised politics as an historical process – that has opened up a political space for the revival of civil society.[17]

This chapter starts with some brief descriptions of global civil society, while recognising that we are not yet in a position to begin to construct definitive guides to it.[18] The notion of civil society is then discussed, showing how it might be applied to global politics, and how it is different from other current concepts in international relations theory and international political economy. Then, the emergence of global civil society is considered as an historical process arising from the conjunction of three changes: first, the 'fading away' of anarchy among states and its replacement by a different type of norm-directed system of global governance, a process partly attributable to the globalisation of liberalism; second, at the functional, micro-level, the inability of states to deal with certain social welfare problems and other aspects of governance, resulting in increasing efforts by non-state actors to address them; and, third, the crumbling of old forms of political identity, centred on the state, and the growth of new forms of political and social identity that are challenging the Gramscian hegemony of statist world politics.

THE CHARACTER OF GLOBAL CIVIL SOCIETY

What exactly is encompassed by the concept of global civil society? To explore it, we have to look for political spaces other than those bounded by the parameters of the nation-state system. The spatial boundaries of global civil society are different, because its autonomy from the constructed boundaries of the state system also allows for the construction of new political spaces.[19] These political spaces are delineated by networks of economic, social and cultural relations, and they are being occupied by the conscious association of actors, in physically separated locations, who link themselves together in networks for particular political and social purposes.[20] The concept of epistemic communities, recently explored by Peter Haas, is one example of such networks although, as defined, epistemic communities are oriented directly toward input into the policymaking processes of the state.[21] While the participants in the networks of global civil society interact with states and governments over particular policy issues, the networks themselves extend across levels of analysis and state borders, and are not constrained by the state system itself. A few examples of such networks will illustrate how they are constituted and who belongs to them.

One political space in which global civil society is particularly visible is that surrounding environmental politics.[22] In the sphere of environmental activities, we see a growing number of transnational networks oriented around common strategies and goals.[23] All of these networks exist under the over-arching rubric of a general environmental ethic – or 'operating system' – although the actors involved in the various networks, and the relations between them vary significantly. Some networks are quite consciously anti-state, others are oriented toward state reform, some simply ignore the state altogether. Greenpeace, for example, constitutes by itself a global network involved in both anti-state and state-reforming tendencies simultaneously; its members participate in actions against state organisations even as they lobby national legislators.[24] The Asian Pacific People's Environmental Network, based in Penang, Malaysia, is made up of both urban and rural organisations, and operates at both international and regional levels. The International Network for Environmental Management is a global industrial association. A growing number of these networks are being organised around concepts of place, nationality, culture, species and specific issues.[25]

Environmental networks are also becoming development networks, and vice versa.[26] In the Third World, a burgeoning number of small-scale organisations, largely independent of the overarching state, provide a vast range of services to marginal and neglected populations.[27] Often, these organisations are tied into the global political system through transnational alliances established with other organizations in the North. One example of such an alliance is the programme 'From the Ground Up,' administered by the Centre for International Development and Environment of the World Resources Institute.[28] NGO activities at the June 1992 UN Conference on Environment and Development were coordinated through extensive transnational alliances and networks of communication. According to some reports, NGOs influenced significantly the tone and content of some of the agreements and charters under negotiation at the conference.[29] The Global Forum taking place in parallel with the conference led to further growth in these networks.[30]

In the sphere of human rights, the example that most immediately comes to mind when we speak of human rights organisations is Amnesty International. But human rights networks are much more extensive than local chapters of Amnesty.[31] A broad range of organisations has come into existence as a response to the global institutionalisation of norms relating to human rights.[32] While the gradual emergence of these norms can be traced back some decades, a major impetus to the development of human rights networks came with the signing of the Helsinki Accords in 1975. One of the three 'baskets' in the agreement specified the observance of human rights by all signatories, including those from the Soviet Bloc, and legitimated the establishment of groups to monitor governmental observance. Although these groups were routinely suppressed by Eastern Bloc governments, many of them, such as Charter 77 in Czechoslovakia, eventually became part of the 'civil societies' that were so instrumental in bringing down the European Communist regimes. One contemporary development is the increasing linkage between human rights groups and environmental organisations. The logic of such an association arises from concerns that large-scale, environmentally destructive projects often displace large numbers of the poor and disempowered, whose rights to land are routinely ignored. The shared objectives of the two different types of groups mean that cooperation makes a great deal of sense. To the extent that health and welfare are also increasingly seen as human rights, the role of environmental degradation in undermining them is another basis for working together.[33]

Another rapidly growing network in global civil society is composed of groups of indigenous people, that is, tribes, clans, societies and cultures that predate the arrival of colonialism and/or the mass urbanisation of populations. For example, in the fall of 1991, Jan de Vos, an anthropologist who works with Indian societies in the Lacandon forest of the southern Mexican state of Chiapas, was invited to a meeting of Lummi Indians in the Pacific Northwest by environmental groups working with the Lummi. At that meeting, he addressed efforts by the Lacandon and Maya Indians to establish new sovereignty claims in Chiapas (more recently given voice in the Zapatista 'uprising' there). The Lummi's purpose in bringing de Vos to the United States was to establish relations with the Indians of Mexico for purposes of political organisation and solidarity.[34] These types of connections among indigenous peoples are steadily growing in number.[35]

Similar global linkages exist or are developing on the basis of a broad range of other social and political issues. There is a well-developed global network of organisations concerned about AIDS.[36] Anti-abortion activists in the United States are establishing linkages with their foreign counterparts, especially in Europe. And transnational linkages among peace and anti-nuclear movements have been noted since the 1950s.[37]

It is, however, legitimate to ask how great the impact of these networks of global civil society really is on the state system. Are they able to influence not only the behaviour of some governments in special circumstances, but also patterns of world politics more generally? Do they somehow alter the anarchic system based on power, wealth and self-reliance? And, if not, why should we pay any attention to this phenomenon? The following section argues that the concept of global civil society is both meaningful and useful, and reflects and helps us to understand rapidly changing world politics.

THE CONCEPT AND HISTORY OF GLOBAL CIVIL SOCIETY

Ken Booth observed recently that:

> Sovereignty is disintegrating. States are less able to perform their traditional functions. Global factors increasingly impinge on all decisions made by governments. Identity patterns are becoming more complex, as people assert local loyalties but want to share in global values and lifestyles. The traditional distinction between 'foreign' and 'domestic' policy is less tenable than ever. And there is growing awareness that we are sharing a common world history....The [metaphor for the] international system which is now developing...is of an egg-box containing the shells of sovereignty; but alongside it a global community omelette is cooking.[38]

Booth's omelette includes a variety of ingredients: international regimes, international society, diplomatic culture and neo-liberal institutions, all the components of what Buzan might call a 'maturing – if not mature – anarchy'.[39] Why should global civil society be added to what is, already, a fairly piquant recipe?

All of these concepts are, in the final analysis, overwhelmingly state-centric. All are part of the menu of choices available to national governments as they struggle to retain elements of their sovereignty that are slowly diffusing away. Although the concept of international regime has not, after twenty years of debate, been clearly defined, international regimes do seem to be artifacts of state power, inasmuch as they serve the specific interests of state and governments.[40] Hedley Bull, of course, wrote about an 'international society' and, although he suggested that alternative future world orders might be 'neo-medieval' in form, his conception of international society remained centred on states.[41] Diplomatic culture is an idea whose use and utility seem to have waned. Once it could be applied to an elite society of cultured, educated diplomats, who as representatives of their states' interests frequently met in a variety of different venues to deal with a wide range of issues. While such diplomats can be found, even today, most have been replaced by technically competent experts whose knowledge and experience are limited to very few issue areas, and who do not have the cultural background evident in the old diplomacy.[42] Neo-liberal institutions, according to Robert O. Keohane, simply represent the increasing socialisation of states, such that 'much behavior [in international politics] is recognised by participants as reflecting established rules, norms, and conventions, and its meaning is interpreted in light of these understandings.'[43] But who, except the most shortsighted realist has ever suggested that states were never socialised? Buzan's notion of a maturing anarchy, in which rules and mutual respect for sovereignty become the norm, comes much closer to an accurate, and realistic, description of international politics today.[44]

Global civil society differs from all of these. It has to recognise states, but it is not state-centric. The notion of civil society – from the Latin *civilis societas* – was originally used to refer not to those societies that existed within individual states or organised polities, but to the condition of living in a 'civilised' community sufficiently advanced to have its own legal codes – *jus civile* – above that of individual states. Thus, barbarian and pre-urban cultures were not considered civil societies. Subsequently, the concept underwent a bifurcation as it was adapted to meet the needs of various political theorists. Locke contrasted political or civil society with the paternal authority of the state, whereas for Hegel and Marx, civil society, or *burgerliche Gesellschaft*, referred to the state of human development reached by advanced peoples, where the economic and social order moved according to its own largely selfish principles and ends, independent of the ethical demands of law and political association. Unlike Locke, Hegel and Marx thought civil society to be self-seeking and lacking in the moral cohesion of primitive societies. Current usages focus mostly on the social, cultural, economic and ethical arrangements of modern industrial society considered apart from the state, and regard civil society as a realm that is somewhat autonomous of state control and, in particular, totalitarian control.[45]

Returning to the original Latin concept of civil society, a *civilis societas*, a civilised community is defined as having its own legal codes, as opposed to those of individual states. The networks that I have described here are all united, more or less, by common norms or codes of behaviour that have emerged in reaction to the legal and other socially constructed fictions of the nation-state system. The end of the Cold War has also given a particular impetus to the emergence of global civil society. As James Mayall has argued, albeit in a somewhat different context, the universalisation of the state after 1945 represented an attempt to '"freeze" the political map and bring history to an end...[which] seems unlikely to succeed'.[46] The Cold War brought some degree of stability by freezing the political map, but its end signalled the restarting of history and the appearance of new forms of political action. One result is that a politics of collective identity is developing around the world. In some places, such politics are expressed via nationalism; in others, through identities based in civil society.

While global civil society must interact with states, the code of global civil society denies the primacy of states or *their* sovereign rights over the 'sovereign' rights of individuals and communities.[47] This civil society is 'global' not only because of those connections that cross national boundaries and operate within the 'global, nonterritorial region',[48] but also as a result of a growing element of global consciousness in the way the members of global civil society act. This is most evident in what Daniel Deudney has called 'green culture as earth nationalism',[49] but was also visible in the peace movement of the 1980s, as well as other contemporary networks, such as those organised around indigenous peoples, AIDS and human rights, as described above. These functional and conceptual processes lead to what Alberto Melucci calls the 'planetarization' of action, creating a 'transsocietal order' that 'challenges not only the cultural shape of international relations but the logic governing them.'[50]

Why is global civil society emerging at this historical juncture?[51] We can account for the phenomenon in three linked ways. Historically, at the end of the twentieth century we see the diffusing away of sovereignty from the state both upwards, to supranational institutions, and downwards, to subnational ones. This is first, in part, the culmination of the long-term socialisation of all remaining geographical territory (including some ocean and excluding Antarctica) into nation-states, and shorter-term integrative processes set loose in the aftermath of the Second World War,[52] as well as a consequence of a shift away from anarchy as the central organising principle of the international system. Second, global civil society is emerging as a functional response to the decreasing ability and willingness of governments to undertake a variety of welfare functions, for example, environmental conservation and restoration or the provision of basic health services, at the same time as there is a growing demand for new forms of governance at a multiplicity of levels ranging from the local to the global. Finally, global civil society can be seen as a form of large-scale resistance to the Gramscian hegemony of the current international system. These points will be considered in the rest of the chapter.

NOT ANARCHY BUT SOCIETY

Anarchy often appears to be a fact of international life, akin to an enduring physical – if not metaphysical – constant of the international system; that, at least, is a position of many scholars of international relations. But is it? Contrary to common uses, anarchy is a word with multiple meanings. It comes from the Greek *anarkhos*, meaning 'without a ruler.' In everyday conversation, we take it to mean political disorder and chaos whereas, in the language of international relations, it implies the absence of an overarching sovereign or ruler. The condition of international anarchy has, we are told, certain implications for the behaviour of states, especially 'self-help'.[53] Neo-realists see anarchy as an enduring feature of the international system. By implication, only a world state, the emergence of which is unlikely in a system regulated by the balance of power, could put an end to anarchy.

But anarchy has another meaning: the absence of any cohering principle, as in a common standard or purpose.[54] The conventional assumption in international politics and law is that if a system of rule does not have a centralised body enforcing the rules or law, there can be no cohering principles. This assumption of anarchy is maintained even when such a set of principles does exist and is subscribed to by a majority, because, it is argued, it is impossible to protect against 'defection' and the 'free rider'.[55] But neither markets nor the international state system are anarchic in this second sense; rather, they can be regarded as being strongly institutionalised.[56] Indeed, states in a so-called anarchy do not operate in an empty social vacuum; international political space is permeated with norms and rules, albeit ones we often pretend not to see. Alexander Wendt argues that even 'self-help' is a rule, or rather, an institution, that is endogenous to what appears to be an anarchic system.[57] This implies that states, or their sovereigns, must agree that self-help will be a rule, and they can only reach such an agreement if they already have a basis for concluding such a contract. By doing so they establish another social rule.

In fact, if we look closely, we can begin to see that the 'international system' is not the unordered anarchy posited by Kenneth Waltz and other neo-realists. As Friedrich Kratochwil, Nicholas Onuf and Wendt have noted, it is characterised by a great deal of order, explicit as well as implicit.[58] It may be more accurate, in fact, to describe the rules of this system in terms of the concept of *governance*. James Rosenau defines governance as:

> [R]eferring to activities backed by shared goals that may or may not derive from legal and formally prescribed responsibilities and that do not necessarily rely on police powers to overcome defiance and attain compliance....It embraces governmental institutions, but it also subsumes informal, non-governmental mechanisms....[It is] a system of rule that is as dependent on intersubjective meanings as on formally sanctioned constitutions and charters.[59]

The implication of this conception of rule is that, although there is not yet a world government (and it is unlikely that there ever will be one), there is a great deal of rule-governed activity going on. Governance includes, of course, explicit arrangements such as regimes, international treaties, and so on; it also incorporates some that are less obvious, including sets of norms governing human rights and human treatment of the environment. This system of governance, operating on the basis of an almost universally-shared set of norms, provides political space to global civil society in a manner similar to that provided by the state (or, rather, most states, if not all of them.) More to the point, because of the diffusion of sovereignty, on the one hand, and the inability of existing political institutions to provide governance at all levels, on the other, global civil society is, in many instances, filling this gap.

It is the global diffusion of the norms of liberalism that has made this mode of governance possible and feasible. These norms, especially those associated with human rights (and individual self-interest), have become, during the past few decades, a central focus of international politics.[60] The state remains a principal political institution in global politics but, under Western norms, the individual is sovereign. Such an assertion is not meant to suggest the 'end of history' – indeed, it is the momentary triumph of this set of overarching norms that also leads to the resistance to the growing penetration of societies by a globalising economic system and state-led development programmes. This resistance is evident, as well, in other forms, including the increase in ethnic conflict seen during the past few years. Nonetheless, one consequence of the winding down of the Cold War is a commitment to one particular form of social organisation overriding all other possibilities and, for the moment, the alternatives seem to have vanished.[61] This means, therefore, that the particular function filled by the state in the global system – mediation between international and domestic realms – is being transformed. The state may continue to fulfill other functions but, even here, there is a growing tendency to slough off such functions.

This newly dominant governance, or 'operating system', in global politics – liberalism with the individual at its core – has come to fill a role similar to the system of rules and rule promulgated by the Catholic Church prior to Westphalia. However, unlike the rules of the Church, the norms of liberalism have little to say about everyday social and ethical behaviour, except to place *homo economicus* at the centre of the world. But the notion of human rights does set standards for behaviour. Furthermore, the openness of liberalism's rules means that a high degree of diversity and heterogeneity, and a broad number of activities, are possible. The principles of liberalism thus come to represent something like the *jus civile* of the civilised community, existing above the laws of individual states.

However, it should be recognised that the dominance of the norms of liberalism does not mean that everyone is committed to them or that they should be regarded as innately or universally beneficial: resistance to the implications of governance under these norms is being expressed in the cultural sphere as much as the political one. But what the dominance of liberalism does do is to begin to make possible the substitution of new global social constructions in place of the older one of anarchy. It is under the umbrella of these emerging social constructions that global civil society is emerging.

STATE INCOMPETENCE, GOVERNANCE AND SOCIAL COMPETENCE

A second cause for the emergence of global civil society is functional in nature, resulting from what states – more precisely, national governments – are able and willing to do in this changing global system, and may have also to do with the 'demand' for governance in realms and issue-areas that were heretofore not addressed by existing institutions.[62] In contrast to this, as many have noted, civil society has become increasingly competent and willing to take on a variety of tasks. Paradoxically, this transfer of 'competence' has its origins in the industrialised state's attempt to accumulate greater power and control with respect to society.

In the effort to accomplish total mobilisation during the Second World War – a process that established a model for governing in the future – the industrial state made available to its citizens the tools and skills that would ultimately begin to empower society with respect to the state. Originally, in the course of pursuing security and territorial expansion, sovereigns found it expedient to conclude compacts with their populations offering protection in exchange for the revenues and manpower to fight wars of state security. The advent of mass mobilisation and large-scale warfare during the nineteenth and early twentieth centuries also led to the emergence of the welfare state. This amendment to the original compact between state and society, was, in part, a result of the Industrial Revolution and its spread throughout Europe. If citizens were to fulfil their part of the deal, they had to be able-bodied, not yoked to the land through feudal relations, and willing to support government and state. Hence, states increasingly found it necessary to intervene in the workings of the economy to ensure that support from their populations would be forthcoming. This meant better working conditions and higher living standards, as well as mass education to achieve socialisation and training compatible with developing technology. Since the middle of the twentieth century, as the security-and-protection function of the state became easier to flaunt but more and more difficult to fulfil (for although new armaments, promising greater levels of protection and deterrence, could always be procured, the possibilities of actually securing populations in the event of war decreased), the welfare function of the state came to dominate, reaching its apogee in the countries of Western Europe.

At some point, however, a problem begins to emerge: growing state incompetence as against growing societal competence. Although anti-statist ideology has been alive and well in liberal democracies for many decades, the general trend following the Second World War was of growing expectations in terms of the quantity and breadth of services provided by government bureaucracies. The paradox here is that the increasing cost of providing such services, ultimately paid through the tax base, has now begun to generate a backlash among those who provide the revenues. Furthermore, the commitment to economic liberalism and efficiency prevalent in the last decade has put further pressure on governments to balance budgets and reduce welfare expenditures. As the shortfall between revenues and costs increase, cutbacks in the welfare function follow, with the result that services deteriorate. This, in turn, leads to a gradual delegitimation of the state and a growing reliance on society to find other ways of fulfilling the welfare function.[63]

The state has also begun to fall short in yet another way. As it loses competence, and begins to shed functions, it also loses the ability to manage and govern. This is especially true when governments are responsible for a vast range of highly complex problems rather than just the more traditional ones, such as war and finance, a point seen most clearly in terms of environmental quality and protection. While the state's provision of environmental protection is relatively recent, this service has come about as a direct result of the growing welfare function and public pressure discussed above. The first generation of environmental protection functions in the industrialised world tended to focus on industrial externalities, such as air and water pollution. A second generation has more to do with the maintenance of the 'resource base' that underpins global civilisation, including protection of the atmosphere, soil and forests. (A third generation will, probably, involve major changes in economic practices, which may further undermine the state.) In maintaining the resource base, the problem is not so much pollution as it is depletion of renewable resources, such as forests, and lack of control over poisons that unintentionally waft across national borders, such as the nuclear radiation from Chernobyl.

The appropriation of resources generally takes place under property rights arrangements developed or sanctioned by the state and, in some cases, via delivery systems managed by state agencies. These agencies have been established by state bureaucracies for managing the exploitation of supply rather than the reduction or modification of demand.[64] As a result, they suffer from an institutional inability to respond to depletion in such a way as to ensure the protection of the resource and the long-term sustenance of the material base. This occurs even as failure to do so promises to have serious health and welfare effects over the longer term. Consequently, environmental degradation is fuelling a growing demand for services that governments are ill-equipped to afford and which, in many instances, go against the property rights arrangements sanctioned by those governments.[65] This is true at the international level, as well. Regimes and international organisations provide some help in this regard but, to a growing degree, NGOs have become necessary to global governance. More paradoxical, perhaps, is the fact that particular forms of non-institutionalised governance are becoming necessary at the *local* and *regional* levels of states, as well. Often, moreover, such governance, as manifested in the environment and development projects and alliances of non-governmental organisations extends between the local to the global, crossing levels of government in the process.

The growing incompetence of national governments, and their difficulties with governance, are not, however, matched by a similar process within the societies they govern. This phenomenon can be explained by reference to a set of dynamics which were initiated earlier in the twentieth century but culminated during the Cold War. The mobilisation of manpower, industry and technology during the Second World War placed a premium on the creation of a class of technical and bureaucratic managers to operate government agencies and research institutions, and this need grew during the decades that followed.[66] The extension of American national interest to all parts of the globe during this period meant, as well, that a trained cadre with specialised knowledge about foreign societies and their politics and economics was essential if the 'free world' was to be managed for the benefit of the United States. Finally, the emergence of a scientific problem-solving paradigm, as the dominant model for managing the new global system, created a need for large numbers of individuals trained in a variety of scientific disciplines. This approach also became the basis for the prosecution of the Cold War, as various educational and technical operations were integrated into the national 'defence'.[67]

To meet this demand, the system of higher education in the United States grew enormously. Growing numbers of highly skilled individuals were trained and graduated, with the expectation that they would find employment in universities, the corporate world, or government. The growth in educated cadres was not limited to the United States, because the American model was universalised. Foreigners were encouraged to come to the United States – indeed, their way was often paid – to acquire the skills and training necessary to rationalise their own societies.[68] Other countries began to recognise the prestige inherent in systems of higher education, as well as their need for trained individuals in order to compete in this new global system.

James Rosenau has taken particular note of the growing analytical skills and capabilities of what he calls 'powerful people', arguing that:

> The advent of postinternational politics...has developed...from fundamental and enduring changes in the analytic skills and cathetic capacities of people. It is not the attitudes of citizens toward politics that are transforming world politics, but their ability to employ, articulate, direct, and implement whatever their attitudes may be.[69]

Frequently, the rise of 'powerful people' is attributed to the 'communication/computer/information revolution', as though the simple absorption of data and precedent is all that would be necessary to effect the political mobilisation described by Rosenau. This is an incomplete explanation of the phenomenon. It is not the contact itself but the ability to use data as *knowledge* that is the critical element – data are the electronic bits transmitted by communication systems; knowledge involves having the skills to use the data toward specified ends. The relevant skills have been spread, perhaps unwittingly, by the growth in post-secondary educational institutions around the world, as well as by changes in the world economy. Because political systems are so diverse, the particular channels of articulation of this new competence vary from one country to the next. However, the general effect is one of the creation of networks of global political activity in parallel to the state system. These networks are not totally insulated or isolated from the state system, since states are omnipresent, and often seem almost omnipotent. They do, however, enjoy a certain degree of autonomy precisely because states are not omnicompetent. States that seek to suppress the activities of these networks often find themselves criticised, and sometimes isolated, by others.

The technologies that may have had the most effect on generating 'people power' and global civil society are those that have produced inexpensive global transportation. The proliferation of jets and air travel since the 1960s has created an era of relatively cheap and easy global travel.[70] This has allowed a significant number of people the opportunity for long-distance travel which led to cross-cultural fertilisation and activities. Travel introduces people to new ways of doing things, including new forms of social organisation, and they come to see the costs of old ways of doing things. Information is taken back home and used to change ways of life and patterns of social activity. People discover that there are other ways to live, and other places to live in, and they do both.[71]

Travel of the sort suggested here is more than just a means of getting about, it is a process of knowledge exchange – not just data transmission – that allows all kinds of political and social transactions to take place outside of the purview or control of governments. This process has enough local consequences to affect global politics.[72] This argument is, in a sense, an extension of Rosenau's 'powerful people' paradigm mentioned above. The key difference between his explanation and mine is not the utility of new information or technologies, but the discovery of new ways of doing things, of acting, of engaging in political and other activities. It is new forms of social organisation and social practice, and not hardware alone, that have global political effects. Finally, even if the total number of people engaged in these practices is limited, their cumulative impact may be substantial because of their dominant role in production and the reproduction of societies.

PRODUCTION AND REPRODUCTION

A third cause for the emergence of global civil society can be found in the spheres of material production and social reproduction. In a recent book, Kenichi Ohmae exalts what he calls the 'borderless world'.[73] In this world, he claims, the state and its borders are no longer important. What is important is consumption, and consumption knows no borders. In this 'borderless world', we are all consumers; indeed, we begin to define ourselves by what we consume, and it becomes central that we have free access to information about products. As Ohmae puts it:

> Today, of course, people everywhere are more and more able to get the information they want directly from all corners of the world. They can see for themselves what the tastes and preferences are in other countries, the styles of clothing now in fashion, the sports, the life-styles.[74]

This does not mean that preferences are universal; clearly they differ, for example, among Japan, Europe and the United States. But it does suggest that, rather that being identified by our country of origin, we are, or somehow will become, defined by our brand names: the Pepsi Generation, Bennetton kids or part of the Gap. Do Ohmae's views make any sense? Does it seem logical that under the principles of liberalism we would replace national loyalty with brand loyalty?[75] David Harvey has written that:

> the shifting social construction of time and space as a result of the restless search for profit creates severe problems of identity: To what space do I as an individual belong? Do I express my idea of citizenship in my neighborhood, city, region, nation, or world?[76]

In the final analysis, brands fail to offer a sufficient anchor for identity, for either groups or individuals. Even if we wear brand names on the outside of our clothing, it hardly seems plausible that all the owners of Levi's Jeans will organise as a political or social force. The construction of identity through the consumption of mass-produced goods creates an undifferentiated agglomeration and, ultimately, fails to serve even individual self-interest.

Flexible production, touted as a means of meeting differentiated wants, and thereby creating differentiated identities, does little better. Stuart Hall has suggested that these new systems of production associated with the globalisation of liberalism actually serve to destroy or undermine the older bases of political and social identity. He observes that:

> 'Post-Fordism' is also associated with broader social and cultural changes. For example, [among these are] greater fragmentation and pluralism, the weakening of older collective solidarities and block identities and the emergence of new identities associated with greater work flexibility, the maximization of individual choices through personal consumption....In part, it is us who are being 're-made'....The 'self' is experienced as more fragmented and incomplete, composed of multiple 'selves' or identities in relation to the different social worlds we inhabit....[77]

This fragmentation of self, Hall goes on to observe, has led to an

> enormous expansion of 'civil society,' caused by the diversification of the different social worlds in which men and women can operate....Of course, 'civil society' is no ideal realm of pure freedom. Its micro-worlds include the multiplication of points of power and conflict. More and more our everyday lives are caught up with these forms of power, and their lines of intersection. Far from there being no resistance to the system, there has been a proliferation of new points of antagonism, new social movements of resistance organized around them, and, consequently, a generalization of 'politics' to spheres which hitherto the left assumed to be apolitical....[78]

As the ideas and modes of production of liberalism have become the 'operating system' in the West, South and, now, the East, identification with the nation-state as the primary social grouping has begun to wither. Yet, individualised identity, based on consumption and the market, is an insufficient basis for establishing new identities. As a result, therefore, we see the rise of new forms of collective identity. In those places where the nation has been suppressed, or where 'nations' have not existed for decades if not centuries (e.g., from a more positive perspective, Catalonia; from a less positive one, Bosnia), we see the stirrings of new nationalisms. In places where nationality does not map simply on to territory, or in social realms where nationalism is often not a respectable basis for identity (especially among the intelligentsia), we see new forms of group identity being created, including some that are very cosmopolitan. Examples of these include the human rights and environmental groups described earlier, as well as feminism, gay and lesbian identities and religious fundamentalism. These new identities are part and parcel of the emergence of global civil society.[79]

What, ultimately, is the cumulative effect of global civil society on world politics? Here we need to turn to theories of social reproduction and transformation. Robert Cox's work on production and historical structures provides one possible way of understanding this process.[80] 'Production', according to Cox,

> creates the material base for all forms of social existence, and the ways in which human efforts are combined in productive processes affect all other aspects of social life, including the polity. Production generates the capacity to exercise power, but power determines the manner in which production takes place.[81]

This is the basis for his understanding of world order and how it changes. Elsewhere in his work he characterises his approach as one based on the notion of historical structures, one that:

> focuses on the structures that constitute the framework or parameters for action and that shape the characters of individual actors....Actors are conditioned by the resources, norms, expectations, and institutions of the societies in which they grow up. They are limited by the social-economic and military-political pressures of their environment. They are products of history.[82]

Historical structures are those institutional practices that make up the fabric of any society. They prescribe what is expected and proscribe what is forbidden. They condition human behaviour, if not its nature, and exercise a constraining influence over the possibilities for individual action in history.[83] Historical structures, according to Cox, exist in the *longue durée* described by Fernand Braudel. Cox also suggests that:

> Participants in a mode of social relations of production share a mental picture of the mode in ideas of what is normal, expected behavior and in how people arrange their lives with regard to work and income.... Specific social groups tend to evolve a collective mentality, that is, a typical way of perceiving and interpreting the world that provides orientation to action for members of the group.

The first set of ideas are 'ethics'; the second, 'rationalities'.[84] Ethics and rationalities are 'intersubjective' in that they can only be really understood from within the classes and social groups that practice them. Traditional Marxism would argue that ethics and rationalities are simply superstructure determined by the material substructure. But Cox and his colleague, Stephen Gill, argue that the process of social change is as much a function of 'progressive self-consciousness' as of structural constraints and material conditions.[85] As an example of this, Cox points to the potential emergence of 'whole segments of societies [that have] become attached, through active participation and developed loyalties, to social institutions engaged in collective activities', which he and Gill call 'counter-hegemonic' or, drawing on Gramsci, 'historic blocs'. This is happening, according to Gill, because the contradictions of economic globalisation and political change have created a crisis of the old hegemonic structures and forms of political consent, which are now coming apart and providing an opportunity for, among other things, the emergence of a transnational civil society.[86] Ultimately, according to Cox,

> The condition for a restructuring of society and polity in this sense would be to build a new historic bloc capable of sustaining a long war of position until it is strong enough to become an alternative basis of polity. This effort would have to be grounded in the popular strata. The activities that comprise it will not likely initially be directed to the state because of the degree of depoliticisation and alienation from the state among these strata. They will more likely be directed to local authorities and to collective self-help. They will in many cases be local responses to global problems–to problems of the environment, of organising production of providing welfare, of migration. If they are ultimately to result in new kinds of state, these forms of state will arise from the practice of non-state popular collective action rather than from extensions of existing types of administrative control.[87]

I should add that, while I find the general argument persuasive, I have my doubts about whether global civil society as I have described it above is truly a counter-hegemonic bloc wherein lie the seeds for a new polity. I think Cox and Gill may give too much emphasis to the relations of production and not enough to the flexibility of the relations of *social reproduction* associated with political institutions, especially under the long-term conditions characteristic of, in particular, many environmental problems. While the transformation of modes of production is well underway, the threat to the material base – the environment – is not immediately obvious, but is likely to emerge over the next 50 years. In the meantime, as the system of material production begins to operate in a more faltering fashion and is less and less able to meet the needs, wants and 'ethics' of the society, then the 'real' interests of society may become obvious to some, who will begin to make an effort to reform or reconstruct the social system. In such an instance, we are likely to see frantic efforts to restore equilibrium, to bring society back to where it once was. The current debates in the United States over free trade versus protectionism have this character as do increasingly vociferous discussions of economics and environment.[88] One side argues that free trade will create new jobs, by implication re-employing those thrown out of work by the new 'social structure of accumulation'. The other claims that such re-employment can only occur if barriers to trade are re-established, which will allow American industries to retool and rehire. The disagreement here is over means, and not ends. What we see being discussed in this instance is a crisis of means towards an agreed end, and not a crisis of the system as a whole.

If the threat to the material base is not immediate, but only emerges over the longer term,[89] it is likely that structures of reproduction and legitimation will be challenged by those who are slowly becoming aware of this crisis as a result of their training and their relationship to the state, that is, the intelligentsia, the educated, and the 'powerful people'. From the source of social legitimation – social elites – there emerges a challenge to the social order and the Gramscian hegemony of the elites. In the long term, it is these types of challenges, and not only changes in the modes of production, that serve to alter political practices. Ultimately, it is simultaneous individual resistance to the consumer culture of global capitalism and collective resistance to its short- and long-term effects that give life and power to global civil society.

SOME CONCLUDING THOUGHTS ON GLOBAL CIVIL SOCIETY

In this paper, I have suggested that the emergence of global civil society can be explained by interacting phenomena, at the macro, or structural, level, and at the micro, or agency, level. At the structural level, I argued that anarchy, as the organising principle of the international system, is withering away. This is the result not so much of sudden changes in the global political scene – a shift from bipolarity to multipolarity or unipolarity – as the long-term acceptance of liberalism as a global 'operating system', with all the short- and long-term contradictions that such a shift may entail. Moreover, the provision of security by states has become problematic not only because of the destructiveness of military technology but also because of the growing 'density' of the global system. This, paradoxically, provides the political space for non-state actors to create alliances and linkages across borders and around the globe that, in the longer term, may serve to undermine particular 'historical structures' and create visible changes in world politics.

At the level of agency, national governments are unable, or loath, to provide the kind of welfare services demanded by citizens, who are more and more aware of what they want and how they might get it. The micro response is to find new ways of providing these services, and citizens are increasingly capable of doing this. Moreover, while many of these efforts are locally focused, they are not limited in terms of adopting forms of social organisation applied elsewhere around the world. Indeed, the transfer of knowledge is facilitated by the various types of communication and transportation hardware that are also a consequence of the conditions of post-Second World War global structure. The results are networks of skilled individuals and groups, operating in newly politicised issue areas, who are helping to modify the state system. Thus, we see the interaction of agency and structure contributing to the emergence and growth of global civil society.

It should be noted, however, that the emergence of global civil society will not necessarily lead to a more peaceful or unified world. On the one hand, it is entirely possible that the effect may be the opposite: the emergence of a neo-medieval world with high levels of conflict and confrontation.[90] On the other hand, there may be promise in this for the future. As Stephen Gill has suggested, some of the processes discussed here could:

> open up new potential for counterhegemonic and progressive forces to begin to make transnational links, and thereby to insert themselves in a more differentiated, multilateral world order. This would be a way to advance the process of democratization of an emerging global civil society and system of international political authority....This might then provide the political space and social possibility to begin to mobilize for the solution to deep-seated problems of social inequality, intolerance, environmental degradation and the militarization of the planet.[91]

In the final analysis, it is important for us to begin to recognise such possibilities, for it is in describing them that we can begin to undertake the reconstruction of world politics that will make them possible.

NOTES

Earlier versions of this paper were presented at the annual meeting of the International Studies Association, Atlanta, Georgia, USA 31 March–4 April, 1992 and appeared in *Millennium* (Vol. 21, No. 3, Winter 1992). In writing it I have benefited from discussions with many people, including members of the Board of Studies in Politics at University of California at Santa Cruz, David Meyer, Paul Wapner, Dan Deudney, Alan Durning, Judith Mayer, James Rosenau, Michael Barnett, Beverly Crawford, Ole Wæver, Alan Gilbert, James Der Derian, Rick Fawn and Jeremy Larkins.

1. Marshall Berman, *All That is Solid Melts Into Air* (New York, NY: Simon and Schuster, 1982), p. 15.
2. Alan Wolfe, 'Three Paths to Development: Market, State, and Civil Society', Paper presented to the International Meeting of NGOs and the UN System Agencies, Rio de Janeiro, 6–9 August 1991, p. 1.
3. An example of the latest stage in this debate – between constructivism and realism – can be found in Alexander Wendt, 'Anarchy is What States Make of It: The Social Construction of Power Politics', *International Organization* (Vol. 46, No. 2, Spring 1992), pp. 391–425; and Markus Fischer, 'Feudal Europe, 800–1300: Communal Discourse and Conflictual Practices', *International Organization* (Vol. 46, No. 2, Spring 1992), pp. 427–66, and citations therein, and the exchange of commentaries in *International Organization* (Vol. 47, No. 3, Summer 1993), pp. 479–500.
4. See, for example, Fischer, 'Feudal Europe'; Stephen D. Krasner, 'Westphalia and All That', pp. 235–264, in Judith Goldstein and Robert O. Koehane (eds.), *Ideas and Foreign Policy: Beliefs, Institutions and Political Change*, (Ithaca, NY: Cornell University Press, 1993); John G. Ruggie, 'Territoriality and Beyond: Problematizing Modernity in International Relations', *International Organization* (Vol. 47, No.1, Winter 1993), pp. 141–76. Ken Booth observes, somewhat tongue in cheek, that 'By the 1980s, the academic study of international politics had itself become an anarchical society.' 'Security in Anarchy: Utopian Realism in Theory and Practice,' *International Affairs* (Vol. 67, No. 3, July 1991), p. 530.
5. This notion is borrowed from Barry Buzan, *People, States and Fear*, 2nd edn (Boulder, CO: Lynne Rienner, 1991). I will also argue below that anarchy is, in fact, a fiction. A discussion of the history of transnational activity can be found in Craig N. Murphy, *International Organizations and Industrial Change: Global Governance since 1850* (New York, NY: Oxford University Press, 1994).
6. Hedley Bull, *The Anarchical Society: A Study of Order in World Politics* (New York, NY: Columbia University Press, 1977), pp. 254–76.
7. James N. Rosenau, *Turbulence in World Politics: A Theory of Change and Continuity* (Princeton, NJ: Princeton University Press, 1990).

8. See, among others, Stephen Gill, 'Reflections on Global Order and Sociohistorical Time', *Alternatives* (Vol. 16, No.3, Summer 1991), p. 311, where he uses the term global civil society; Ken Booth, 'Security in Anarchy'; Paul Wapner, 'Ecological Activism and World Civic Politics', Paper prepared for a panel on the Role of NGOs in International Environmental Cooperation and Security, International Studies Association Conference, Atlanta, 31 March–4 April 1992; and Paul Ghils, 'International Civil Society: International Non-Governmental Organizations in the International System', *International Social Science Journal* (Vol. 133, August 1992), pp. 417–29.
9. 'Heteronomous', in this case, implies that these networks are differentiated from each other in terms of specialisations: there is not a single network, but many, each fulfilling a different function. For a discussion of the term in the medieval context, see John G. Ruggie, 'Continuity and Transformation in the World Polity: Toward a Neorealist Synthesis', *World Politics* (Vol. 35, No. 2, January 1983), pp. 273–4.
10. The term is from Benedict Anderson who writes: 'Communities are to be distinguished, not by their falsity/genuineness, but by the style in which they are imagined. Javanese villagers have always known that they are connected to people they have never seen, but these ties were once imagined particularistically – as indefinitely stretchable nets of kinship and clientship.' *Imagined Communities: Reflections on the Origin and Spread of Nationalism*, 2nd edn (London: Verso, 1991), p. 6.
11. Wolfe, 'Three Paths', p. 1.
12. Crawford Young, *The Politics of Cultural Pluralism* (Madison, WI: University of Wisconsin Press, 1976), p. 66. The state-centred systemic model is a 'transforming theory' or model that originates in the practices of state diplomacy, is appropriated by those who study these practices and which, in turn, influences those practices. See David Dessler, 'The Use and Abuse of Social Science for Policy', *SAIS Review* (Vol. 9, No. 2, Summer–Fall 1989), pp. 222–3.
13. See, for example, Jonathan Schell, 'Introduction,' in Adam Michnik, *Letters from Prison and Other Essays* (Berkeley, CA: University of California Press, 1985); and Zbigniew Rau (ed.), *The Reemergence of Civil Society in Eastern Europe and the Soviet Union* (Boulder, CO: Westview, 1991).
14. See, for example, the attack on 'local foreign policies' by Peter J. Spiro, 'Taking Foreign Policy Away from the Feds', *Washington Quarterly* (Vol. 11, No. 1, Winter 1988), pp. 191–203.
15. But, see David Skidmore and Valerie M. Hudson (eds), *The Limits of State Autonomy: Societal Groups and Foreign Policy Formulation* (Boulder, CO: Westview Press, 1993).
16. See the critique of this notion in Michael Walzer, 'The Civil Society Argument', pp. 89–107, in Chantal Mouffe (ed.), *Dimensions of Radical Democracy: Pluralism, Citizenship, Community* (London: Verso, 1992).

17. Stuart Hall has developed this idea in detail. See, for example, 'Brave New World', *Socialist Review* (Vol. 21, No. 1, 1991). pp. 57–64, and especially pp. 62–3.
18. Hall suggests that there may be no map but, rather, '[A] network of strategies and powers and their articulations....' *Ibid.*, p. 64.
19. 'Ecological issues are in many respects politically and ideologically unoccupied territory; and thus the object of attention from diverse ideological standpoints.' Alan Scott, *Ideology and the New Social Movements* (London: Unwin Hyman, 1990), p. 107. I would not, however, want to underestimate the residual force of nationalism in the expression of ecological and other social movements.
20. See Hall, 'Brave New World', p. 63. I am not referring to 'social movements' in the general sense, although they do constitute part of global civil society; rather I am focusing on networks of action and knowledge that are much broader in scope. A general overview of global social movements is provided by Paul Elkins, *A New World Order: Grassroots Movements for Global Change* (London: Routledge, 1992).
21. Peter Haas (ed.), 'Knowledge, Power, and International Policy Coordination', *International Organization* (Vol. 46, No. 1, Winter 1992), special issue.
22. This aspect of global civil society is explored in detail Ronnie D. Lipschutz, 'Learn of the Green World: Global Environmental Change, Global Civil Society and Social Learning', *Transnational Associations* (No. 3, 1993), pp. 124–138,
23. The notion of networks is briefly addressed by Sidney Tarrow, 'National Politics and Collective Action: Recent Theory and Research in Western Europe and the United States', *Annual Review of Sociology* (Vol. 14, 1988), pp. 431–3. It is discussed in greater detail in Kathryn Sikkink, 'Human rights, principled issue-networks, and sovereignty in Latin America', *International Organization* (Vol. 47, No. 3, Summer 1993), pp. 411–42; and Sheldon Annis, 'Evolving Connectedness Among Environmental Groups and Grassroots Organizations in Protected Areas of Central America', *World Development* (Vol. 20, No. 4, 1992), pp. 587–95. For a more formalistic description of networks, see David Knoke, *Political Networks: The Structural Perspective* (Cambridge: Cambridge University Press, 1990), esp. pp. 76–81.
24. See, for example, Paul Wapner, *Making States Biodegradable: Ecological Activism and World Politics*, Draft Manuscript (Albany, NY: SUNY Press, 1994).
25. See Gareth Porter and Janet Welsh Brown, *Global Environmental Politics* (Boulder, CO: Westview, 1991), pp. 56–60.
26. Dharam Ghai and Jessica M. Vivian (eds), *Grassroots Environmental Action: People's Participation in Sustainable Development* (London: Routledge, 1992).

27. There is a growing literature on the importance of such groups in a local context. See, for example, David Korten, *Getting to the 21st Century: Voluntary Action and the Global Agenda* (West Hartford, CT: Kumarian Press, 1990); Alan B. During, *Action at the Grassroots: Fighting Poverty and Environmental Decline* (Washington, DC: Worldwatch Institute, Jan. 1989); and Robin Broad, John Cavanagh and Walden Bello, 'Development: The Market is Not Enough', *Foreign Policy* (Vol. 81, Winter 1990–91), pp. 152–60.
28. See the informational brochure provided by Centre for International Development and Environment of the World Resources Institute, 'From the Ground Up: Improving Natural Resource Management by Documenting Grassroots Experience in Sustainable Development', no date; and also issues of the *NGO Networker*, a newsletter published by the World Resources Institute (Washington, DC).
29. Conversation with Frances Spivy-Weber, Director, UNCED US Citizens Working Group on Forests, 7 March 1992. See also Lawrence T. Woods, 'Nongovernmental Organizations and the United Nations System: Reflecting Upon the Earth Summit Experience', *International Studies Notes* (Vol. 18, No. 1, Winter 1993), pp. 9–15.
30. Nina Broner Worcman, 'Local Groups Think Globally', *Technology Review* (Vol. 95, No. 7, October 1992), p. 36.
31. Sikkink, 'Human Rights'.
32. See, for example, Edward A. Gargan, 'India Rights Group's Cry: Police Rape and Torture', *New York Times*, 14 October 1992.
33. For an overview of the roles of non-governmental organisations in human rights work, see Henry J. Steiner, *Diverse Partners: Non-Governmental Organizations in the Human Rights Movement* (Cambridge, MA: Harvard Law School/Human Rights Internet, 1991).
34. Jan De Vos, seminar, University of California, Santa Cruz. De Vos' work is only in Spanish. See, for example, *La pas de Dios y del rey: la conquista de la selva lacandona, 1525–1821*, 2nd edn (Mexico, DF: Secretariat of Education and Culture of Chiapas, Foundation of Economic Culture, 1988). What is ironic about efforts by the Maya to consolidate their sovereignty claims along North American Indian lines is the fact that the sovereign Indian tribes of North America did not possess territorial sovereignty, or even a tribal identity, prior to the arrival of Europeans. The governments of Britain, France and the United States more or less 'created' them via the various treaties concluded during the nineteenth century. The loop does not end there. Various 'nations', such as the Iroquois, did exist prior to the European arrival. To a large degree, however, Europeans imposed (or imagined) sovereignty and territory where none had previously existed. But it is interesting to note the claim that the Iroquois 'created' the United States, proposing that it be developed along federal lines. See Jack Weatherford, *Indian Givers: How the Indians of the Americas Transformed*

the World (New York, NY: Crown, 1988).

35. John Brown Childs, 'Rooted Cosmopolitanism: The Transnational Character of Indigenous Particularity', Stevenson Programme on Global Security Colloquium, University of California at Santa Cruz, 19 October 1992; Franke Wilmer, *The Indigenous Voice in World Politics* (Beverly Hills: Sage, 1993), pp. 127–161; Bice Maiguashca, 'The Role of Ideas in a Changing World Order: The Case of the International Indigenous Movement, 1975–91', Paper prepared for the International Conference on 'Changing World Order and the United Nations System', Yokohama, Japan, 24–27 March 1992.

36. See, for example, Roger Coate and Kurt Will, 'Social Networks Responding to Aids: Travel Restrictions and the San Francisco Boycott', Paper prepared for delivery at the Annual Meeting of the International Studies Association, Atlanta, Georgia, 31 March–4 April, 1992.

37. See, for example, Skidmore and Hudson (eds), *Limits of State Autonomy*; David Meyer's paper, 'How the Cold War was Really Won: A View From Below', Paper prepared for delivery at the Annual Meeting of the International Studies Association, Vancouver, British Columbia, 1991; and David Meyer and Sam Marullo, 'Grassroots Mobilization and International Politics: Peace Protest and the End of the Cold War', *Research in Social Movements, Conflict and Change* (Vol. 14, 1992), pp. 99–140. A number of other observers and writers have begun to speculate on action within these political spaces. See Chadwick F. Alger, 'The World Relations of Cities: Closing the Gap Between Social Science Paradigms and Everyday Human Experience', *International Studies Quarterly* (Vol. 34, No. 4, 1990), p. 494; and Paul Wapner, 'Ecological Activism'.

38. Booth, 'Security in Anarchy,' p. 542.

39. Buzan, *People, States and Fear*, pp. 174–81.

40. Stephen Krasner (ed.), *International Regimes* (Ithaca, NY: Cornell University Press, 1983). The concept of 'regime' can, of course, be applied in many contexts, domestic as well as international. Indeed, according to Oran R. Young, a regime is simply one form of social institution that has been given a distinctive name. See *Resource Regimes: Natural Resources and Social Institutions* (Berkeley, CA: University of California Press, 1982). To be sure, there are international regimes administered by non-governmental organisations (for example, the CITES regime), but they are still the creation of states.

41. Bull, *Anarchical Society*, pp. 13 and 264–76. A recent exploration of the difference between 'international system' and 'international society' can be found in Barry Buzan, 'From International System to International Society: Structural Realism and Regime Theory Meet the English School', *International Organization* (Vol. 47, No. 3, Summer 1993), pp. 327–52.

42. Indeed, Raymond Cohen has recently argued that, because of the spread of the state system beyond Europe, the notion of diplomatic culture is no longer very useful at all. See *Negotiating Across Cultures* (Washington, DC: US Institute of Peace, 1991).
43. 'Neoliberal Institutionalism: A Perspective on World Politics', pp. 1–20, in Robert O. Keohane, *International Institutions and State Power* (Boulder, CO: Westview Press, 1989), p. 1.
44. See Buzan, 'From International System to International Society'. Other provocative analyses of the 'globalization' of politics are: Evan Luard, *The Globalization of Politics: The Changed Focus of Political Action in the Modern World* (London: Macmillan, 1990); and Leslie Sklair, *Sociology of the Global System: Social Change in Global Perspective* (Baltimore, MD: Johns Hopkins University Press, 1991). Luard maintains a focus on the primacy of the state; Sklair uses neo-marxist ideas to describe the ongoing battle of societies against global capitalism.
45. I owe most of the content of this paragraph to consultations with J. Peter Euben and Robert Meister, but have also drawn on Wolfe, 'Three Paths,' and Walzer, 'The Civil Society Argument'. However, in today's world, civil society is never completely insulated from the state, since it tends to occupy those 'spaces' not controlled by the state.
46. James Mayall, *Nationalism and International Society* (Cambridge: Cambridge University Press, 1990), p. 56.
47. This point was suggested to me by Alan Gilbert, and it is particularly evident in the movement to restore rights of sovereignty to 'indigenous peoples'. As argued below, global civil society may be a reaction to the Gramscian hegemony of the state system.
48. John G. Ruggie, 'International Structure and International Transformation: Space, Time, and Method,' in E.O. Czempiel and James N. Rosenau (eds), *Global Changes and Theoretical Challenges* (Lexington, MA: Lexington Books, 1989), p. 31.
49. Daniel Deudney, 'Global Environmental Rescue and the Emergence of World Domestic Politics', in Ronnie D. Lipschutz and Ken Conca (eds), *The State and Social Power in Global Environmental Politics* (New York, NY: Columbia University Press, 1993), pp. 280–305.
50. Alberto Melucci, *Nomads of the Present: Social Movements and Individual Needs in Contemporary Society*, in J. Keane and Paul Mier (eds), (London: Hutchinson Radius, 1989), pp. 74 and 86.
51. It is conceivable that global civil societies existed in earlier times, in the form of the Church, medical and missionary organisations, as well as the slavery abolitionist movements of the nineteenth century. What is important is the leakage of sovereignty and responsibility away from the state to other actors, imbuing the latter with constitutive rights – in much the same way as seems to have been the case in medieval society. On constitutive rules and rights, see, for example, Ruggie, 'International Structure'; David

Dessler, 'What's at Stake in the Agent-Structure Debate,' *International Organization* (Vol. 43, No. 3, Summer 1989), pp. 441–73; and Ronnie D. Lipschutz and Judith Mayer, 'Not Seeing the Forest for the Trees: Rights, Rules, and the Renegotiation of Resource Management Regimes', pp. 246–273, in Lipschutz and Conca (eds), *The State and Social Power*.

52. The globalisation of liberalism, along with a number of other integrative processes, is actively transforming the classical nation-state. This process and recognition of it is not new, but it does seems much more conspicuous than it once was. See Roland Robertson, 'Mapping the Global Condition: Globalization as a Central Concept', pp. 15–30, in Mike Featherstone, (ed.), *Global Culture* (London: Sage, 1991).

53. See, for example, Kenneth N. Waltz, *Man, the State and War: A Theoretical Analysis* (New York, NY: Columbia University Press, 1959).

54. These definitions of anarchy are taken from *The American Heritage Dictionary of the English Language* (Boston, MA: Houghton-Mifflin, 1981).

55. On the difficulties of collective action, see Mancur Olsen, *The Logic of Collective Action* (Cambridge, MA: Harvard University Press, 1971); and Russell Hardin, *Collective Action* (Baltimore, MD: Johns Hopkins University Press, 1982). For critiques, see Elinor Ostrom, *Governing the Commons: The Evolution of Institutions for Collective Action* (Cambridge: Cambridge University Press, 1990), ch. 1. On the possibilities of cooperation under anarchy, see the work of Robert Axelrod, *The Evolution of Cooperation* (New York, NY: Basic, 1984).

56. On the market as a social institution, see Robert Heilbroner, 'Behind the Veil of Economics', in *Behind the Veil of Economics: Essays in the Worldly Philosophy*, (New York, NY: W.W. Norton, 1988), pp. 13–34. For a more general discussion of the nature of social institutions, see Oran Young, *Resource Regimes*. See also Ronnie D. Lipschutz, *When Nations Clash: Raw Materials, Ideology and Foreign Policy*, (New York, NY: Ballinger/Harper & Row, 1989), p. 244.

57. Alexander Wendt, 'Anarchy is What States Make of It', pp. 391–426.

58. Friedrich Kratochwil, *Rules, Norms, and Decisions: On the Conditions of Practical and Legal Reasoning in International Relations and Domestic Affairs* (Cambridge: Cambridge University Press, 1990); and Nicholas Greenwood Onuf, *World of Our Making: Rules and Rule in Social Theory and International Relations* (Columbia, SC: University of South Carolina Press, 1989); and Wendt, 'Anarchy is What States Make of It'.

59. James N. Rosenau, 'Governance, Order, and Change in World Politics', pp. 1–29, in James N. Rosenau and E.O. Czempiel (eds), *Governance without Government: Order and Change in World Politics*, (Cambridge: Cambridge University Press, 1992), p. 4.

60. A view somewhat critical of this liberal perspective – perhaps with some justification – is offered by Laura MacDonald, 'Globalizing Civil Society: Interpreting International NGOs in Central America', Paper prepared for

presentation to the International Studies Association, Acapulco, 24–27 March 1993.

61. This is not to suggest that peace is necessarily at hand; only that inter-state war is becoming much less common, while intra-state war is increasing in frequency. Conflict may also be reconstituted in other, non-state spheres of human social relations, for example culture. For provocative explorations of this, see William S. Lind, 'Defending Western Culture', *Foreign Policy* (No. 84, Fall 1991), pp. 40–50; Samuel P. Huntington, 'The Clash of Civilizations', *Foreign Affairs* (Vol. 72, No. 3, Summer 1993), pp. 22–49; and responses to Huntington in *Foreign Affairs* (Vol. 72, No. 4, Sept./Oct. 1993), pp. 2–26.
62. It is possible that the emergence of the universal norms of liberalism – which places a premium on individual 'self-help' – is a driving force behind the declining competence and willingness of governments. It seems more likely, however, that governments and states simply cannot cope with the multitude of demands placed on them.
63. Thus, the growing move toward privatisation of municipal services in the United States, as well as efforts to privatise health services in Britain and reduce welfare services in Scandinavia.
64. This contradiction was evident in the central command bureaucracies of the old Soviet Union. Many of the original management agencies, such as the United States Forest Service, were established to conserve resources through rationalised management, but not for purposes of protection. See, for example, Samuel P. Hays, *Conservation and the Gospel of Efficiency* (New York, NY: Atheneum, 1980).
65. This point is developed in greater detail in Lipschutz, 'Learn of the Green World'; Ronnie D. Lipschutz, 'Networks of Knowledge and Practice: Global Civil Society and the Protection of the Global Environment', in L. Anathea Brooks and Stacy Van Deveer (eds), *Saving the Seas: Science, Values, and International Governance*, (work in progress).
66. Note that the upper echelons remained in elite hands until well into the 1960s and even 1970s; see, for a discussion of this, Richard Barnet, *Roots of War* (Baltimore, MD: Penguin, 1972).
67. Enrico Augelli and Craig Murphy, *America's Quest for Supremacy and the Third World*, (London: Pinter, 1988), pp. 66–70.
68. This continues to be the case today, as evidenced by the high proportion of non-American citizens receiving doctorates in scientific and engineering fields.
69. Rosenau, *Turbulence in World Politics*, p. 334.
70. Alger, 'The World Relations of Cities'.
71. This does not imply a homogenisation of culture, however, since new forms of social organisation are often adapted for local conditions. For a fascinating exposition of this process, see Arjun Appadurai, 'Disjuncture and Difference in the Global Cultural Economy', pp. 295–310, in Mike

Featherstone (ed.), *Global Culture*.

72. See Saskia Sassen, *The Mobility of Labour and Capital: A Study in International Investment and Labor Flow* (Cambridge: Cambridge University Press, 1988).

73. Kenichi Ohmae, *The Borderless World: Power and Strategy in the Interlinked Economy* (New York, NY: HarperCollins, 1990).

74. Ibid., p. 19.

75. Certainly, this seemed to be the stance of Michael Jordan at the Barcelona Olympics, when he refused to wear the United States national uniform because it was supplied by Nike and not by the company that he endorsed.

76. David Harvey, 'Flexibility: Threat or Opportunity', *Socialist Review* (Vol. 21, No. 1, January 1991), p. 77.

77. 'Brave New World' *Socialist Review*, p. 58.

78. Ibid., p. 63.

79. Because the new 'nationalisms' are directed toward the acquisition of a state, they do not fall under the rubric of global civil society.

80. What follows is informed and inspired by Robert W. Cox, *Power, Production and World Order* (New York, NY: Columbia University Press, 1987); Stephen Gill, Robert Cox and Kees Van Der Pijl, 'Structural Change and Globalising Elites: Political Economy Perspectives in the Emerging World Order', Prepared for the International Conference on Changing World Order and the United Nations System, Yokohama, Japan, 24–27 March 1992; Stephen Gill, 'Reflections of Global Order', pp. 275–314; and Eric Laferrière, 'The Globalization of Politics: Environmental Degradation and North-South Relations', Paper presented at the annual Conference of the Canadian Political Science Association, University of Prince Edward Island, Charlottetown, 31 May–2 June 1992.

81. Cox, *Power, Production and World Order*, p. 1.

82. Ibid., p. 38.

83. Ibid.; see also, Lipschutz, *When Nations Clash*, ch. 2.

84. Cox, *Power, Production and World Order*, pp. 22 and 25.

85. Stephen Gill, 'Epistemology, Ontology and the "Italian School"', pp. 21–48, in Stephen Gill (ed.), *Gramsci, Historical Materialism and International Relations* (Cambridge: Cambridge University Press, 1993), pp. 36–7. See also Robert W. Cox, 'Structural Issues of Global Governance: Implications for Europe', pp. 259–89, in Gill, ibid.

86. Ibid., pp. 32–3.

87. Cox, 'Structural Issues', p. 272.

88. See, for example, Durwood Zaelke, Paul Orbuch and Robert F. Housman (eds), *Trade and the Environment: Law, Economics, and Policy* (Washington, DC: Island Press, 1993); and Allan Schnaiberg and Kenneth Alan Gould, *Environment and Society: The Enduring Conflict*, (New York: St. Martin's Press, 1994).

89. I should note, however, that in many parts of the world, the threat to the material base is immediate. Because of social complexity, however, these parts lack the autonomy to address those threats in an immediate fashion. For an explanation of 'social complexity', see Lipschutz, 'Learn of the Green World'; and 'Networks of Knowledge and Practice'.
90. In retrospect, Hedley Bull's characterisation of the 'new mediaevalism' seems quite accurate. *The Anarchical Society*, pp. 254–5 and 264–76. The neo-medieval world will be a patchwork, a pastiche of political and economic actors, engaged with each other, and in conflict, too. Global civil society may well be only one part of this world. See also Booth's discussion of medievalism in 'Security in Anarchy'.
91. Gill, 'Reflections on Global Order,' p. 311.

Part III
Practical Implications

7 Humanitarian Intervention and State Practice at the End of the Cold War

Nicholas J. Wheeler and Justin Morris

INTRODUCTION

Traditional political theory assumes that the state provides for the security and welfare of its citizens while accepting a plurality of conceptions of what constitutes the 'good life'. So long as states fulfil their domestic obligations towards their citizens, and abide by the norms of non-intervention and non-aggression in their external behaviour, then no conflict occurs between the requirements of international order and individual justice. This is the essential morality of the society of states.[1] However, this underlying justification for the division of the world into sovereign states is critically challenged by the reality that, in all too many parts of the world, states are the principal threat to and not the ultimate guardian of their citizens' security.[2] Consequently, this gives rise to a conflict between the requirements of inter-state order and individual justice, with the principle of non-intervention standing as a barrier to the development of effective means of protecting individual human rights. This conflict between order and justice is revealed in its starkest form in those exceptional cases of human suffering that are triggered either by the breakdown of the state into anarchy and civil war, or by the genocidal practices of governments and ethnic militias competing for control of the state. In these situations can the society of states remain passive or should it legitimise humanitarian intervention inside state borders?

The legitimacy of humanitarian intervention in a society of states built on the principle of non-intervention has long been a subject of controversy among international lawyers and moral philosophers. While humanitarian intervention can take the form of coercive, non-military intervention (some might even argue that diplomatic censure and isolation constitute intervention), we will confine our remarks to the question of military intervention.[3] Our working definition of humanitarian intervention is: unsolicited military intervention in another state's internal affairs with the primary intention of alleviating the suffering of some or all within its borders.[4] Historically, state practice has given little support to the legitimacy of such action, but at the end of the Cold War, some commentators argue that recent cases demonstrate a new-found acceptance of the concept, and argue furthermore that such a development is to be welcomed on the grounds that it strengthens the normative value of the society of states.

Through a comparative study of emergent state practice in the Cold War and post-Cold War eras we will critically assess both of these claims. The descriptive claim that there is a new norm of humanitarian intervention will be questioned on the grounds that none of the post-Cold War cases represent clear-cut examples of humanitarian intervention as defined above. The normative claim that this is a welcome development will be challenged on the grounds that the moral value of the order provided by an international society, predicated upon the principle of non-intervention, has to be judged not only in relation to the impotence of the society of states in the face of immediate human suffering, but also in terms of the potential moral consequences of a long-term and generalised erosion of this principle.

The argument will proceed in three stages. We will begin by setting out the standard arguments for and against humanitarian intervention. Next, we will briefly consider how far state practice during the Cold War recognised the legitimacy of such a right. This will be followed by a study of the responses of the 'international community' to the Kurdish, Somali and Rwandan crises, and an assessment of the extent to which an emergent norm of humanitarian intervention has developed.[5] We have chosen these three cases for specific consideration because they are examples of armed intervention which most clearly illustrate the problems associated with legitimising a right of humanitarian intervention. Our omission of detailed analysis of cases such as Haiti and, more notably, the former Yugoslavia may seem surprising, but limits of space aside, we feel that these cases reflect less directly upon the central themes of this chapter.

ARGUMENTS AGAINST HUMANITARIAN INTERVENTION

There are five principal objections to humanitarian intervention. The first is that disagreement on the moral questions is sufficiently pervasive and intractable that a consensus on the principles governing humanitarian intervention is unlikely to be achieved. In the absence of such agreement, legitimising a right of humanitarian intervention could lead individual states to act on their particular moral principles, thereby undermining an international order based on the principles of sovereignty, non-intervention and non-use of force. Genocide provides a good example of the problem of securing international consensus. Whilst at first sight it might seem that the outlawing of the practice reflects a consensual moral principle, the legal prohibition fails to determine what constitutes genocide in practice. Writing in the *International Herald Tribune* in September 1992, Charles Krauthammer suggested that humanitarian intervention was legitimate in cases of genocide, but then asserted against the views of other commentators that Serbian war crimes in Bosnia do not constitute such practice.[6] Since the arbitrary nature of quantitative criteria mean that it cannot provide a basis for adjudicating between cases, the question remains: at what point does the international community say that enough is enough, and agree to overturn the principles of non-intervention and non-use of force? As yet, the international community appears unable to provide an answer to this question.

The second argument against humanitarian intervention contends that even if a consensus could be established, states will apply the principles selectively, thus resulting in what may be perceived as inconsistency in policy. Because states will be governed by what they judge to be their national interest, they will intervene only when they deem this to be at stake. The problem of selectivity arises when an agreed moral principle is at stake in more than one situation, but national interest dictates a divergence of response. A good example of this is the claim by Muslim states that the West is guilty of double standards in failing to respond as effectively to the plight of Bosnian Muslims as it had to the case of the Iraqi Kurds. Since the principles may be applied selectively, they are likely to be viewed with suspicion by the 'targets' of intervention, and by those states wedded to the concept of sovereignty, thereby undermining the fragile normative foundations of the society of states.

The problem of selectivity is likely to be compounded by the third objection, that of abuse. Thomas Franck and Nigel Rodley have highlighted this problem with their contention that the prohibition of the use of force is already vulnerable to states abusing it in the name of self-defence, and that a right of humanitarian intervention would only provide further scope for abuse.[7] In the absence of an impartial mechanism for deciding when humanitarian intervention was permissible, states might espouse humanitarian motives as a pretext to cover the pursuit of national self-interest. Accepting the ethical appeal of a right of humanitarian intervention, they contend that

> [i]n theory no moral person can take exception to a rule which, in the absence of an effective international system to secure human rights,

> permits disinterested states to intervene surgically to protect severely endangered human rights and lives, wherever the need may arise.[8]

However, having examined a number of cases in which humanitarian motives were claimed to be primary, they conclude that:

> A study of interventions in practice...reveals that most have occurred in situations where the humanitarian motive is at least balanced, if not outweighed, by a desire to...reinforce sociopolitical and economic instruments of the status quo.[9]

Problems of selectivity and abuse are predicated on the assumption that states may intervene for reasons of national self-interest. However, the next objection to humanitarian intervention posits that states will only ever act for reasons of self-interest; they will never be driven to act for primarily humanitarian reasons. This argument has two components, descriptive and normative. With regard to the former, the claim is made that there is no support in state practice for the idea of humanitarian intervention. An examination of cases often cited as examples of humanitarian intervention (such as the three Cold War examples considered later in this chapter) indicates that the humanitarian motive was only one factor in a complex equation involving numerous stimuli. Mason and Wheeler note that 'most of the cases which can plausibly be regarded as examples of humanitarian intervention involve mixed motives: that is, they are cases in which humanitarian objectives and self-interest coincide, and both serve to drive policy.'[10] Indeed, it is most unlikely that humanitarian motives will ever be paramount, but the fact that a state intervenes for primarily self-interested motives does not necessarily obviate humanitarian benefits, though it does of course place such an action outside of our definition of humanitarian intervention. Moreover, since in practice it will be extremely difficult, if not impossible, to distinguish between the motives, there is always the danger as noted above that states will disguise national self-interest in humanitarian rhetoric.

Even if state leaders were willing to consider military intervention on primarily humanitarian grounds, the second part of this objection makes the normative claim of Realists that such a course of action should be rejected since their primary responsibility is to protect the security of their citizens, including those who serve in the armed forces. The only moral justification for risking soldiers' lives is in defence of the national interest. Krauthammer writes: 'Statesmen...do not have the right to launch their nation into large unfathomable military adventures, to risk not their lives but the lives of their countrymen, purely out of humanitarian feeling.'[11]

The final objection goes under the umbrella heading of prudence. We identify four types of prudence and adopt Robert H. Jackson's labels of 'self-regarding' and 'other-regarding' to categorise them. The latter is predicated upon the idea that when state leaders formulate policy, their primary consideration should be the 'rights, interests and welfare' of others.[12] Other-regarding or normative prudence can take two forms. The first is that the non-intervention principle should be respected on grounds of rule-consequentialism.[13] General well-being is better served by upholding the principle of non-intervention than by allowing humanitarian intervention in the face of disagreements about what constitutes extreme human rights violations in global international society. This brings us back to the first objection and has been dealt with above.

The second line of reasoning relates to the utility of armed humanitarian intervention, leading Adam Roberts to ask the question whether 'humanitarian war' is an oxymoron.[14] He suggests that military intervention 'may come to involve a range of policies and activities which go beyond, or even conflict with, the label "humanitarian"'.[15] Military intervention designed to save lives is likely to involve loss of life – including the lives of the intervening soldiers and possibly those of innocent civilians killed as a consequence of military operations. Since, as Ken Booth observes, the 'injection of international military force, to impose a resolution of a bitter conflict, is likely to be a slippery slope, and probably an ineffective instrument',[16] such loss of life is likely to be a meaningless sacrifice. State leaders must be sensitive to these dangers, and before embarking on the use of force must be clear as to what the political and military objectives of humanitarian intervention are, and what price they are prepared to pay to see these goals achieved.

In contrast to 'other-regarding prudence', 'self-regarding prudence' is where 'leaders are only thinking of themselves or their regimes'.[17] Again, there are two types. The first relates to the fear of precedent-setting. States remain jealous of their sovereign perogatives, fearing the consequences of setting precedents for humanitarian intervention which may be employed against them at some future date. This is particularly true in the case of those non-Western states which accord little constitutional respect for civil and political rights. Self-regarding prudence is also a factor in policy-making in liberal-democratic states where state leaders are continually sensitive to public opinion and the fickle nature of the media and the domestic electorate. While governments have to respond to short-term demands for action – fuelled by the media bombardment of harrowing pictures of human suffering – they must be wary of commiting themselves to foreign adventures which will drain tax revenues and cost lives. The 'CNN factor' is a double-edged sword: it can pressurise governments into hastily conceived and open-ended military interventions, yet with equal rapidity, pictures of 'body-bags' arriving home can lead to public disillusionment and calls for withdrawal.[18]

These four objections are not mutually exclusive; indeed opponents of humanitarian intervention – be they commentators or policy-makers – are most likely to cite them in combination. This resistance to humanitarian intervention is reflected in the existence of an international legal framework which many jurists – labelled 'restrictionists' – claim prohibits the use of force to protect human rights.[19] The lack of a clear legal basis in either treaty or customary international law may itself be seen as yet a further objection to humanitarian intervention.

ARGUMENTS IN FAVOUR OF HUMANITARIAN INTERVENTION

The fundamental argument in favour of humanitarian intervention is that the principles of sovereignty and non-intervention – the cornerstones of the international legal order – cannot be sacrosanct in the face of massive human suffering caused by either the collapse of a state into civil war and anarchy or a government's oppression of its people. Those who espouse a duty of humanitarian intervention do so on the grounds that we all have moral obligations to do what we can to alleviate human suffering wherever it occurs. This is predicated on the cosmopolitanist claim that our identity as citizens of sovereign states does not exhaust our obligations as collective subjects of humanity.[20] Refuting the scepticism of those who believe that we can never arrive at universally agreed moral principles, cosmopolitanists assert that a consensus on universal human rights is attainable, though they recognise that not all statist elites respect these rights.

There is, however, divergence within the cosmopolitanist tradition over the extent to which it is the responsibility of states to enforce these universal moral principles. Some within the tradition reject the notion of 'humanitarian war' as an oxymoron and claim that the use of force to relieve gross human suffering may fit the category of a 'just war'.[21] If the judgement is made by state leaders that more lives will be saved by military intervention than will be lost by a policy of non-intervention, and that overall the good brought about by intervening will outweigh the evil done in accomplishing this, then on grounds of utilitarian or consequentialist reasoning, intervention is permissible. As Hugh Beach writes, '[t]he practicality of what is proposed is a crucial ingredient in formulating the ethical judgement...this...is not pragmatism set against morality, but an essential ingredient in the moral judgement itself'.[22] This moral defence of 'humanitarian war' rejects the normative claim that state leaders have an exclusive duty of responsibility to their citizens. Such a duty places what is surely too stringent an obligation on state leaders, since it is absurd to say that nothing should be done to relieve the suffering of thousands, or even millions, if such an action places just one soldier's life at risk. A state may have its strongest obligations to its citizens, but it can nevertheless discharge obligations to non-citizens without violating its primary ethic of responsibility.[23]

Advocates of a moral duty of humanitarian intervention find support among a small number of jurists who, challenging the 'restrictionist' interpretation of international law, contend that a legal right of humanitarian intervention exists. These 'counter-restrictionists' identify the United Nations (UN) as the principal body for the promotion and protection of human rights. Two lines of reasoning underpin this position. The first is that human rights violations may constitute a threat to international peace and security, thereby enabling the Security Council to take enforcement action under Article 39 of the Charter.[24] The second contention is that preventing gross human rights abuses is itself legitimate grounds for intervention. According to Fernando Teson, 'the promotion of human rights is as important a purpose in the Charter as is the control of international conflict'.[25] Hence it is contended by the 'counter-restrictionists' that the UN has a legal right to overturn the rule which prohibits the Organisation from becoming involved in the internal affairs of member states – Article 2 (7) of the Charter. As with the right to self-defence, humanitarian intervention is seen here as a legitimate exception to the non-use of force principle found in Article 2 (4) of the UN Charter.

Some jurists are prepared to go even further, asserting that if the UN fails to take remedial action – as was so often the case during the Cold War – individual states may intervene with force to reduce human suffering. Reisman and McDougal assert that the human rights provisions of the Charter (Articles 1 (3), 55 and 56) provide a basis for unilateral action. They claim that were this not the case it 'would be suicidally destructive of the explicit purposes for which the United Nations was established'.[26] An alternative grounding for a legal right of unilateral humanitarian intervention is found in the assertion that a residual customary right exists independent of the Charter, although this remains very controversal among jurists.

STATE PRACTICE DURING THE COLD WAR

This section assesses the extent to which state practice during the Cold War recognised the legitimacy of humanitarian intervention. Here, we will focus upon the three cases in the post-1945 period where interventionary action by a neighbouring state led to the ending of genocidal behaviour: India's 1971 intervention in East Pakistan; Tanzania's 1978 intervention in Uganda; and Vietnam's 1979 intervention in Cambodia.

As Justin Morris has pointed out in his study of these cases, the international community chose to condemn all three interventions as breaches of the principles of non-intervention and non-use of force, although the international response was to a large degree conditioned by the political and strategic imperatives of the Cold War.[27] The case where armed intervention was arguably most justifiable on humanitarian grounds – Vietnam's intervention to overthrow the Pol Pot regime in Cambodia – received the greatest censure. Rather than legitimise Hanoi's overturning of the norm of non-intervention on humanitarian grounds, Vietnam was castigated by both the US-led Western bloc and China for acting as an agent of Soviet imperialism.[28] In contrast, Tanzania's overthrow of Idi Amin received little more than ritualistic public denunciation from the Cold War protagonists, with the new Ugandan Government rapidly receiving widespread recognition and financial aid from a number of foreign governments. With the exception of the majority of African states which roundly condemned its actions, the rest of the international community reacted in a way which amounted to what Caroline Thomas has described as 'almost tacit approval'.[29] This would suggest that Cold War geopolitics were not as strong a motivating influence in this case, and that, Amin had almost totally alienated the Soviet Union, his superpower patron and only ally.

In the face of international condemnation, each of the intervening states argued that they were acting in self-defence – the legitimate right of all states under Article 51 of the UN Charter. Tanzania, Vietnam and India all claimed, with some legitimacy, that they were the victims of armed aggression. Both Uganda and Cambodia had undertaken cross-border incursions in the months prior to the invasions, while India claimed that its national security was in part threatened by limited Pakistani air strikes, but more significantly by 'demographic aggression' caused by the huge refugee flows across its borders from East Pakistan. What is striking about these cases is that while the interventions resulted in a cessation of genocidal practices, none of the intervening states attempted to justify their actions on humanitarian grounds, although India and Tanzania did allude to the tyrannical nature of the regimes against which they acted. Their reluctance to advance humanitarian justifications for their actions essentially reflected the fact that none of them acted primarily for such reasons. Gary Klintworth's study of these three cases led him to conclude:

> Vietnam, of course, did not undertake its long and costly occupation of Kampuchea for altruistic humanitarian motives. And nor did India or Tanzania, undertake their respective actions just to rescue fellow human beings....While saving human beings from being killed was an inevitable consequence of intervention by Vietnam, and earlier by Tanzania and India, it was always secondary to the overriding priority imposed by concern for vital security interests.[30]

A further reason for the unwillingness of the intervening states to claim a right of humanitarian intervention has been suggested by Adam Roberts. He writes, 'there was probably also a thought that to sanctify a doctrine of humanitarian intervention would be to store up trouble for themselves or their friends'.[31] Here, Roberts is referring to what, in our discussion of 'self-regarding prudence', we called the fear of 'precedent-setting'. There is some evidence to support this claim in the case of India, with Delhi fearing international censure over its human-rights policies in Kashmir and Punjab. However, there is no available evidence to substantiate the claim in relation to Vietnam, while in the case of Tanzania, statements made by the then President Julius Nyerere suggest that no such concern existed. Indeed, among Black African leaders, Nyerere was a rare and outspoken exponent of humanitarian values.

An alternative explanation is offered by Hedley Bull, who suggests that the members of international society, including the three intervening states themselves, were sensitive to the risks involved in taking actions which eroded the principle of non-intervention. This concern centred on the dangers to international order of implementing particular conceptions of justice in a world where there is no shared understanding of what justice entails, and no consensus on what level of human suffering would justify humanitarian intervention. Writing in the mid-1980s, Bull stated:

> As regards the right of so-called humanitarian intervention...there is no present tendency for states to claim, or for the international community to recognise, any such right. The reluctance evident in the international community even to experiment with the conception of a right of humanitarian intervention reflects not only an unwillingness to jeopardise the rules of sovereignty and non-intervention by conceding

> such a right to individual states, but also the lack of any agreed doctrine as to what human rights are.[32]

Thus, while Roberts contends that the fear of 'precedent-setting' lay behind the reluctance of state leaders to justify their actions in humanitarian terms, Bull's analysis is based upon what we have earlier called 'other-regarding' prudence, and more specifically rule-consequentialism. These two explanations are not mutually exclusive, and within the Cold War context in which Bull worked, such an approach was probably inescapable.

Despite the illegitimacy of the idea of humanitarian intervention in post-1945 international politics, there are growing suggestions that at the end of the Cold War the international community – or at least certain states within it – is beginning to challenge the taboo of humanitarian intervention. We now turn to the three cases which we wish to consider in our analysis of the claim that humanitarian intervention is gaining legitimacy in the post-Cold War era: the interventions into Kurdistan, Somalia and Rwanda.

STATE PRACTICE IN THE POST-COLD WAR ERA

The Crisis in Iraqi Kurdistan

Saddam Hussein's invasion of Kuwait in August 1990 set in motion a series of events which were trumpeted by many statesmen, journalists and academics as heralding the beginning of a 'New World Order'. This new phase in international politics was to be predicated upon a degree of great-power cooperation which had not been seen since the Concert of Europe, and it was to provide not only a more orderly world but also a more just one. However, the fact that such cooperation has not lived up to initial expectations is not surprising if one considers more carefully the nature of the political coalition upon which this new order was to be built. Whilst a high degree of consensus was (eventually) evident during the conflict phase of the Gulf crisis, the 'humanitarian' operation to assist the Kurds was carried out against a backdrop of political disagreement. Thomas Pickering, former US Ambassador to the UN, exaggerated the degree of consensus attained during the international intervention in Kurdistan, when he boldly asserted that:

> [I]n the case of Iraq's treatment of its Kurdish minority, the international community came firmly to the view that the non-intervention doctrine could not shield genocidal and other practices which were themselves prohibited by international law and treaties.

> While the world has seen the sovereign exercise of butchery before, this is the first time that a significant number of governments have rejected a state's right to do so and acted using military forces to prevent it by providing humanitarian assistance and protection directly for the victims.[33]

While similar sentiments were echoed by the G-7 in its political declaration issued at the London Summit in July 1991, we should be cautious before jumping to the conclusion that the Western powers' intervention in Northern Iraq had the wide backing of the international community, or that it set a clear precedent for future humanitarian interventions. Despite the attempts of Western governments to present the Kurdish safe havens as legitimate in the eyes of the wider international community, it has to be recognised that there was little or no support among the UN Security Council's non-Western members for military intervention to protect the Kurds.

On 5 April 1991, the Security Council narrowly passed Resolution 688 with China, a veto-bearing member of the Council, abstaining along with India, while Cuba, Yemen and Zimbabwe voted against. This resolution declared that the refugee problem on the Iraqi-Turkish border, caused by Saddam's oppression of the Kurds, constituted a 'threat to international peace and security'.[34] It called upon the Iraqi Government to stop oppressing its people (human rights abuses were also taking place at this time against the Shi'a in the south) and to allow UN relief agencies to operate inside its territorial borders. However, it was not passed under the collective security provisions of Chapter VII of the Charter, and did not provide for military enforcement.[35] The Western allies were unable to get Security Council backing for such a resolution since it was clear that Beijing would use its veto power to block any resolution which went beyond mere declaratory condemnation. It also seems probable that Moscow would have done likewise, since the USSR, along with China and other states on the Council such as India and Romania, were fearful that anything stronger might set a precedent for humanitarian intervention.

Since UN action to respond to threats to international peace and security constitutes a legitimate exception to the non-intervention principle in Article 2 (7) of the Charter, military intervention to assist the Kurds could technically have been undertaken without breaching existing Charter law. However, the above-mentioned states were not prepared to take the risk of sanctioning any action which in practice could have been perceived as threatening the norm of non-intervention. This may have reflected concerns of rule-consequentialism as alluded to by Bull, or it may be that those

Council members most strongly opposed to military action based their objections on self-regarding prudential fears of 'precedent-setting'. Despite the lack of any provision for military action, the resolution did nevertheless break new ground in that the Security Council accepted that the manner in which a state treats its own citizens can have repercussions for international security. The Security Council determined, in accordance with Article 39 of the Charter, that the flow of Kurdish refugees amounted to 'a threat to international peace and security'. This was in stark contrast to its inaction in the face of India's claim in 1971 that it was a victim of 'demographic aggression', and as such may represent an evolutionary step towards the collective policing of the human rights policies of sovereign states.

Once Resolution 688 was passed, attention moved to establishing some form of safe area for the Kurds. On 7 April, the US Defence Secretary, Dick Cheney, announced that the US was considering returning to the Security Council to seek authorisation for the establishment of such areas. Cheney seemed to have little chance of realising his plans since it was becoming clear that opposition to the idea was insurmountable. Nevertheless, on 8 April, the British Prime Minister John Major proposed at a meeting of EC leaders that enclaves be created under UN protection, arguing that existing Security Council resolutions provided the legal authority for such a scheme.

France and the other EC states were immediately supportive of the idea, but the initial US response was cool. This stemmed partly from the fact that the UK had not consulted Washington prior to announcing the plan, but more significantly it was thought that it would have adverse implications for regional stability, since it threatened Iraq's sovereignty and future as a politically and territorially integral entity. In an attempt to gather wider support, London began to stress the project's humanitarian character, playing down its military and legal aspects. The term 'enclave' – with its associated legal connotations – was dropped in favour of the 'safe havens' label. These moves, coupled with domestic pressure, brought American acceptance, and thus Britain, France, Italy and the Netherlands were joined by the US in establishing the 'safe havens' in mid-April 1991. While the Western powers claimed that Resolution 688 provided legal authority for the 'safe havens' project, it is easy to agree with Roberts that the intervention stretched 'the elastic of Security Council resolutions close to breaking point'.[36] Dick Cheney's desire to return to the Security Council for a specific mandate would further seem to strengthen this assertion, and it was the view reportedly taken by Eric Suy, the UN Secretary-General's Special Envoy to Iraq, and by the Secretary-General himself.[37]

If the Western powers did not have the backing of UN Charter law for their intervention, what are we to make of Christopher Greenwood's claim that they were 'asserting a right of humanitarian intervention of some kind?'[38] Hiding behind the fig-leaf of Resolution 688, Western leaders were able to avoid the debate as to whether the 'safe havens' could be justified as an exercise of the customary legal right of humanitarian intervention. However, the British Foreign Secretary, Douglas Hurd, was forced to argue that such a right existed when defending the establishment by Britain, France and the US of the southern 'no-fly zone' over Iraq in August 1992. The purpose of the zone was to monitor Iraq's compliance with Resolution 688 with regard to its treatment of the Shi'a in the South, but there was no specific Security Council resolution authorising it. When questioned on the zone's legality, Hurd's response was:

> we operate under international law. Not every action that a British government or an American government or a French government takes has to be underwritten by a specific provision in a UN resolution provided we comply with international law. International law recognises extreme humanitarian need....We are on strong legal as well as humanitarian ground in setting up this 'no-fly' zone.[39]

The Foreign Secretary appeared to be claiming that the Western powers did not need UN Security Council authority to create the southern 'no-fly zone' because there existed a right of humanitarian intervention under customary international law. The difficulty with this claim is that in accordance with Article 38 of the Statute of the International Court of Justice, customary international law depends, *inter alia*, upon state practice, but as we have seen there is very little to suggest that such a right is recognised by the international community. Both the West's intervention in Northern Iraq in April 1991, and its creation of the southern 'no-fly zone' in late 1992, appear to be built upon the shakiest of legal foundations. As such they are open to the charge that they represent the Western powers playing fast and loose with the cardinal rules of international society – the principles of sovereignty and non-intervention. There is of course an alternative assertion which posits that these actions represent the international community's embryonic acceptance of an emergent right of humanitarian intervention. While this may soothe the conscience of the West, and initially be morally appealing, the evidence of the Iraqi case suggests that it is fallacious. It is undermined by the limited nature of the international backing which the 'safe havens' project received, and also by its selectivity. Why did the Western states stop at establishing a 'no-fly zone' in the southern part of Iraq when they had created 'safe havens' for the Kurdish population in the north? The answer seems two-fold: first, there was a perception that support for the Shi'a would lead to an unwanted increase in Iranian influence in the region; second, their cries for help, unlike those of the Kurds, received relatively little media attention and thus Western governments were not forced into taking such decisive action. As James Mayall argues, action was only taken to protect the Kurds 'because the attention devoted by the Western media to the plight of the Kurds threatened the political dividends Western governments had secured from their conduct of the war itself'.[40]

For Mayall, the obligation to assist the Kurds does not derive from a general obligation to protect basic human rights wherever they are threatened, but from a specific responsibility incurred by the Western powers as a consequence of acts taken during the war itself.[41] Certainly, had the repression of the Kurds occurred in any other circumstances than as a result of the Gulf War, it is inconceivable that Western governments would have responded in the way they did. The Western intervention in Iraqi Kurdistan is an example of governments responding to the humanitarian sentiments of public opinion. While this does not necesarily obviate an ethic of global responsibility on the part of Western leaders, the case would nevertheless appear to be an example of liberal-democratic governments pursuing populist policies on grounds of 'self-regarding prudence'. Moreover, against a defeated Iraqi army, there was little risk to soldiers' lives in providing humanitarian aid to the Kurds, and the preceding Gulf War ensured that forces and logistics were readily available, making the operation relatively inexpensive.

'Operation Safe Haven' enjoyed initial success in dealing with the refugee problem and clearly saved lives. However, as the media spotlight began to shift elsewhere and public interest waned, so did the commitment of Western governments to protect the Kurds. While Western air forces continue to police a 'no-fly zone' over northern Iraq extending limited protection, the intervening states were eager to hand over the running of the 'safe havens' to what they knew was an ill-equipped and badly supported UN relief operation. This faces enormous problems given Iraq's enduring hostility towards its Kurdish minority. Despite its success in alleviating the immediate suffering of the Kurds, four years later the intervention appears to have been little more than a short-term palliative which has failed to address their long-term plight.[42]

Somalia

At first sight the UN-mandated, US-led intervention in Somalia in

December 1992 looks like a classic case of humanitarian intervention. The Somali people faced a terrible famine, and while food aid was arriving at the port of Mogadishu throughout 1992, its delivery was dependent upon the different clans and warlords that controlled the country. The chaos which gripped Somalia resulted from a series of uprisings against the government of President Siad Barre in December 1990 and January 1991, and was compounded by drought. As the central government collapsed, a variety of groups took control of parts of the country, some claiming independence, others authority over the whole state.

The Organisation of the Islamic Conference, the Organisation of African Unity and the League of Arab States all attempted to bring stability to the country, but without success. Eventually in January 1992 the UN became involved, with the Security Council unanimously adopting Resolution 733. This declared that the conflict in Somalia constituted 'a threat to international peace and security', establised an arms embargo under Chapter VII of the Charter, and called for an increase in humanitarian assistance.[43] As the situation in Somalia deteriorated further, and the magnitude of human suffering increased, the Council adopted Resolution 794 without dissent. This reaffirmed the Article 39 determination made in Resolution 733, and under Chapter VII of the Charter, authorised member states to use 'all necessary means' to create a secure environment for the delivery of humanitarian aid, thus permitting the use of military force by member states.[44]

Although both resolutions found that the humanitarian crisis in Somalia represented a threat to international security, their rationale for doing so was different. Resolution 733 concentrated predominantly upon the civil war in Somalia, and the extent to which the conflict threatened regional peace and stability. In contrast, Resolution 794 represented a sharp break in existing practice, for as Christopher Greenwood notes, 'it was the plight of the Somali people which was given as the reason for invoking Chapter VII of the Charter and authorising intervention'.[45] The preamble to the Resolution states:

> Determining that the magnitude of human tragedy caused by the conflict in Somalia, further exacerbated by the obstacles to the distribution of humanitarian assistance, constitutes a threat to international peace and security.[46]

Roberts accepts that the Security Council had some grounds for finding a threat to international security, but he asserts that its concerns were primarily humanitarian.[47] Jackson goes further in pointing to what he sees as the specious nature of the claim that the human suffering in Somali threatened international security. He argues that the real motivation was humanitarian, and that both the Secretary-General and the Security Council engaged in

> a political fudge, presumably designed to comply with the rules of the UN Charter and at the same time mollify Third World and particularly African states who might be alarmed at what could easily be seen by them as a new form of colonialism under UN auspices.[48]

Western leaders certainly espoused humanitarian sympathies. Dick Cheney stated that '[t]he mission is very clear indeed. It is a humanitarian mission'.[49] Such sentiments may have been sincere, and there is no evidence to suggest that in the case of Somalia, Washington was covertly pursuing national self-interest behind the figleaf of humanitarianism. Nevertheless, there is little doubt that the primary driving force behind US policy was the desire to placate a public opinion saturated by media coverage of suffering Somalis. As in the case of Kurdistan, 'self-regarding prudence' appears to have been the decisive factor in the intervention, although this does not necessarily negate sentiments of common humanity on the part of US policy-makers. However, for other states on the Security Council, the influence of humanitarian ideals seems less clear. For example, while in contrast to its stance over Resolution 688, China voted in favour of Resolution 794, it is not clear how far humanitarian considerations lay behind this.

The most positive explanation for Beijing's change of position is that it is willing to cooperate with the international community as it begins to experiment with a limited conception of collective intervention to protect human rights. Perhaps the attitude of China reinforces Jackson's claim that the case of Somalia shows how 'norms of humanitarian intervention are operative in contemporary international society'.[50] However, it is easy to exaggerate the degree to which such experiments are finding collective endorsement in the wider society of states. China is at best only just becoming receptive to the idea that sovereignty and non-intervention can be compromised in the name of protecting human rights. In part, this stems from Beijing's desire to maintain good relations with the West, but the extent to which it reflects the gradual emergence of consensual moral principles in the international community is open to debate.

Our scepticism over the emergence of a new norm is fuelled by the caveats attached to Resolution 794. Although it was innovative in its apparent acceptance that human suffering *per se* can constitute a threat to international peace and security – and as such goes further than any other Security Council resolution to date – its importance was severely undermined by the manner in which it was drafted. For example, immediately prior to noting the relationship between human suffering and threats to international peace and security, the resolution recognises 'the *unique* character of the present situation in Somalia and mindful of its deteriorating, complex and *extraordinary* nature, requiring an immediate and *exceptional* response'.[51]

The use of terms such as 'unique', 'extraordinary' and 'exceptional' have to be seen as an attempt to differentiate the case of Somalia from other cases of internal disorder, hence reducing the chance of 'precedent- setting'. They seem to have been inserted specifically to appease the fears of states such as China which may have otherwise blocked a Chapter VII enforcement action. It was argued in the Council that the Somali case was unique because the state had effectively collapsed. While acknowledging the contentious nature of the proposition, Roberts contends that:

> Somalia is not a case of intervention against the will of the government, but of intervention when there is a lack of a government. Thus Operation Restore Hope could have been justified in terms of the long-standing proposition in international law that when a state completely collapses into chaos, there can be grounds for military intervention by other states if such a course has a serious chance of restoring order.[52]

This argument may have accommodated the divergent views within the Security Council, but it becomes problematic if one considers the legal nature of the principle of non-intervention. It can only be sustained if one of the following lines of reasoning is pursued. Firstly, that the duty of non-intervention did not arise in the case of Somalia because the government had collapsed. However, this line of reasoning fails to accord with the fact that in international law it is states and not governments that are recognised as the 'locus of rights and duties'.[53] The alternative argument is predicated upon the idea that the duty of non-intervention did not arise because the state had ceased to exist. This is correct in so far as it identifies the correct subject of the duty, but must be fallacious since it is predicated upon the contention that the state had collapsed because the government had collapsed. This is tantamount to claiming that a state and its government are synonymous, and as such it fails to accord with the rules of international law which see government as a criteria for, but not wholly constitutive of, statehood.

The fact that Somalia continued to exist in a legal sense does not, however, undermine Robert Jackson's contention that it had 'ceased to exist in any empirical sense'.[54] He makes a distinction between states as juridical and political entities, and it is in the latter sense that Somalia can be said to have collapsed. Liberal political theory justifies statehood on the grounds that the state is of authentic value to its population. This has led some liberal theorists to suggest that where the state fails to provide for the good life, its right to the protection of the norm of non-intervention should be called into question.[55] The political collapse of the state of Somalia placed it within this category, and the international community's sanctioning of intervention there could arguably be said to be symptomatic of its embroyonic willingness to experiment with ideas of humanitarian intervention. Michael Mastanduno and Gene Lyons summarise this point well in suggesting that

> a justification increasingly likely to be recognised as legitimate in international society...[is] intervention in cases of civil-war or other circumstances in which central authority collapses and governments can no longer carry out the functions normally associated with sovereignty, such as providing security or ensuring sustenance to the population or significant parts of it....This justification is compatible with the sovereignty norm on the underlying assumption that sovereignty brings with it certain responsibilities or presupposes some minimal level of governing capacity.[56]

The problem with this claim is that the language employed in Resolution 794, with its emphasis upon the unique nature of the crisis in Somalia, strongly suggests that certain states on the Council remain very reluctant to extend this principle to other cases. This stance is motivated by a fear of eroding Article 2(7) of the Charter. However, from the standpoint of liberal political theory, the case of Somalia is far from unique, with many states failing to function in a manner commensurate with it. As Thomas Weiss points out, the suffering in Sudan in 1992 was just as acute as that in Somalia.[57] The problem for the Council is that while non-Western states such as China reject the liberal conception of the state, its Western members find themselves pressurised by media-fed publics who increasingly expect other governments to respect what they see as basic human rights.

One consequence of these tensions is that the Security Council has been forced, as Roberts states, 'to make the awkward facts of crisis fit the procrustean bed of the UN Charter'.[58] Rather than rewrite the rulebook to accommodate any embroyonic right of collective humanitarian intervention, the fragile consensus in the Security Council has forced it to employ the traditional Chapter VII mechanism. All post-Cold War interventions have been primarily justified on the grounds of threats to international peace and security, the only permissible exception to the non-intervention rule expressly provided for by the Charter. However, while this allows the Security Council to maintain a united front, the price of adopting this approach is that it becomes vulnerable to charges of abuse.

Here abuse does not mean states claiming humanitarian motives as a cover for the pursuit of national self-interest; instead the problem is one of the Council employing its discretionary powers to determine a threat to international peace and security in cases where it is often hard to sustain the argument that such a threat genuinely exists. This tactic has been adopted on a number of occasions by the Western members of the Council, thus providing UN legitimisation for policies which would otherwise breach the cardinal rules of non-intervention and non-use of force. The Charter provides no guidance as to what constitutes threats to international peace and security, but when it was drafted, the framers had in mind traditional cross-border aggression. Since the end of the Cold War, the meaning of the term has been stretched to breaking point; it now covers intra-state security problems like human rights abuses and human displacement. The problem is that if terms and powers are constantly redefined in this way, their legitimacy is undermined as is the collective authority of the Council.

The threat to the Council's authority has to be balanced against the humanitarian benefits of using the Charter in this manner. If, as a result of the Security Council employing its Chapter VII powers, it is able to bring widespread relief to the victims of human rights abuses, this may be morally justifiable, if legally questionable. However, the case of Somalia clearly demonstrates the limits of such an approach and shows how a military mission that begins with the best of humanitarian intentions can all too easily end up escalating the levels of violence in a civil war. Instead of providing aid and stability, such missions may themselves become the catalyst for further violence. One only has to think of media images of US helicopter gunships shooting missiles into the urban areas of southern Mogadishu to understand Victoria Brittain's observation that:

> the US put in 38,000 troops and 10,000 Somalis were killed in four months of clashes with UN peacekeepers or clan fighting according to US intelligence sources. The US lost 68 killed and 262 wounded as the mission muddled its way from famine-relief to war-making.[59]

The UN operation in Somalia was severely compromised after the UN decided that apprehension of clan-leader General Aideed was vital to the stability of Somalia. Although a UN peacekeeping force had replaced the US force in May 1993, the US retained effective control of UN political and military operations in Somalia. The humanitarian rationale for the initial intervention became secondary as the US, with UN authority, embarked upon a hunt for Aideed who was singled out as frustrating the process of disarmament and the distribution of aid. Whatever the arguments for such a partisan stance, it led the US to suffer much-publicised casualties. This fermented growing disillusionment among US public opinion, forcing President Clinton to announce a timetable for the withdrawal of US forces from the UN operation in Somalia.

The loss of US service personnel leaves Washington's policy of intervention in Somalia vulnerable to the realist critique that state leaders violated their primary ethical responsibility to place soldiers at risk only when national self-interest requires it. Ironically, the operation could also be criticised from a cosmopolitanist, consequentialist standpoint, since even if it is accepted that states have obligations to non-citizens which justify risking soldiers' lives, this can only ever be morally permissible if it is believed that general well-being will be increased by such actions. It is hard to justify US actions as maximising general well-being, when they chose to pursue General Aideed, and then withdrew from the UN force in Somalia when the costs proved prohibitive. In providing famine relief, the US intervention in December 1992 undoubtedly saved lives, but as with Kurdistan, military intervention was a short-term palliative which did little to address the long-term problems of the Somali people. The difficulty with making an overall assessment of the intervention in Somalia is that while with retrospect we can calculate the costs and benefits of doing so, we can never know the consequences of a policy of non-intervention.

Rwanda

The shooting-down of the plane carrying the Presidents of Rwanda and Burundi on 6 April 1994 led to a massive upsurge of political violence among the seven million people that inhabit the tiny African state of Rwanda. The country has long been riven by conflict; the 'ethnic' Hutus and Tutsis who make up its population have been vying for control of the state since independence.[60] The Hutu-dominated government of President Juvenal Habyarimana was, prior to his death, under threat from the guerrilla army of the Rwanda Patriotic Front (RPF). This force was made up of Tutsi exiles who had fled to Uganda and other neighbouring states after the majority Hutus overthrew the rule of the minortity Tutsis shortly after independence. The RPF was a disciplined and educated force committed to fighting for a government which would promote ethnic reconcilliation. Under pressure from the international community, Habyarimana and the RPF signed the Arusha Accord in August 1993. This UN-brokered peace agreement led the UN Security Council to dispatch the United Nations Mission in Rwanda (UNAMIR I). This force consisted of 2500 peacekeeping troops and was charged with the task of monitoring the fragile cease-fire and accompanying process of demilitarisation.

Despite strong opposition to the Arusha Accord from Hutu extremists, it appeared to offer the best prospect for long-term peace in Rwanda, but Habyarima's death destroyed these hopes. It not only led to a renewal of the civil war with the RPF, but also to a political vacuum in which elements of the Rwandan government forces, the Presidential Guard and the Hutu youth militias – the Interhamwe – were free to kill Tutsis and moderate Hutu leaders. It now seems that the Interhamwe had prepared lists of those to be killed and that the death of the President was the signal for the carnage to begin.[61] By telling Hutus that the Tutsis in the RPF would steal their land and destroy them, an atmosphere of ethnic hatred was whipped up which led Hutus to engage in the most appalling and indiscriminate acts of mass violence. Some 500 000 Tutsis and moderate Hutus were killed as a result of these genocidal practices.

The RPF's victory in the civil war led hundreds of thousands of Hutus – including those responsible for the killing – to flee the country. Refugee camps on the Rwanda–Zaire border became 'home' for around a million people, and despite the best efforts of the various non-governmental organisations and the United Nations High Commissioner for Refugees, many died for lack of basic subsistence and medical care. It was the harrowing pictures of this suffering which forced the US and other Western governments to provide a more activist programme of humanitarian aid. Against this background of human suffering in Rwanda in 1994, the efforts of Western governments were nevertheless meagre. Only France took upon itself the burden of military intervention, undertaking, with UN authority, 'Operation Turquoise'. This established a secure humanitarian zone in the south-western part of the country, but the rationale and sucess of this intervention are open to question.

Prior to the French deployment, the UN's presence in Rwanda consisted of UNAMIR I. The problem with this peacekeeping force was that it had neither the mandate nor the firepower to stop the killing, and it proved unable to secure a political agreement between the parties. In these circumstances, the UN Secretary-General, Boutros Boutros-Ghali, wrote to the Security Council on 20 April expressing his concern that UNAMIR I 'cannot be left at risk indefinitely when there is no possibility of their performing the tasks for which they were dispatched'.[62] He set out the following options for Security Council consideration: UNAMIR I could be heavily reinforced and given a mandate under Chapter VII to coerce the parties into a peace process and to stop the killing; it could be significantly reduced, serving both as protection for UN mediators working for a cease-fire and assisting in the delivery of humanitarian aid where possible; or, it could be withdrawn totally. After Somalia, there was no enthusiasm among the US or other Western members of the Security Council to risk their soldiers in another messy and open-ended civil war, but at the same time, the Security Council did not want to be seen to be totally washing its hands of Rwanda. Consequently, Resolution 912 of 21 April 1994 took the second option outlined by the Secretary-General, and scaled back UNAMIR I from 2500 to 444.[63]

Not surprisingly, this step did nothing to reduce the level of human suffering in Rwanda. Critics argue that the reduction in troops was a catastrophic blunder. Reflecting on the decision after the RPF's seizure of power, the new Rwandan Prime Minister, Twagiramungu, expressed his disgust that 'instead of protecting the population, the UN's tiny military force ran away'.[64] This judgement of the UN seems harsh since the Organisation can only act at the behest of its member states. The Secretary-General presented the Security Council with a wide spectrum of options, ranging from complete withdrawal to Chapter VII enforcement. It was the member states of the Security Council who chose to reduce the UNAMIR force, and who refused to provide it with a mandate for enforcement action, and thus any blame for the UN's failures in Rwanda lies at their door.

With the benefit of hindsight, the Security Council seems to have regretted its decision to scale back UNAMIR I. Peter Hansen, US Secretary-General for Humanitarian Affairs, is quoted as saying that '[e]ven the Security Council members, officially or unofficially, have come to realise that [Resolution 912] was an over-reaction and a mistake'.[65] Whatever the wisdom behind Resolution 912, the Security Council overturned its earlier decision, and in passing Resolution 918 on 17 May 1994, it authorised an increase in the UN force in Rwanda to 5500. This force, UNAMIR II, was mandated to protect 'civilians at risk in Rwanda' and to 'provide security and support' for humanitarian relief operations, although there was no question of it having the authority to use force other than in self-defence.[66] In the intervening period between the passing of these two resolutions, the Secretary-General appears to have been shocked by the scale of the continuing atrocities in Rwanda. Writing to the Security Council on 13 May 1994, he stated that:

> The world community has witnessed with horror and disbelief the slaughter and suffering of innocent civilians in Rwanda. While the chances for a lasting peace are fundamentally in the hands of the political and military leaders of the country, the international community cannot ignore the atrocious effects of this conflict on innocent civilians.[67]

Accordingly, he strongly recommended that the UN force in Rwanda be substantially strengthened, a stance which was at variance with the more cautious one he had previously adopted. It appeared from the Security Council's unanimous passing of Resolution 918 that its member states were finally willing to implement this course of action. However, while a number of African states came forward with offers of troops for UNAMIR II, the requisite logistic and financial support was not forthcoming. Western governments were the only ones capable of providing such support and thus stand accused of failing to make good the promises which they had made.

The reluctance of the US to act has to be seen in the light of Congressional concerns about US involvement in UN operations after the Somali experience. Nevertheless, Pentagon haggling over the cost of hiring vehicles to UNAMIR II, when the UN is short of $2 billion in unpaid dues from the US, is surely one of the shoddiest aspects of the international response to the Rwandan tragedy. Boutros Boutros-Ghali described the international reaction as a 'scandal'.[68] In a letter to the President of the Security Council on 20 June, he criticised 'the failure of Member States to promptly provide the resources necessary for the implementation of [UNAMIR's] expanded mandate', and added that '[m]eanwhile, the situation in Rwanda has continued to deteriorate and the killing of innocent civilians has not been stopped'.[69]

Given the failure of Western states to provide the requisite support for the deployment of a multinational peacekeeping force, France sought Security Council authorisation to lead a 'humanitarian' mission in which other member states would be invited to participate. The French Government emphasised the 'strictly humanitarian' character of the operation, with French Prime Minister Eduard Balladur arguing that France was obliged to intervene to stop 'one of the most unbearable tragedies in recent history'.[70] He set out five criteria which would underpin the proposed intervention: the operation must have UN authorisation and the support of other countries; all operations should be limited to humanitarian actions; troops should remain near the Zairean border; they should not enter into the heart of Rwanda; and finally, the mission should be limited to a maximum of several weeks before handing over to a strengthened UNAMIR force.

The UN Secretary-General was reportedly enthusiastic about the French initiative, and in his letter of 20 June he invited it to consider mandating French intervention under Chapter VII of the Charter. The next day the Security Council passed Resolution 929 which sanctioned the 'establishment of a temporary operation under national command and control aimed at contributing, in an impartial way, to the security and protection of displaced persons, refugees and civilians at risk in Rwanda'.[71] Acting under Chapter VII it authorised 'Member States cooperating with the Secretary-General to conduct the operation...using all necessary means to achieve the humanitarian objectives'.[72] As had been the case with Somalia, the Security Council stressed that, in authorising this intervention, it was responding to a 'unique case'. Despite the inclusion of this phrase, an examination of Security Council practice in the post-Cold War era demonstrates a recurrent recourse to the claim of exceptional circumstances to justify UN interventionary action. The fact that five states (China, Brazil, Pakistan, Nigeria and New Zealand) abstained on the vote reflects the sensitivity of some Council members to what they see as attempts by the dominant Western states to manipulate the Council and erode Article 2(7) of the Charter.

The slender margin by which the vote was carried can be contrasted with the unanimous support for the US-led intervention in Somalia. The French insisted that their operation was purely humanitarian, François Léotard, Minister for Defence, claiming that '[w]e are not there for a national, French action. We are there to enforce a UN resolution to stop atrocities'.[73] Nevertheless, while the US and to a lesser extent Britain appeared supportive, other states remained sceptical.[74] In the case of Somalia, the US had seemingly acted for humanitarian reasons, although it was prompted to do so by the pressure of public opinion. French policy-makers were similarly responding to an outraged public, but in contrast to Washington's actions in Somalia, there is evidence to suggest that Paris was also covertly pursuing national self-interest behind the figleaf of humanitarianism. While 'self-regarding prudence' was an influencing factor behind French actions, unlike the Kurdish and Somali cases, it was not the primary motivation.

France had a long-standing relationship with the government of Habyarimana, it had propped up the one-party Hutu state for twenty years, and provided troops when the RPF threatened to overrun the country in 1990 and 1993. The French President, François Mitterrand, was reportedly anxious to restore waning French credibility in Africa, and was fearful that an RPF victory in French-speaking Rwanda would result in the country coming under the influence of Anglophones.[75] Victoria Brittain suggests that Paris may also have feared 'that the regional impact (on, for example, unstable Zaire) of an educated and democratic government in Rwanda would be explosive'.[76] President Mobuto's dictatorial regime has been a staunch ally of France and any erosion of his power would further weaken the Elysée's hold over Western Africa, a region traditionally under its sphere of influence. For all these reasons, it is difficult to maintain that France acted on 'strictly humanitarian' grounds, or that its intervention was impartial as required by UN Security Council Resolution 929.

This contention is strengthened by an analysis of France's behaviour in the Security Council, and the timing and nature of its intervention. When, in the immediate aftermath of Habyarimana's death, decisive military action might have stopped the killing, France along with others voted to cut back the UNAMIR force. An unnamed Paris source is quoted as saying that '[w]e said nothing during the massacres and we voted for the UN force in Rwanda to be reduced when the killing started but now that the killing is mostly over, we suddenly find a burning desire to save lives'.[77] While the French intervention was only ever intended to be the first stage of a two-part mission – a holding operation pending the deployment of UNAMIR II – had Paris responded positively to Resolution 918 and provided the support necessary for a rapid deployment of UNAMIR II, the question of unilateral intervention would not have arisen. It could be argued, however, that an immediate deployment of a multinational force may have undermined French attempts to prop up its failing ally, and it is within this context that we should consider France's voting behaviour within the Council.

Further evidence for the partisan nature of the French intervention can be seen in the fact that its relief actions were concentrated in the south-western part of the country on the border with Zaire, where Hutu forces loyal to the ousted government were strongest. While France was the only state willing to commit a substantial number of troops to Rwanda, their deployment pattern ensured that they were never placed in a combat role, with Paris emphasing that it was not at war with the RPF. Their concentration in the south-west compromised their ability to provide humanitarian assistance to the mass population of Rwanda, but it suited France's political agenda.

French behaviour accords with the realist premise that states should only risk their soldiers in defence of the national interest, but it undermines the humanitarian credentials of 'Operation Turquoise'. The fact that the French acted primarily for selfish reasons does not mean that their policy-makers' espousal of humanitarian sentiments were totally insincere. Paris may have been motivated, at least in part, by humanitarian sentiments, but nevertheless this is a clear case of a state abusing the concept of humanitarian intervention. This judgement of abuse is tempered by the fact that the operation was authorised by the UN Security Council, and indeed France stipulated that it would not act without such authority.

A key precondition for Security Council approval was a clear timetable for the withdrawal of French troops. This served both to temper any fears that Paris might be using its intervention to further neo-colonial ambitions in the region, and also to prevent it from becoming embroiled in an open-ended and costly commitment as the US had done in Somalia. Paradoxically though, this timetable served to limit further the beneficial impact of the operation, since when the French came to withdraw in mid-August 1994, some commentators suggested that they left behind them a situation little improved from that which they had first encountered. With the withdrawal of French troops, many of the Rwandans who had sought refuge in the French humanitarian zone attempted to flee over the border into Zaire. The problem with this verdict is that for all of the criticisms made of the French intervention, it may be justified on the grounds that lives were saved. The difficulty with arriving at such a moral judgement is reflected in the response of Lynda Chalker, British Minister for Overseas Aid and Development, who when asked whether the French were right to intervene responded, 'I can't say, its almost impossible...somebody had to stabilise it...[and] by and large it has probably worked'.[78] Even if it is argued that French action in Rwanda represents a case of abuse, the question remains as to whether some form of intervention was morally required. In the words of Paul Webster:

> When the aftermath of the Rwandan affair is analysed and the number of days when massacres were averted totalled up, an answer might emerge to the question of whether it was better to do something, even in self-interest, as the French have done, or whether it was better to stand aside in hesitation and indifference like the rest of the world.[79]

CONCLUSION

The cases of post-Cold War intervention considered in this chapter provide no more than the most tentative support for the descriptive claim that the concept of humanitarian intervention is now seen by the international community as legitimate. There are two key objections to the descriptive claim. The first is that the specific facts of each case are such that they cannot be considered as model examples of humanitarian intervention. In the case of Kurdistan, it is clear that military intervention would not have occurred in any other circumstances than in the context of the Gulf War. Furthermore, the action was on the very edge of legality; the inability of Western states to obtain a Security Council mandate for their military intervention is testament to the wider perception that their actions were illegitimate. In contrast, the Somali case is an example of an intervening state receiving the backing of the international community, but it does not conform to the classical model of intervention against a government's will because the state had effectively collapsed. French intervention in Rwanda enjoyed UN Security Council backing, but unlike the case of Somalia, where Security Council support was unanimous, five Council members abstained on the vote on Resolution 929. In part this reflected suspicion on the part of many states that France was attempting to use the guise of humanitarian intervention to cover actions motivated primarily by national self-interest. Additionally, there was a reluctance to participate in what is coming to be seen as a generalised erosion of the principle of non-intervention. In an attempt to pacify these wider concerns, the Security Council was forced in the case of Rwanda – as it had previously been when voting on Somalia – to emphasise the unique and exceptional circumstances which justified military intervention.

The second weakness of the descriptive claim is that it exaggerates the acceptance in state practice of post-Cold War 'humanitarian interventions'. Analysis of these cases reveals that intervening states were initially compelled to act by media and domestic publics and thus in responding to domestic exigencies their primary motivation appears to have been what we have earlier identified as a form of 'self-regarding prudence'. In the cases of Kurdistan and Somalia the original motivation was to appease domestic publics. Nevertheless, this does not necessarily place these interventions outside of our definition of humanitarian intervention since, once the operations were embarked upon, there is no suggestion that the intervening states were attempting to cloak power-political motives behind the guise of humanitarianism. In this sense, the case of Rwanda differs from the other two for while 'self-regarding prudence' was a factor, pursuit of national self-interest was, throughout the intervention, the dominant motivation, and thus the case cannot be considered to be one of humanitarian intervention.

What emerges from all these cases is that the principal force behind any reassessment of the non-intervention norm is not state leaders imbued with a post-Cold War ethic of humanitarian responsibility, but domestic publics pressurising policy-makers into taking actions to relieve human suffering. Mayall suggests that in the case of the Kurds, British ministers were forced into actions which were 'possibly against their own instincts and in dubious accord with the established rules of international relations'.[80] As he notes, the question is whether breaks with existing practices like the 'safe havens' will lead state leaders to legitimise new practices, or alternatively, whether they will be seen as exceptions to the bedrock rule of non-intervention.

Whatever the limited enthusiasm among Western state leaders for eroding the norm of non-intervention in the defence of human rights, it is clear that any shift on the question of humanitarian intervention is primarily confined to liberal-democratic states. Many non-Western states question the West's (and especially US) motives in advocating humanitarian intervention, seeing it as a new form of 'imperialism' which will leave the weak vulnerable to the cultural preferences of the strong.[81] Third World state leaders may genuinely value the existing 'authoritative' practices of sovereignty and non-intervention as a way of pragmatically coping with cultural differences, but they may also employ this rhetoric to cover the fact that the human rights agenda of Western governments is a threat to their own power. Hence they may oppose legitimising humanitarian intervention for fear of setting precedents which might be employed against them in the future – that is, they may be motivated by the first form of 'self-regarding prudence' identified earlier in the chapter. While the radical reaction of some Western governments to recent humanitarian crises has been substantially influenced by the need to respond to domestic electorates, domestic public opinion is not such a powerful force in those states most hostile to the emerging human rights agenda of the post-Cold War world. Human rights groups within these states struggle to find the space to criticise government polices, often fighting for their very survival in the face of internal repression. Thus they are not in the luxurious position of Western publics, able to criticise and influence their governments on questions of humanitarian intervention. Consequently, while the new-found willingness of some Western states to act with force to protect human rights provides the basis for the descriptive claim that humanitarian intervention is now seen as legitimate, it fails to take into account how far this is limited to media and public opinion in liberal-democratic states, and the hostility of some non-Western states toward such a trend.

The most powerful challenger to post-Cold War Western-sponsored humanitarian interventions has been China. When issues of intervention have arisen, China has proved to be the most cautious of the Security Council's permanent members, though the reason for this remains unclear. It seems unlikely that its concern over the erosion of Article 2(7) stems from a fear that, at some future date, it may itself become the target of intervention. China is protected against such an eventuality by both its veto within the Security Council and a military capability which makes any form of coercive intervention against it wholly untenable. It seems more likely that China's experience at the hands of the colonial powers, coupled with a radically different conception of human rights, lies behind a policy which places sovereignty and non-intervention at the pinnacle of a hierarchy of principles. If this is so, and China is genuinely concerned about eroding Article 2(7) on grounds of rule-consequentialism, then the extent to which humanitarian intervention is likely to gain legitimate status within the UN Security Council will remain very limited.

Hitherto, the problem of securing a Security Council consensus on military intervention to relieve human suffering has been side-stepped by use of the Chapter VII mechanism. Determining that a situation represents a threat to international peace and security remains the only means by which intervention can be legitimised within the existing Charter framework, and therefore serves to placate fears – particularly on the part of Beijing – over intervention. However, utilising Article 39 in this way is likely to prove a finite palliative. The Security Council's continuing broadening of the definition of what constitutes such a threat itself undermines the Charter's non-intervention provision and as such it may eventually be resisted by China and other non-Western Council members. Thus a dilemma exists for those states which, for whatever reasons, are attempting to promote the concept of humanitarian intervention. So long as the Security Council lacks consensus as to what level of human rights violations justifies denying states protection of the norm of non-intervention, the Chapter VII mechanism remains the only means by which intervention can be legitimised. Yet by employing the Charter in this way the willingness of those states which oppose intervention to acquiesce in the Security Council's actions is slowly exhausted.

If Chinese sensitivity over Article 2(7) is a powerful brake on the Security Council mandating intervention in defence of human rights, Beijing's options are, in turn, severely limited by wider political constraints. These dictate that it does not step too far out of line within a Security Council which, since the end of the Cold War and the collapse of the Soviet Union, has been dominated by its three Western permanent members, especially the US. The end of the Cold War promised an era of great-power cooperation, but the disintegration of the USSR undermined the political balance of power which had prevailed for almost fifty years. Consequently, the US enjoys a position of almost unfettered predominance on the international stage, and this is reflected in the manner in which it has been able to establish a position of dominance over the Security Council in the post-Cold War world.

During the Kurdish crisis the political dynamics of the post-Cold War international system had yet to be resolved. With the Soviet Union still in existence, Washington remained wary of antagonising Moscow, for although the Soviet superpower was in terminal decline, it still represented a significant political adversary. Furthermore, the presence of the Soviet Union within the Council meant that China had less fear of being internationally isolated if it opposed intervention. As a result of these factors the resolution passed to assist the Kurds was a weak compromise, the Western allies being unable to obtain the Security Council backing for the direct military intervention which they sought. In contrast, US military intervention in Somalia received unanimous Security Council backing, and furthermore even after the US force was replaced by a UN peacekeeping force (including US forces), it was Washington and not New York which controlled UN military operations in Somalia, leading to the disastrous policy of the 'witch-hunt' against Aideed. It is interesting to speculate how far the US military would have been given such a 'neo-imperialist charter' by the UN Security Council had the US been operating in the political context that existed when it was trying to secure Security Council support for the 'safe havens'.

It was the new political environment prevailing within the Security Council which gave rise to the US intervention in Somalia and the analogous French action in Rwanda. Neither of these operations can be characterised in terms of unilateral or collective interventions; they occupy a grey area between the collectively authorised use of force in defence of human rights and unilateral military actions which threaten not only the non-intervention norm but also the authority of the UN as the collective policing body of the society of states. The 'collective authorisation' model of post-Cold War intervention in Somalia, Rwanda and, more recently, Haiti, reflects the failure of UN member states to give the Organisation the means of global law enforcement set out in the Charter. If the only attainable solution to this lack of commitment is for the UN Security Council to authorise the great powers to use force inside state borders, it is vital that the Security Council and the Secretary-General exercise some control over the conduct of military operations on the ground. Many advocates of humanitarian intervention call for the establishment of a multinational force dedicated to UN operations, and capable of quick deployment at the request of the Secretary-General and Security Council.[82] Yet in the absence of such a force, the international community must develop mechanisms for ensuring that military force employed on behalf of the UN operates according to 'just-war' principles of discrimination and proportionality. The difficulty is that any extension of UN oversight of military operations requires intervening states to delegate to the Security Council command and control over its national forces. This is likely to be heavily resisted by policy-makers and military leaders responsible for the success of intervention and fearful for the safety of their military personnel. The cases of Somalia and Haiti demonstrate the reluctance of US politicians to accept UN jurisdiction over US forces. Some even go so far as to say that unless vital national interests are at stake, the US should not commit troops to risky UN operations.[83] Thus, it is not only the motive of the intervening state which is important when considering the legitimacy of humanitarian intervention, there is also the interrelated question of the conduct of military operations.

The cases of Somalia and Rwanda demonstrate the palpable weaknesses of the 'collective authorisation' model, but its great strength is that it enables the Security Council to sanction military intervention by individual states without issuing a general licence for a right of unilateral humanitarian intervention. In the cases of Kurdistan, Somalia and Rwanda, intervention was conditional upon Security Council authorisation, although in the case of the Kurds, despite Western claims to the contrary, the mandate was exceeded. There were reports that Paris was considering intervention in Rwanda even without Security Council backing, but French policy-makers were emphatic that action was conditional on such a mandate.[84] Thus, it seems that Hedley Bull's judgement on the illegitimacy of unilateral humanitarian intervention – based on grounds of rule-consequentionalism – remains as relevant in the post-Cold War era as it was when he made it in the mid-1980s. The contention that states are no nearer to reaching agreement on the moral principles which would trigger a right of either unilateral or collective humanitarian intervention finds support in the words of Adam Roberts:

> Any attempt to devise a general justification for humanitarian intervention, even if such a doctrine were to limit intervention to very extreme circumstances, would run into difficulty. A blind humanitarianism, which fails to perceive the basic truth that different states perceive social and international problems very differently, can only lead into a blind alley.[85]

A detailed study of state practice in the Kurdish, Somali and Rwandan cases confirms Roberts's pessimistic judgement in relation to the immediate post-Cold War period. However, it is too soon to say, as Roberts implies, that the international community cannot develop such principles in the future. The 'collective authorisation' model of state intervention appears to represent the best that can be hoped for in terms of international intervention to protect human rights at the end of the Cold War. However, if, as seems possible, the Security Council consensus breaks down and there is no UN backing for intervention, should we accept Mark Hoffman's argument that although undesirable, unilateral military intervention 'could be supported...because it may be the only effective option available to stop massive, unwarranted killings'.[86] Notwithstanding Hoffman's claim, state practice indicates that the international community remains resolutely opposed to codifying a legal right of unilateral humanitarian intervention. The weakness of the normative claim in support of a right of unilateral humanitarian intervention is that in focusing on individual cases of human suffering it fails to see that issuing a licence for humanitarian intervention is likely to bring about a generalised erosion of the norms of non-intervention and non-use of force, and with it a long-term reduction in general well-being. The logic of this rule-consequentialist position is that even if military intervention could prevent or stop genocide, the absence of Security Council approval renders such an action not only illegal, but also illegitimate.

The moral consequences for general well-being of states championing a right of humanitarian intervention might be justified if previous military interventions gave credence to the normative assumption that general well-being will be increased by intervening. If this were the case, the highly questionable legitimacy of such a practice might be overlooked on the grounds that intervention is justifiable in moral terms. However, the short-term experience of intervention in Kurdistan and more especially Somalia suggests that even where the relief of human suffering is the primary operational motive, the normative case for humanitarian intervention is far from proven. The self-interested French intervention in Rwanda does little to dispel this conclusion. Even if one sets aside initial French motives and the intrinsically linked issue of the rapidity of their withdrawal, the subsequent difficulties of the UN operation serve only to question the assertion that intervention can have long-term beneficial results.

If military intervention in humanitarian crises is always condemned to be a short-term palliative, is it the most appropriate form of intervention? The problem in the three cases studied here is that the initial determination to employ force in defence of humanitarian goals has not been backed up by a long-term political, economic and social commitment to the interventionary project. Thomas Weiss accepts that humanitarian intervention 'raises the levels of violence in the short run...[and makes] reconciliation more difficult in the longer term', but he asserts that 'to halt genocide, massive abuse of human rights, and starvation...is absolutely essential'.[87] The difficulty with Weiss's moral absolutism is that after the sincerest moral and prudential calculations, state leaders may intervene in the belief that they will stop the killing and save lives, but end up after months, years or decades with a situation where more lives have been lost than saved. There may be no alternative to consequentialist moral reasoning in judging the success or failure of military intervention, but the predicament for state leaders is that while they do not have the luxury of hindsight, they still have to shoulder the moral burden of juggling conflicting moral imperatives.

NOTES

The authors would like to express their appreciation to Andrew Mason and especially Timothy Dunne for their very helpful comments on an earlier draft of this article.

1. Robert H. Jackson, 'Martin Wight, International Theory and the Good Life', *Millennium: Journal of International Studies* (Vol. 19, No. 2, Summer 1990), pp. 265–7.
2. See Richard Falk, *Human Rights and State Sovereignty* (New York: Holmes and Meier, 1981); and Ken Booth, 'Security and Emancipation', *Review of International Studies* (Vol. 17, No. 4, October 1991), pp. 313–26.
3. For a recent discussion of definitions of humanitarian intervention, see Jack Donnelly, 'Human Rights, Humanitarian Crisis, and Humanitarian Intervention', *International Journal* (Vol. XLVIII, Autumn 1993), pp. 607–40.
4. This definition of humanitarian intervention does not include interventions to rescue and defend foreign nationals.
5. International community is the term generally used by state leaders when they explain and justify their policies to domestic and international publics. The term international society has a more specialised meaning and is used by scholars to denote the existence of common interests and common values among states.
6. Charles Krauthammer, 'In Bosnia, Partition Might Do', *International Herald Tribune*, 9 September 1992.
7. Thomas M. Franck and Nigel S. Rodley, 'After Bangladesh: The Law of Humanitarian Intervention by Force', *American Journal of International Law* (Vol. 67, 1973), pp. 275–305.
8. Ibid., p. 278.
9. Ibid.
10. Andrew Mason and Nicholas J. Wheeler, 'Realist Objections to Humanitarian Intervention', in Barry Holden (ed.), *The Ethical Dimensions of Global Change* (London: Macmillan, 1996).

11. Krauthammer, 'In Bosnia'.
12. Robert H. Jackson, 'The Situational Ethics of Statecraft', paper presented to a conference on Ethics and Statecraft sponsored by the Carnegie Council on Ethics and International Affairs, University of British Columbia, Vancouver, 1994, p. 12.
13. Mason and Wheeler, 'Realist Objections'.
14. Adam Roberts, 'Humanitarian War: Military Intervention and Human Rights', *International Affairs* (Vol. 69, No. 3, July 1993), pp. 429–51.
15. Ibid., p. 448.
16. Ken Booth, 'Human Wrongs and International Relations' (the Second John Vincent Memorial Lecture, delivered at Keele University, 6 May 1994).
17. Jackson,'Martin Wight', p. 12.
18. The 'CNN factor' is discussed in Thomas G. Weiss, 'Triage: Humanitarian Interventions in a New Era', *World Policy Journal* (Vol. XI, No. 1, Spring 1994), p. 63.
19. For the classic 'restrictionist' view, see Ian Brownlie, *International Law and the Use of Force by States* (Oxford: Clarendon Press, 1963). Also see Ian Brownlie, 'Thoughts on Kind-hearted Gunmen', in Richard Lillich (ed.), *Humanitarian Intervention and the United Nations* (Charlottesville, VA: University Press of Virginia, 1973), pp. 139–48. For a general discussion of the 'restrictionist' view see Anthony C. Arend and Robert J. Beck, *International Law and the Use of Force* (London: Routledge, 1993).
20. See Bhikhu Parekh, 'Beyond Humanitarian Intervention'. Paper given to the Conference on Individual and Collective Rights in a National Context (School of Slovonic and East European Studies, University of London, 1994); Andrew Linklater, *Men and Citizens in the Theory of International Relations* (London: Macmillan, 1982); and Alan Gerwith, 'Ethical Universalism and Particularism', *The Journal of Philosophy* (Vol. LXXXV, No. 6, June 1988), pp. 283–302.
21. See Michael Walzer, *Just and Unjust Wars* (London: Allen Lane, 1977), pp. 107–8; Bhikhu Parekh, ibid.; Jarat Chopra and Thomas G. Weiss, 'Sovereignty Is No Longer Sacrosanct: Codifying Humanitarian Intervention', *Ethics and International Affairs* (Vol. 6, 1992), pp. 95–117; and Nick Lewer and Oliver Ramsbotham, *'Something Must be Done': Towards an Ethical Framework for Humanitarian Intervention in International Social Conflict'*, Peace Research Report No. 33, University of Bradford, Department of Peace Studies, August 1993, pp. 1–50.
22. Hugh Beach, 'Just Intervention'. Pamphlet of Council for Arms Control, 1993, p. 6.
23. Mason and Wheeler, 'Realist Objections'.
24. For the 'counter-restrictionist' view see M. Reissman and M. McDougal, 'Humanitarian Intervention to Protect the Ibos' in Lillich, *Humanitarian Intervention and the United Nations*, pp. 167–95; and Arend and Beck, *International Law*, pp. 132–6.

25. Quoted in Arend and Beck, *International Law*, p. 132.
26. Quoted in ibid. p. 133.
27. Justin Morris, 'The Concept of Humanitarian Intervention in International Relations', MA Dissertation (University of Hull, 1991), pp. 11–30.
28. Caroline Thomas, *New States, Sovereignty and Intervention* (Aldershot: Gower, 1985), p. 113; and Arend and Beck, *International Law*, pp. 122–3.
29. Thomas, *New States*, p. 113.
30. Gary Klintworth, *Vietnam's Intervention in Cambodia in International Law* (Canberra: AGPS Press, 1989), p. 59.
31. Roberts, *'Humanitarian War'* p. 434.
32. Hedley Bull (ed.), *Intervention in World Politics* (Oxford: Clarendon Press, 1984), p. 193. For a fuller analysis of Bull's views on humanitarian intervention see Nicholas J. Wheeler, 'Pluralist and Solidarist Conceptions of International Society: Bull and Vincent on Humanitarian Intervention', *Millennium: Journal of International Studies* (Vol. 21, No. 3, Winter 1992), pp. 463–89.
33. Richard N. Gardner, 'International Law and the Use of Force', *New Dimensions in International Security* (London: IISS, Adelphi Paper No. 266, Winter 1991/92), pp. 71–2.
34. UNSC Res, 46 SCOR (1991) of 5 April 1991; see also K.C. Wellens (ed.), *Resolutions and Statements of the United Nations Security Council (1946–1992)* (Dordrecht: Martinus Nijhoff, 1993, 2nd edn), pp. 578–80.
35. Christopher Greenwood, 'Is there a Right of Humanitarian Intervention?', *The World Today* (February 1993), p. 36.
36. Roberts, 'Humanitarian War', p. 438.
37. Morris, 'The Concept of Humanitarian Intervention', p. 37.
38. Greenwood, 'Is There a Right', p. 36.
39. Quoted in ibid., p. 36.
40. James Mayall, 'Non-Intervention, Self-Determination and the "New World Order"', *International Affairs* (Vol. 67, No. 3, July 1991), p. 426.
41. Ibid., p. 428.
42. For a view which is more positive on the long-term results of the intervention to protect the Kurds, see Weiss, 'Triage', p. 66.
43. UNSC Res, 733, 47 UN SCOR (1992) of 23 January 1992.
44. UNSC Res, 794, 47 UN SCOR (1992) of 3 December 1992.
45. Grenwood, 'Is There a Right', p. 37.
46. UNSC Res, 794, 47 UN SCOR (1992) of 3 December 1994.
47. Roberts, 'Humanitarian War', p. 440.
48. Robert H. Jackson, 'Armed Humanitarianism', *International Journal* (Vol. XLVIII, Autumn 1993), p. 596.
49. Quoted in Roberts, 'Humanitarian War', p. 441.
50. Jackson, 'Armed Humanitarianism', p. 604.
51. UNSC Res, 794, 47 UN SCOR (1992) of 3 December 1992 (emphasis added).

52. Roberts, 'Humanitarian War', p. 440.
53. See Roger Cotterell, *The Sociology of Law* (London: Butterworths, 1984), p. 138.
54. Jackson, 'Armed Humanitarianism', p. 594.
55. See R.J. Vincent and Peter Wilson, 'Beyond Non-Intervention', in Ian Forbes and Mark Hoffmann (eds), *Political Theory, International Relations and the Ethics of Intervention* (London: Macmillan, 1993), p. 125; and Parekh, 'Beyond Humanitarian Intervention', pp. 20 & 26–8.
56. Michael Mastanduno and Gene Lyons, 'Beyond Westphalia? International Intervention, State Sovereignty, and The Future Of International Society' (Summary of a conference held at Dartmouth College, Hanover, New Hampshire, 18–20 May, 1992), pp. 27–8.
57. Weiss, 'Triage', p. 61.
58. Roberts, 'Humanitarian War', p. 440.
59. Victoria Brittain, 'France's Fatal Impact', *The Guardian*, 24 June 1994.
60. Some commentators question how far the Tutsi-Hutu conflict is an 'ethnic' one, arguing that the conflictual 'ethnic' identities of Hutus and Tutsis are a social construct of the colonial era. An example of this is Robert Block's 'The Tragedy of Rwanda', *The New York Review of Books* (20 October 1994), pp. 3–8.
61. Alex de Waal, 'Rwandan genocide took four years to plan', *The Times*, 18 June 1994.
62. UN Doc.S/1994/470, 20 April 1994.
63. UNSC Res, 912, 49 UN SCOR (1994) of 21 April 1994.
64. David Beresford, 'Who is Guilty for Africa's Holocaust?, *The Guardian*, 30–31 July 1994.
65. Quoted in ibid.
66. UNSC Res. 918, 49 UN SCOR (1994) of 17 May 1994.
67. UN Doc.S/1994/565, 13 May 1994.
68. James Bone and Michael Binyon, 'UN Ready to Back French Intervention in Rwanda', *The Times*, 21 June 1994.
69. UN Doc. S/1994/728/, 20 April 1994.
70. Julian Nundy, 'Balladur takes a moral stance on intervention', *The Independent*, 23 June 1994.
71. UNSC Res. 929, 49 UN SCOR (1994) of 22 June 1994.
72. Ibid.
73. Andrew Gumbel and Mark Tran, 'UN Backs French Intervention in Rwanda in spite of Doubts over "Humanitarian" Motives', *The Guardian*, 23 June 1994.
74. Ibid.
75. Richard Dowden, 'French Press on with Rwanda Mission', *The Independent*, 21 June 1994.
76. Victoria Brittain, 'France's Fatal Impact', *The Guardian*, 24 June 1994.
77. Richard Dowden, 'French Press on with Rwanda Mission'.

78. David Beresford, 'Who is Guilty '.
79. Paul Webster, 'France Ducks as the Shells Whistle in', *The Guardian*, 7 July 1994.
80. Mayall, 'Non-Intervention, Self-Determination' p. 425.
81. See Caroline Thomas, 'The Pragmatic Case Against Intervention', in Forbes and Hoffman (eds), *Poltical Theory*, pp. 95 & 100.
82. The idea of a standing UN force, comprised of volunteer military personnel has been advanced by Sir Brian Urquhart. See 'For a UN Volunteer Military Force', *New York Review of Books* (10 June 1993), pp. 3–4, and discussions of the idea in subsequent issues.
83. Jurek Martin, 'Dole in Move over US Troops', *The Financial Times*, 19 October 1993; and Ian Brodie and David Adams, 'Clinton Keeps Control of UN Missions', *The Times*, 21 October 1993.
84. Richard Dowden, 'French "Invasion" of Rwanda Under Way', *The Independent*, 22 June 1994.
85. Roberts, 'Humanitarian War', p. 448.
86. Mark Hoffman, 'Agency, Identity and Intervention', in Forbes and Hoffman (eds), *Poltical Theory*, p. 206.
87. Weiss, 'Triage', p. 62.

8 Can International Society Be Green?

Robert H. Jackson

NORMATIVE PLURALISM IN INTERNATIONAL RELATIONS

Can theorists of international society come to grips with the normative problems that the environment presents to contemporary world politics? The question arises because the society of states is often seen as a fundamental obstacle to the solutions to many problems of our time, including environmental problems, which extend beyond international boundaries and thus seem to call for transnational, cosmopolitan or global conceptions of social obligations. Robert Goodin considers 'that the traditional structure of international law – guided as it is by notions of autonomous national actors with strong rights that all other national actors similarly share – is wildly inappropriate to many of these new environmental challenges. A system of shared duties or, better yet, shared responsibilities is a more fitting model, given the nature of the tasks at hand.'[1]

International society is, of course, a society of states based on negative liberties – sovereign immunities – of its members. But it is also a society of humankind which postulates human rights, a world society which presupposes international social welfare, and a global society which posits a network of transnational relations. One could readily identify other international norms – such as minority rights, aboriginal status or gender claims, all of which are emerging or re-emerging today. Global environmentalism which presupposes the health of the planet Earth as a moral value should now also be included among those norms. International society and the diplomatic and legal practices from which it springs is more flexible and adaptable than Goodin implies. It is a *pluralistic* sphere consisting of different and in some cases diverging norms which figure in the choices of statesmen and stateswomen.[2] This means that the international sphere, like most other spheres of human conduct, is fraught with normative tensions, anomalies and conflicts.

The concept of international normative pluralism may call for a few clarifying comments. I refer here to 'ethical pluralism' or, in other words, the normative diversity of international relations.[3] I am not referring to the 'pluralist' conception of international society in which states are the exclusive right-and-duty-bearing units, as contrasted with the 'solidarist' conception in which individual human beings are the ultimate subjects of international law.[4] States obviously are no longer the sole constituents of international society, if they ever were; but to suggest that individuals enjoy that standing to the exclusion of all other normative categories is similarly misleading. The fact of the matter is that international society consists of diverse normative units none of which can arbitrarily be ruled out of any analysis.

There are both advantages and disadvantages to an approach which directs our attention to the various and often contradictory justifications that may be given for international actions. Moral and legal philosophers might not be satisfied unless we conceptualise international norms in terms of a systematic framework in which a basic norm is identified from which all others can be derived.[5] We should of course seek to understand not only the choices that are made but also the grounds for justifying or condemning them: one cannot question the philosophical drive for coherence. But we must search for those grounds in the subject we are studying. In the world of international relations as experienced by the people involved, the various norms do not interlock in a systematic way as they would, for example, in a normative hierarchy: the immunities of sovereign states may conflict with human rights which may be at odds with global economic welfare which may, in turn, clash with environmental values.

As a working hypothesis it is reasonable to assume that international norms can collide at certain points thereby obliging state-leaders and other international agents to make what can often amount to difficult normative choices. One of the fundamental aims of normative studies in international relations should be to understand such choices and this is a basic goal of the traditional International Society approach. Hedley Bull hit the nail on the head when he once defined that approach as 'characterized above all by explicit reliance upon the exercise of judgement'.[6]

To sum up: international society is a changing, indeed an evolving, normative sphere and not a static or strictly limiting one; in other words, it is an historical and sociological concept. International norms cannot be stipulated by academic theorists sitting in their university offices; they can only be disclosed by the actions of the particular people involved in that sphere of human activity, the most important of whom still are public officials. Empirical rootedness is the theory's main strength: the richness of the idea of international society in that regard should be acknowledged. I believe this strength more than balances the principal weakness of the approach: its lack of philosophical grounding.

INTERNATIONAL SOCIETY AND ENVIRONMENTAL NORMS

It is important to distinguish between the environment in the scientific sense, as a concept of nature, and the environment in the social or historical sense, as a habitat which is invested with intrinsic meaning and value.[7] The former concept is necessary to deal with the environment on an instrumental basis. The latter concept is required to justify whatever human actions in relation to the environment are made possible by science, technology and industry. The underlying assumption is that humans now have the power to affect significantly the environment, for better or for worse, and therefore the responsibility that goes with that power. In particular, the despoliation or destruction of the environment is now recognised to be not only dysfunctional or unwise but also wrong. It must therefore be justified. That, of course, involves balancing environmental values with other values, such as economic development, human rights or national sovereignty.

Here, I will be concerned only with the latter concept in which the environment can lay claim to human accountability: a candidate for recognition, protection, reclamation and preservation.[8] Thus the environment today, somewhat like foreigners and particularly 'barbarians' and 'savages' in times past, is brought within the normative compass of what R.G. Collingwood refers to as 'civilisation' in which 'the other' can no longer be 'exploited' but must be 'respected' as a matter of social consciousness and social responsibility.[9] Since the environment is a habitat for humans and other species, and patently is not comparable to human 'others', and since environmental problems go beyond national boundaries, the appropriate moral stance that one should adopt would seem to be stewardship, trusteeship or some other version of global paternalism. But I cannot explore the distinctive character of environmental ethics here.

The special significance of environmental norms for practitioners and theorists of international relations stems from the obvious reality that environmental problems are not confined within the territorial boundaries of independent states. Air and water pollution is blind to state jurisdiction; depletion of the ozone layer and global warming know nothing of state sovereignty; the destruction of tropical rain forests is an ecological loss to the world. These international environmental problems, and many others that one could mention, are widely recognised nowadays by practitioners and theorists alike. Indeed, the expansion of environmental awareness, from a mere object of science, technology and industry to an authentic subject of human responsibility (including legal accountability), has been extraordinary in recent decades.

The environment is increasingly a subject of international law. Among the many topics brought within the orbit of such law are ozone depletion, decline of biological diversity, global warming, toxic wastes, air and water pollution, acid rain, destruction of forests and population explosion. Among the general pronouncements on environmental norms are the Stockholm Declaration (1972), the Report of the World Commission on Environment and Development (Brundtland Report, 1987), and the Rio Declaration (1992).[10] There are already numerous specialised treaties, including the Geneva Convention on Long-Range Transboundary Air Pollution, the Vienna Convention and Montreal Protocol on the Ozone Layer, the Basel Convention on Hazardous Wastes, the Nordic Environmental Protection Convention, the London Convention on Marine Pollution, and the UN Convention on the Law of the Sea. I cannot here review the extensive legal literature on environmental problems which is a huge subject and one that is still expanding rapidly.[11] I simply note in passing the extent to which there is a greening of international society in the diplomatic and legal sphere.

The significance of this development is, of course, a subject of debate. The argument, already noted, that the environment presents normative problems to which representatives and agents of sovereign states cannot respond in the usual terms of state sovereignty and international law is quite widespread today and calls for some comment. Protection of the environment obviously does not readily fit with the freedom of states to do whatever they will inside their own jurisdiction. Environmental degradation cannot be confined within state boundaries but readily spills over them: for example, once airborne pollution is released into the atmosphere it moves unhindered with the weather. Other kinds of environmental degradation, such as ozone depletion or marine pollution, have similar effects. Thus, the normative logic of state sovereignty appears inconsistent and perhaps even at odds with the normative logic of environmental protection, which requires cooperation across international boundaries.

Robert Goodin, as indicated, sees state sovereignty as a significant obstacle to dealing responsibly and effectively with international environmental problems and calls, instead, for a regime of 'shared duties' and 'shared responsibilities' in which sovereign states would be morally and legally bound to address such problems.[12] He regards the 1987 Montreal Protocol on Substances that Deplete the Ozone Layer – which comes into force when ratified by two thirds of the countries that cause the problem – as an example of such a regime because it imposes 'rather onerous burdens' specifically on those states which are responsible. In short it links responsibility with power and agency.

But is a cooperative arrangement, such as the Montreal Protocol, inconsistent with the pluralistic idea of an international society outlined above? I do not believe it is. There is nothing in existing international practice which bars cooperation on environmental issues or any other common problems or joint concerns. As already indicated, international society does not rest exclusively on a conception of sovereign rights; it merely recognises that states are fundamental right-and-duty-bearing units in world politics and consequently sovereignty and non-intervention are basic preemptory norms. States are obliged not to harm fellow states without cause; and while they are not obliged to cooperate, except for the pursuit of peace and prevention of aggression as mandated by Chapter VII of the UN Charter, they are not prevented from cooperating either. International society theory recognises that even though states are sovereign that does not release them from their duties and responsibilities to other states; nor does it stop them from engaging in collaborative action to deal with joint or common problems.[13] Contemporary international relations is honeycombed with virtually countless international organisations and non-governmental organisations which deal with a remarkable variety of joint substantive problems and concerns.[14] The environment is fast emerging as one of the most important.[15]

Whether or not representatives or agents of states take joint action to protect the environment is thus dictated not by international law but, rather, by their conception of responsibility, usually in the face of competing claims on their conduct in the circumstances in which they find themselves. That conception is social and situational: it is influenced by their membership and participation in international society. That is surely what the Montreal Protocol is indicative of: the recognition by state leaders that joint action by the parties who are responsible – the polluting states – is the only effective and justifiable way to address the problem of ozone depletion which is caused by greenhouse gases which are produced almost entirely by developed countries. One obviously could not reasonably place that responsibility on countries which are not the source of the problem or on all countries equally; responsibilities in that regard must be differentiable, just as responsibilities for peace fall most heavily on the great powers. State-leaders are not here acting out of any sense of a binding legal obligation but out of the recognition of a common interest or concern that such action is necessary and right. A polluting state could deny its share of responsibility, and refuse to sign the accord, but it could not in that way escape from bearing responsibility for the problem which is established not volitionally but rather by scientific evidence.

Goodin and similar critics of the existing state sovereignty regime seem to take the view that environmental norms must be legally binding to be effective. Anything else 'is still very much a second-best solution, morally'.[16] That view has a domestic parallel in which government-mandated and enforced laws have been found necessary for environmental protection and clean-up within state jurisdictions. However, international society cannot be equated with domestic society: there are no authorities and agencies comparable to those of the state to enforce international law; the UN Environmental Programme and similar bodies do not have the legal authority or enforcement powers of domestic environmental protection agencies. If environmental protection were to become an international obligation comparable to that of non-intervention, that would constitute a revolutionary change which would transform international relations into something entirely different in which states would no longer be sovereign in the classical negative liberty meaning of the term. A system of shared-responsibilities, legally mandated and enforced, would be a brave new world with revolutionary implications for international life which would not stop at the environment. The possibility of anything like that happening in the near future is remote.

Hedley Bull had little to say about the environment. But he was aware of the argument that the existing state-centric organisation of international society was an obstacle to environmental protection and preservation. He regarded it as 'unhelpful':

> The states system...and the sense of common interests and values that underlies it...is the principal expression of human unity or solidarity that exists at the present time, and such hopes as we may entertain for the emergence of a more cohesive world society are bound up with its preservation and development.[17]

To this one should add that that system is anything but monolithic or normatively rigid as its critics seem to imply. On the contrary, it is pluralistic and flexible – as one would expect from any practical and non-ideological system of norms that is historically open to change. It is this characteristic of international society which makes it possible for international agents to extend old norms (as with the international law of damages) and to evolve new norms (as with international collaboration) to address novel substantive problems of international relations, including environmental problems.[18] What is increasingly noticeable is an international variant of ordinary legal and political activity in which existing practices are applied to new problems and vice versa: what Michael

Oakeshott refers to as the 'correction of anomalies' and (more obscurely) the 'pursuit of intimations' which can only occur within – and thus presupposes – a practical normative framework of some kind.[19] Here one also cannot help but recall Burke: international society, being traditional or conventional, is necessarily subject to evolutionary change; 'in what we improve, we are never wholly new; in what we retain, we are never wholly obsolete.'[20]

INTERNATIONAL ENVIRONMENTAL NORMS

My claim that international society can be green is evident from a necessarily brief glance at current principles and practices of international environmental law. The existence of such norms – setting aside the question of their practical efficacy – suggests at a minimum that there is room – arguably ample room – in international society for addressing environmental concerns. Classical international law has not obstructed or even discouraged environmental concerns; on the contrary, it has been employed and adjusted to accommodate and indeed to promote such concerns, to fit them into received legal principles and practices. In the 1941 Trail (British Columbia) Smelter case international legality was combined with diplomatic compromise to address the problem of transborder pollution to the evident satisfaction or at least endorsement of the states parties and the interests they represented – namely the United States which suffered from the pollution caused by the smelter, and Canada in whose territory the polluting firm operated. The international tribunal, established with the consent of each state to adjudicate the case, saw its role as one of balancing the conflicting interests involved: permitting the smelter to continue in production 'but under such restrictions and limitations as would, as far as reasonable, prevent damage to the United States'.[21] This ruling is consistent with the traditional principle of state responsibility for international damages caused to neighbouring states: the pollution 'could be characterized as an "invasion" (however modest) of US sovereignty'.[22] It also discloses collaboration between the United States and Canada in so far as the adjudication process was set up by agreement between the two countries. One could speculate whether the same solution would have been found if the polluter had been located on the American side of the border. But there is an extensive array of cross-border collaborative arrangements, legal and quasi-legal, between the United States and Canada on a host of joint substantive problems from fisheries to trade – among the most prominent being the International Joint Commission and the Free Trade Agreement dispute panels.

Similar normative reasoning and concern is conspicuous in efforts by 'downwind' states, such as the Scandinavian countries, Austria, Switzerland and Canada, to invoke a general norm of international responsibility for damages caused by industrial activities which produce acid rain in neighbouring countries. This obviously challenges the view that such effects are merely accidents of geography and thus impose no obligations on the polluter – a misfortune and not misconduct. The same normative logic is evident in the 'polluter-pays principle': that those who pollute bear the responsibility of compensating for damages they cause others – including other states. There are today various international conventions which address questions of civil liability concerning the transboundary movements of hazardous wastes, marine pollution by dumping wastes, oil-pollution damage, and oil-pollution damage resulting from seabed exploration and exploitation. Such norms are consistent with the traditional idea of state responsibility in international law. International compensation for environmental damage caused by the intentional or negligent polluting actions of a neighbouring state is, in principle, no different from any other kind of transborder damages.

An important caveat is necessary at this stage. Patricia Birnie is at some pains to emphasise that 'there are serious difficulties with the application of state responsibility in the field of environmental law....None of the conventions relating to environment protection...does more than state that principles of liability should be developed'.[23] But my point here is simply that normative reasoning which focuses on state sovereignty and liability is consistent with the theory of international society. What international law provides, in this regard, is a convenient and appropriate point of departure for conceiving, promoting, and, if possible, instituting international environmental norms. How far international liability can be extended into the environmental sphere is undoubtedly a practical problem. But it surely is not a theoretical problem.

There is a long history of international conferences and commissions in which representatives of states assemble from time to time to address joint substantive problems or concerns. In the past such international collaboration was provoked by preoccupations with security or trade or communications but there is, at least in principle, no reason why they cannot concern environmental problems. As indicated, in recent decades there have been major international conferences and commissions on the environment: the 1972 Stockholm Conference, the 1983 World Commission on Environment and Development, and the 1992 Rio Conference. All of them have attempted to articulate and initiate international environmental norms either as quasi-legal precepts or as law.

The principle of state sovereignty has not been, arguably could not be, abandoned by recent endeavours at international conferences to promote global environmental protection. On the contrary, it would have to be a central postulate and point of reference – if environmental problems were to be considered by the representatives and delegates of sovereign states in attendance. And it is exactly that. The themes of international conferences – including conferences on the environment – cannot wander very far from the preoccupations of sovereign states, the core of which is state sovereignty. Principle 21 of the Stockholm Declaration on the Human Environment gave sovereignty a central place in its normative proposals, while acknowledging that states must nevertheless assume responsibility for international pollution. The Rio Declaration (Principle 2) likewise emphasises 'the sovereign right [of states] to exploit their own resources pursuant to their own environmental and developmental policies'. Whether this signals a step backward from international environmental responsibility is a subject of current debate.[24] That sovereignty continues to be a central norm to which environmental concerns must be adjusted cannot be doubted.

Conferences and commissions of this sort – unlike peace conferences which follow major wars – are not called to reconstitute international society or remake international law. They are in the business of 'helping define' issues, proposing 'strategies', making 'recommendations', considering 'ways and means', and so forth, to increase international cooperation with a view to promoting environmental protection.[25] In other words, this is entirely consistent with the traditional international practice of adapting the available tools of international society for the purpose of addressing newly-perceived international problems and concerns. States have already set up a large number of international bodies – from the Commission for the Conservation of Antarctic Marine Living Resources to the United Nations Environment Programme – concerned with environmental problems. Of course, what any international conference or commission can achieve on any subject will always depend on the willingness and ability of the participants, particularly the leading states, to enter into commitments or to cooperate in other ways. The environment is no different.

Most commentators draw attention to the limits of this sort of international action for dealing with environmental problems. By bringing together all interested and concerned parties, including those who wish to promote environmental values as well as those who want to resist them, the developed countries as well as the developing countries, such international arrangements obviously restrict what can be achieved. By operating with the principle that all parties can have a voice in the matter – even if that voice is differentially weighted, for example, by the criteria of affected interests or degree of responsibility – the arrangement must still accommodate diverse views if the states system is to be open, as it should be, to the interests and concerns of all its members. Such an arrangement is fundamentally political. Furthermore, what can be accomplished in any political assembly, domestic or international, is always limited to what those involved are prepared to accept and undertake. The recent Rio Conference is a good example: not only did it reaffirm the fundamental principle of state sovereignty, but it also insisted on 'common but differentiated responsibilities' in which it was acknowledged that responsibility must be tied to the different capacities of states, and thus developing countries must not be subjected to the same standards as developed countries. In other words, the Rio conference, to get a joint declaration, found it necessary to reconcile environmental and developmental norms.[26]

Restricted as they may be, such international activities – together with the actions of non-governmental organisations which inevitably accompany them – are the only realistic basis for addressing common environmental problems. Any alternative arrangements that one could imagine, such as international agencies with the authority and power to enforce environmental protection laws, are at the present time difficult to distinguish from utopianism.

TWO SPHERES OF INTERNATIONAL ENVIRONMENTALISM

The theory of international society affords a way of thinking in a realistic vein about environmental problems – including not only acts of pollution which are damaging to a neighbouring state or group of states (and which can thus be understood in reciprocal terms of the traditional obligation to refrain from causing harm to sovereign neighbours), but also acts of pollution which are damaging to everybody (and must be understood in cooperative or global terms). One way to theorise both types of environmental problems is via the conception of international society as comprising two coexisting spheres: a primary and obligatory regime of negative liberties – international civil association – and a secondary and voluntary regime of positive liberties – international enterprise association.[27]

Classical international society, at least since the Treaty of Westphalia (1648), has postulated negative liberties of states based on sovereignty and non-intervention: *Rex est imperator in regno suo* (the king is emperor in his own realm). State-leaders are bound to respect each other's sovereignty unless they have valid reasons to do otherwise. That injunction is captured in classical international law as embodied today in the United Nations Charter, Article 2(4), which declares that 'All members shall refrain in their international relations from the threat or use of force against the territorial integrity or political independence of any State'. As a rule states are responsible for any damages they inflict without cause, either intentionally or negligently, on their neighbours.

But this first regime is accompanied by a second regime of positive liberties whereby state leaders are free to cooperate to pursue and promote common substantive ends, such as joint defence, mutual economic development, scientific collaboration, technological cooperation, regulated broadcasting frequencies, standardised weights and measures, transportation regulations, customs unions, weather forecasting. The second regime is a voluntary sphere of international activity which in most cases derives from common interests or shared concerns of states. By 'voluntary' I mean that states, as a condition of being sovereign, are not bound to enter into such arrangements. If they do enter they are, of course, then bound to honour them.

The second regime is none the less important, and has always been evident, because although states are independent they are not and never have been either totally isolated or entirely self-sufficient; on the contrary, they live in most cases geographically cheek-by-jowl and face common problems, many of which they can only address satisfactorily through cooperation. Those problems arguably increase as their power to affect each other, both beneficially and adversely, expands in the course of scientific advance and economic development. Transborder environmental pollution is an example of such a spillover problem which stems from the adverse and often unforeseen and unintended consequences of the expanding technological and industrial power of modern states.

Protection of the environment can readily be understood in terms of these two spheres of international society. The sovereign right of non-intervention and the corresponding responsibility to forbear from action that is likely to harm or damage another state, can address environmental problems. Thus, for example, transborder acid rain or downstream river pollution is an international environmental problem whose normative logic is consistent with the classical norm of sovereignty. Likewise, the joint action of states to address the common problems of ozone depletion or hazardous waste disposal or conservation of wildlife or preservation of rain forests or the protection of biodiversity, is consistent with their positive freedom to collaborate for common purposes to deal with problems that could not be dealt with satisfactorily by each one alone.

The argument so far contends, contrary to a popular critique of traditional international society, that environmental norms are not precluded by the received practices of international relations based on state sovereignty. They can accordingly be brought within the compass of that theory which seeks to comprehend such practices and reflect upon them: the theory of international society. Objections to this claim, which usually call for a radical change of international norms in which traditional state sovereignty is reduced in significance, focus on the fact that states cannot be obliged by law to take positive actions, such as protecting the global environment. States can only be required to refrain from taking actions which are harmful to other states. This voluntarist method of responding to common problems cannot override or 'trump' state sovereignty. That appears to be the objection of Robert Goodin and others who share his view. Much of this regime consists in 'soft' international legal norms that cannot bind states to standards of environmental protection in the same way that domestic law can bind private organisations to take actions that reduce pollution. Thus, international environmental norms remain inferior to state sovereignty which is a 'hard' norm. Hence the assumption that the transborder environment thereby goes largely unprotected.

What is well-founded about this objection is the obvious fact that sovereignty remains a pre-emptory norm in international relations: state leaders cannot in the normal course of their relations issue authoritative commands to each other; they can only try to influence each other in non-prohibited ways. What seems to be missing is the fact that although states are sovereign, they are not isolated from each other; on the contrary, they are in contact with each other, they trade with each other, almost all of them are in dialogue with each other, and virtually all are members of a common society. State leaders are socialised into this society and its responsibilities even though they of course remain responsible first and foremost for the well-being of their own country and its people. There is also 'international public opinion', which can give expression to various international normative concerns that state-leaders can ignore only at the risk of being subjected to negative evaluation and, in extreme cases, being isolated from the rest of international society. Like most other people, state-leaders, as a rule, have little desire to be subjected to negative appraisals and actions if they can possibly avoid it. As a matter of historical fact, very few states freely pursue policies of self-isolation from other states or international society at large. On the contrary, the vast majority endeavour to be involved in the activities of international bodies where they can voice their concerns.

In short, if state leaders desire to be international citizens, and enjoy the esteem of other states and favourable international public opinion, they must within reason be attentive and responsive to the concerns of other state leaders, and also non-governmental organisations. 'Reason' would signify a commitment or contribution to international society that does not involve self-sacrifice. This 'Lockean' limit arguably still makes possible a wide array of international collaborative activities on matters of common concern. The environment is one such concern that has emerged into the bright light of international publicity in recent decades. There are of course other concerns, such as economic development or national security or human rights, which compete and very likely will from time to time conflict with the protection of the environment. One of the main responsibilities of state leaders is to face up to such normative conflicts and make the best decision that circumstances permit. The theory of international society presupposes an applied ethics of statecraft that operates roughly along these lines.

ENVIRONMENTAL NORMS IN OPERATION

Environmental norms should thus be seen not as standing in isolation from, but rather, as running alongside other international norms which compete with each other as claims on decisions and policies of state-leaders and other international agents. The environment is certainly no more privileged in moral terms than national independence, human rights or economic welfare, all of which lay claim to the responsibilities of such people. Instead, it adds yet another dimension to the evolving normative pluralism which has characterised international ethics for a very long time.

Because international norms are bound to conflict in certain circumstances, agents who are responsible for making important normative choices will face dilemmas and search for ways out of or around them. Important examples of such normative conflicts in contemporary international relations would include environmental norms versus sovereign rights and environmentalism versus development. These conflicts link up or overlap with other fundamental international cleavages, such as the gap between developed and developing countries. Confronted by such normative conflicts, state leaders and other members of what is today a global international society naturally want to avoid open breaches and thus seek to find common ground, practical expedients, diplomatic compromises, or even, if necessary, political fudges to deal with them.

One prominent example is the response to the discord between environmental protection and national development that goes by the imaginative name 'sustainable development'. This term obviously denotes the attempt to reconcile, in a way that is politically acceptable, the normative tension between environmental protection, on the one hand, and economic development, on the other. Principle 4 of the Rio Declaration proclaims: 'in order to achieve sustainable development, environmental protection shall constitute an integral part of the development process and cannot be considered in isolation from it'. Legal scholars who have scrutinised the text have drawn different conclusions. Some have argued that '"sustainable development" undermines the autonomy of environmental law as a body of rules and standards designed to restrain and prevent the environmentally destructive effects of certain kinds of economic activity'.[28] Others argue that it is the sort of reconciliation that one should expect in a world that is still organised fundamentally in terms of independent states and is still divided equally fundamentally between developed and developing countries.[29] The following at least is clear: environmental norms, in actual practice, have to be fitted into the normative framework and practices of an on-going and thus historical international society.

Another example is the response to the reality of unequal capabilities between countries both in producing environmental damage and taking responsibility for preventing any further damage and repairing that which has already been caused. The global environment is a common responsibility of everyone on earth and particularly every national government which possesses the power to alter it for better or for worse. But this does not mean that everyone's responsibility is the same. Obviously, a large country like the United States has contributed far more to the greenhouse effect than a small country like Denmark. Equally, developed countries, both individually and collectively, are more capable of environmental clean-up than developing countries.

How have state leaders and other international agents responded to these conflicts? One noteworthy response, again embodied in the Rio Declaration, is the concept of 'common but differentiated responsibilities' which attempts to take the foregoing distinctions into account. The Declaration recognised the differential capacities of states both for doing environmental damage and for repairing it. Rio thus justified environmental standards among states that were sensitive to their different capacities; it also characterised the normative basis for transferring environmental technologies from developed to developing countries as an 'obligation' rather than 'aid' (Principle 7). This arguably is a significant step in the development of normative international relations. The evident grounds for construing this as an international obligation derives from the fact that everyone, including developed countries, will benefit from such transfers which cannot therefore be regarded as charity. In these examples environmental norms have been incorporated into the ongoing pattern of international relations.

A specific organisational instance of this process is the articulation of environmental standards as one condition for World Bank loans. Again the force and significance of environmental conditionality is a matter of debate: Jake Werksman, for example, sees it as introducing environmental accountability into international lending and thus 'qualifying the concept of sovereignty'.[30] Andrew Hurrell agrees that environmental conditionality 'can play a significant role in the promotion of sustainable development' but points out that it involves 'political opposition' from borrowing countries that could very well increase in the future – precisely because it is, after all, a form of external intervention.[31]

This is not to suggest that sovereignty has been circumscribed, because states can still refuse World Bank loans even if the opportunity cost is high. Rather, it suggests that some sovereign countries, namely those which seek such loans, must now accept environmental conditions in addition to the usual economic and financial conditions if they are to access those funds. Perhaps at this point we catch a glimpse of the convergence between environmental conditionality and the above-noted obligation to transfer environmental technology: reciprocity. In other words, if environmental conditions are now applied to international borrowers, mainly developing countries, then technology transfers which make it possible for those countries to observe such conditions must be accepted as an obligation by international lenders, mainly developed countries. That would seem to be a 'reasonable' compromise in the Lockean meaning of the term. This does not 'qualify' the institution of sovereignty – at least not in any way that intimates a fundamental normative change; rather, it incorporates environmental norms into the reciprocal financial relations of sovereign states embodied in the Bretton Woods institutions and international financial practice generally.

In these examples international norms and international politics are entangled with each other, almost to the point of being indistinguishable. There is surely a very good reason for that: the adoption of new norms is a profoundly political question because it affects what the parties involved are prepared to accept and undertake – what is reasonable. This is evident, for example, in efforts taken to incorporate environmental norms into the legal institutions of the European Community, which was initially established in 1957 as a trading community. Norms to reconcile trade and environmental concerns have been incorporated subsequently. Although the

European Court of Justice has been involved in adjudicating cases involving conflicts between trade and environmental norms, it is still largely European community politics which determines what level of environmental protection will be instituted.[32] What has been achieved to date has depended on what member states are prepared to accept and undertake. Thus, even in Western Europe – where international 'community' is arguably more developed and where environmental concerns and green politics have advanced further than almost anywhere else – the environment is only one norm alongside others. But it is now installed as a norm which figures in the actions of state leaders and other international agents – and for the theory of international society that is the most significant point.

The foregoing discussion hopefully gives an intimation of how environmental norms are predicated in concrete international practice. Perhaps this can be taken a step farther by what must be only a cursory glance at the place of such norms in the (second) war in the Persian Gulf (1990–1).[33] This case is interesting because war places a severe test on most values apart from security and survival; in other words military values have such overriding importance that it is difficult not to reduce all other values to secondary or tertiary considerations, or simply to abandon them. There is evidence of military expediency in the Gulf War, but there is also evidence of a widespread international preoccupation with basic normative concerns – such as the justifications for embarking on armed conflict (*jus ad bellum*) and for conducting armed conflict (*jus in bello*) against Iraq.[34]

In the course of that war Iraq resorted to military expedients that involved large-scale oil spillages and incineration of oil-fields which, in turn, resulted in considerable transborder environmental damage. This Iraqi action was in express violation of international environmental laws, such as the 1978 Convention on the Protection of the Marine Environment in the Gulf, to which Iraq was a party. The UN Environmental Programme later reported on the extent of the damage and the problems of clean-up. A 1991 Ottawa Conference of Experts agreed that Iraq was obliged to pay compensation for any environmental damages it had caused. One of the most significant UN Security Council Resolutions on the Gulf conflict, Resolution 687, although primarily concerned with eliminating Iraq's nuclear, chemical and biological weapons capacity, also 'reaffirmed' that Iraq was 'liable under international law' for 'environmental damage and the depletion of natural resources'. That is suggestive if not indicative of an environmental norm in warfare: the environment as part of *jus in bello*. It must of course be understood in the context of Iraq as a defeated power: the story might have been different if Iraq had won. But perhaps the more significant point is the fact that Iraq was defeated not merely by another power but, rather, by a broad coalition of powers acting on behalf of the UN Security Council which acknowledged and affirmed environmental protection as an operative norm, among others, in the Gulf War.

CONCLUSION: SECURITY OR SOCIETY?

How should we explain the greening of international relations? I have tried to account for environmental values in terms of the theory of international society. However, there is one other theoretical perspective which must be considered before we can draw any conclusions from my analysis: the environment understood in terms of security. In this account, environmental damage or destruction is construed as a source of international threat comparable to that of military violence or economic embargo. This argument rests on the assumption that individuals and states depend for their own well-being upon a safe environment which obviously can be interfered with by others, including other states, in such a way as to threaten or cause harm. One version of this 'Realist' logic – the international legal version – is the law of international liability for damages inflicted by states on one another. Here the environment becomes merely another legal norm in the international law of state responsibility. This version is thus part of the International Society approach outlined above.

However, a more prominent version posits international relations as driven by security interests and concerns which all states share as a consequence of the anarchical condition of international politics. Here the concept of security includes not only military security or economic security but also environmental security. The environment is thus conceived in terms of the balance of power and international order: part of the recurrent problem of national security in conditions of anarchy. If we take this idea to its logical conclusion we can even conceive of threats to the 'balance of nature' which would raise unprecedented problems in international relations and call upon 'Realist' statecraft of the highest order – i.e. state leaders who include environmental security in their power-politics calculations.[35]

Does it make sense to think of the environment in terms of national or international security? I do not believe it does, and for several reasons. First, evidence does not support the claim that environmental cooperation between states arises from the logic of self-interest or power politics more generally.[36] State leaders who cooperate or conflict over environmental questions are doing that for various reasons but not for reasons of security. The environment can of course be used as a source of threat or harm--as Iraq used it in the Gulf War. But fear is not the main motive for regulating the environment: that motive has far more to do with a sense of responsibility. Second, one cannot thus conceive of armed intervention based on perceived threats to environmental security, particularly collective environmental security. The degradation of the environment may be a threat to all of us, but it is only perceived that way in the longest of terms. The time horizon for the generation of apprehension by environmental threat or damage is too remote for it to work as part of the logic of security. Third, to expand the concept of 'national security' to include the environment is to 'drain the term of any meaning.'[37] Not only that, it is also to muddle the logic of security which is one of human action and human reaction rooted in self-interest. Ultimately, this is the self-regarding logic of Hobbes' state of nature: the logic of international anarchy. Finally, this position obscures the idea of the environment in human affairs which, as indicated above, is that of a habitat for which humans are responsible since they have the industrial power to damage it and (hopefully) also the scientific genius to repair at least some of the damage or forestall any further destruction.

The environment is not only a self-regarding value but also an other-regarding value, and at that point Realism fails to understand it. The other-regarding aspect of the environment makes it a far better candidate for theorising in terms of international society. However, as indicated, 'The other' in the case of the environment is not only other individuals or other states who share a dependency on the natural habitat but also other animals, species, and forms of life; environmental responsibility thus spreads well beyond the human family.[38] This gives applied environmental ethics its character of stewardship or trusteeship. Yet being a natural phenomenon, the environment is significantly independent of human reason and human will: it is not under the control of human beings in the same way that security is under their control.[39] Nature (or God) plays an important part in determining the health of the environment. In other words, to that extent there is a limit to human responsibility for the environment. But there is absolutely no doubt that considerable and expanding human power over the environment does now exist which posits human responsibility for that part of the environment within its reach. Because that human reach extends across national boundaries, environmental responsibility is international; because it extends beyond national jurisdictions into the 'global commons', environmental responsibility is also planetary. That normative reasoning, it seems to me, is the kernel of good sense in the International Society approach.

NOTES

1. Robert Goodin, 'International Ethics and the Environment Crisis', *Ethics & International Affairs* (Vol. 4, 1990), p. 93.
2. In one of his earliest works Hedley Bull commented that 'the world is very much more complicated than the [academic] arguments' which seek to comprehend it. *The Control of the Arms Race* (London: Weidenfeld & Nicolson, 1961), p. 212.
3. The *Shorter Oxford English Dictionary* gives the following definition of 'pluralism': '2...A system of thought which recognises more than one ultimate principle; opp. to MONISM'. For further comments on this idea see my 'Pluralism in International Relations', *Review of International Studies* (Vol. 18, No. 3, July 1992), pp. 271–81.
4. The latter idea is discussed by Nicholas J. Wheeler in 'Pluralist or Solidarist Conceptions of International Society: Bull and Vincent on Humanitarian Intervention', *Millennium: Journal of International Studies* (Vol. 21, No. 3, Winter 1992), pp. 463–87.
5. Charles Beitz attempts this by applying John Rawls's theory of justice to international relations. See his *Political Theory and International Relations* (Princeton, NJ: Princeton University Press, 1979).
6. Hedley Bull, 'International Theory: The Case for a Classical Approach', in Klaus Knorr and James N. Rosenau (eds), *Contending Approaches to International Politics* (Princeton, NJ: Princeton University Press, 1969), p. 20.
7. For a philosophical analysis, see R.G. Collingwood, *The Idea of History* (London: Oxford University Press, 1956), part V.
8. I shall avoid getting into the question of whether the environment has moral value independent of its value for human beings. When I speak of environmental norms I am referring to standards of conduct which humans are bound to respect.
9. See R.G. Collingwood, *The New Leviathan* (New York, NY: Crowell, 1971), Part III.
10. See *Our Common Future* (Oxford: Oxford University Press, 1987).
11. For a comprehensive recent survey, see Andrew Hurrell and Benedict Kingsbury (eds), *The International Politics of the Environment* (Oxford: Clarendon Press, 1992).
12. Goodin, 'International Ethics and the Environmental Crisis', p. 94.
13. Patricia Birnie argues, convincingly in my view, that 'ample techniques derived from traditional sources of international law are available for development of regulations to protect the environment.' 'International Environment Law: Its Adequacy for Present and Future Needs', in Hurrell and Kingsbury (eds), *The International Politics of the Environment*, p. 82.

14. Numerous studies have mapped these expanding international organizations and their activities. For a particularly insightful account, see Evan Luard, *International Agencies* (London: Macmillan, 1977).
15. See the succinct discussion by Ronnie D. Lipschutz in ch. 6 of this volume.
16. Goodin, 'International Ethics and the Environmental Crisis,' p. 105.
17. Hedley Bull, *The Anarchical Society* (London: Macmillan, 1977), p. 295.
18. Michael Oakeshott, *Rationalism in Politics and Other Essays*, new and expanded edition (Indianapolis, IN: Liberty Press, 1991).
19. See 'Rationalism in Politics' and 'Political Education' in ibid.
20. Reflections on the Revolution in France as quoted by L.I. Bredvold and R.G. Ross (eds), *The Philosophy of Edmund Burke* (Ann Arbor, MI: University of Michigan Press, 1967), p. 157.
21. Quoted by Allen L. Springer, 'International Environmental Law After Rio,' *Ethics & International Affairs* (Vol. 7, 1993), p. 118.
22. Christopher D. Stone, 'Defending the Global Commons,' in P. Sands (ed.), *Greening International Law* (London: Earthscan, 1993), p. 37.
23. Birnie, 'International Environmental Law', pp. 66–7.
24. See M. Pallemaerts, 'International Environmental Law From Stockholm to Rio: Back to the Future?' and I.M. Porras, 'The Rio Declaration', in Sands (ed.), *Greening International Law*, pp. 1–33.
25. This was the language of the terms of reference which the UN General Assembly gave to Gro Harlem Brundtland who was asked to chair the World Commission on Environment and Development. See *Our Common Future*, p. ix.
26. See Porras, 'The Rio Declaration'.
27. This expression of a very old idea in political theory is from Michael Oakeshott, *On Human Conduct* (Oxford: Clarendon Press, 1975). It has been explored in terms of international society by Terry Nardin, *Law, Morality and the Relations of States* (Princeton, NJ: Princeton University Press, 1983). I have also applied the distinction in *Quasi-States: Sovereignty, International Relations and the Third World* (Cambridge: Cambridge University Press, 1990).
28. Pallemaerts, 'International Environmental Law', pp. 18–19.
29. Porras, 'The Rio Declaration', pp. 32–3.
30. Jacob D. Werksman, 'Greening Bretton Woods,' in Sands (ed.), *Greening International Law*, p. 75.
31. Andrew Hurrell, 'Green Conditionality' (typescript to be published by the Overseas Development Council, Washington), pp. 50–2.
32. See Marina Wheeler, 'Greening the EEC Treaty,' in Sands (ed.), *Greening International Law*, pp. 85–99.
33. See the pertinent documents in M. Weller (ed.), *Iraq and Kuwait: The Hostilities and their Aftermath* (Cambridge: Grotius Publications, 1993), pp. 302–3 and 334–56.

34. See Robert H. Jackson, 'Dialectical Justice and the Gulf War', *Review of International Studies* (Vol. 18, No. 4, October 1992), pp. 335–54.
35. See Maurice Keens-Soper, 'From the Balance of Power to the Balance of Nature' (unpublished paper delivered at the Seminar on International Political Theory, Department of International Relations, London School of Economics and Political Science, 7 December 1990), p. 12.
36. See Peter M. Haas with Jan Sundgren, 'Evolving International Environment Law' (publisher unknown), p. 413.
37. Daniel Deudney, 'The Case Against Linking Environmental Degradation and National Security', *Millennium: Journal of International Studies* (Vol. 19, No. 3, Winter 1990), p. 465.
38. I cannot pursue this controversial aspect of environmental ethics here.
39. This argument is derived from R.G. Collingwood, 'Human Nature and Human History,' in *The Idea of History* (Oxford: Oxford University Press, 1956), pp. 205–31.

9 Recognition, Self-Determination and Secession in Post-Cold War International Society

Rick Fawn and James Mayall

INTRODUCTION

Traditional international society was one of dynastic sovereign states. Since 1919, it has ostensibly been based on a principle of popular sovereignty, namely national self-determination. In practice, of course, the attempt to base the criterion of membership on a democratic test of opinion (which is seemingly implied by invoking the principle) has been honoured more often in the breach than in the observance. After the First World War, new states were created out of the debris of the European dynastic empires, theoretically along national lines but with little attention to their democratic credentials; after the Second World War, the Cold War froze the political map in Europe and decolonisation had much the same effect in Asia and Africa. On neither occasion was the right of secessionist self-determination recognised; nor in most places and in the majority of cases did the seizure of power by the military, or in general by unconstitutional means, have any consequences for the state's right to participate in the institutional life of international society. Notwithstanding the universal commitment to uphold universal human rights, the reach of international law stopped abruptly at the boundary.

The disintegration of the Soviet Union, the dismemberment of two East European federations and the collapse of the communism as a political ideology claiming universal validity and ostensibly offering alternative principles for the organisation of international society, have reopened questions about its basis and constitution.

The state may not be the sole actor in the international system but it is certainly the most commonly recognised. Its elements are delineated by the Montevideo Convention as defined territory; a permanent population; independent government; and capacity to engage in relations with other international persons.[1] International society is generally understood as the consensus which binds states together through a common commitment to certain minimum values such as sovereign independence and respect for international law. It thus goes beyond, even though it overlaps with, mere co-existence and systemic interaction which is possible between ideological enemies.[2] Prominent among the values that states share is the principle of territorial integrity. Indeed, so strong is the attachment to this principle that even at the height of the Cold War, trace elements of international society could be detected across the ideological divide.

Within the Montevideo criteria control of territory can be said to be implicit. Control becomes an issue, however, when secessionist movements seek to break away from a non-consenting metropole. Traditionally, the question would have been decided by force and the outcome would have been recognised within international society *ex post facto*. It is by no means certain that the situation has fundamentally changed, but the fact that the use of force as an instrument of foreign policy is proscribed under the UN Charter suggests that there is an urgent need to identify alternative criteria for state recognition.

From time to time, economic viability has been proposed as an appropriate test. However, what constitutes 'viability' is itself problematic. Even two of the most demographically and territorially substantial European states, Ukraine and Russia, both the result of systemic change, have routinely been called unviable since achieving independence in 1991.[3] Moreover, while the demand that new states be economically viable has often been advanced by reluctant decolonisers, historically it has been abandoned. This is easily demonstrated by reference to the statehood of several Oceanic islands or even a number of African countries which cannot finance their own continued existence.

Since the end of the Cold War two other questions about the future composition and expansion of the states-system have generated more interest. The first is the extent to which there is a necessary relationship between democracy and the right to self-determination. The second involves the circumstances under which a secessionist right of self-determination might be deemed to exist, which should in turn trigger international recognition by the international community. These questions are interrelated. A democratic basis for the claim to self-determination might constitute one criterion for recognising secession. In practice, invoking this principle in an uncontentious way has proved almost as difficult since the end of the Cold War as after 1918. Consequently, other reasons have been advanced to justify recognition and non-recognition.

This chapter considers the contradictions in the application of a democratic test to self-determination. It first looks at the extent to which democratic credentials influence a decision to recognise a right of secession, by establishing three categories of secessionist claims together with the responses offered in each case by international society. These are: democracy but no recognition; no democracy but recognition; and democracy explicitly demanded as the criterion for recognition. The democratic basis of secessionism is taken here as some form of representative vote by the secessionist population. A vote for secession by the entire population may seem a legitimate criterion, but it is unlikely, not least in countries where the democratic nature of elections is generally suspect and where secessionism occurs in part because of the overall political conditions of the regime. Indeed, the chapter will suggest that consent of the metropole to secessionist movements is no longer strictly required for international recognition – albeit alongside other circumstances – to be granted. The chapter will also occasionally consider the democratic nature of a prospective country in addition to the democratic credentials of its secessionist efforts. It seems, nevertheless, that the prospects of conditioning the future democratic character of new polities, particularly through the 'conditioning' of international institutions, weighs lightly in considerations of recognition.[4]

After appraising the democratic basis for secession, the chapter then proceeds to examine four sets of factors which in practice governed recognition and non-recognition. These are, first, the extent to which the recognition by some states or supranational bodies can influence the decision to withhold or grant recognition; second, cases where national interests, including the pursuit of advantages from nascent states, are responsible for recognition; third, the pragmatism of recognising successor states when the centre is simply seen as moribund; and finally, the strategic reasons for withholding recognition.

The processes discussed in this chapter are by no means confined to Eastern Europe.[5] The recognition of Eritrea, for example, required an internationally observed referendum but did not extend to the limitations imposed by the victors on the formation of new political parties. Nevertheless, we have chosen to examine the issues of secession and recognition in the context of Eastern Europe and the former Soviet Union. There are three reasons for this decision.

First, international society is being re-examined precisely in light of changes initiated by and occurring in Eastern Europe. Second, Eastern Europe, once the defining threat which fashioned Western policy, remains a key, even predominant policy concern because of the risks and opportunities the region now presents. Indeed, paradoxically, the end of the Cold War has not changed the dominance of East-West over North-South relations in Western political agendas. The third reason is that while one case of fusion has resulted in Eastern Europe, namely Germany, secessionism has spawned 22 countries in place of three. Nor is it clear that the process of fission has run its course: Tatarstan, Chechen-Ingushetia, Mordovia, Mari-el, Chuvashia and Komi-Permyak declared independence from the Russian Federation; Abkhazia and South Ossetia sought autonomy from Georgia, and Transdniester and Gagauzia pursued the same from Moldova. Even though some secessionist movements may have retreated or been defeated and the potential for reintegration, particularly in the post-Soviet space, cannot be discounted, the possibility of further fragmentation also remains high. Regardless of future developments, the former Soviet bloc is clearly the chief global producer of new states.

DEMOCRACY AND SELF-DETERMINATION

There is an implicit assumption that an international society based on the principle of national self-determination implies a commitment by the member states to democratic government. More generally it is based on liberal theory with its respect for negative liberties, that is, those actions which states agree *not* to undertake both internally and externally.

This assumption derives from the understanding of self-determination as an expression of political freedom which entitles 'a people to choose its political allegiance, to influence the political order under which it lives, and to preserve its cultural, ethnic, historical, or territorial identity'.[6] This supposition is predicated on the internal dimension of self-determination which 'makes 'the people' (the citizens) the source of state legitimacy and thus requires a democratic form of government. In this sense, self-determination is analogous to the existence of popular sovereignty'.[7] If self-determination implies the right of a group to conduct its own affairs according to its own wishes, nothing in the concept of self-determination dictates the form of political organisation that must be adopted. However, as the international community can withhold recognition of a prospective state's sovereignty, certain criteria can be demanded.

The attempt to link democracy to self-determination is a development most notable in the rhetoric surrounding the debate over a post-Cold War 'New World Order'. An ill-defined term, the 'New World Order' was taken by many to mean the universal expansion of democracy, even at the expense of international stability. Advocates of this view characteristically exhibit, in the words of one commentator, 'enthusiasm for secessionist movements in the Soviet Union'.[8] Nevertheless, there are grounds for asserting that the connection between democracy and self-determination is more than abstract normative liberal theory. In practical terms, self-determination must necessarily be expressed in certain ways. Assuming that the identification of the relevant population is not itself a problem (which unhappily it very often is), what is required to legitimise the secessionist claim is a plebiscite, or at least a full election in which the issue of self-determination is the central issue. Once self-determination has received this kind of legitimacy, the new state should then also ensure the protection of rights of all citizens within its nascent boundaries. While protection need not be provided on a collective basis, the rights of individuals need to be ensured.

Although the world political map has been largely drawn by force, in recent years the international community, particularly Euro-American states, have adopted these normative aspirations into policy. The Council of Europe and the CSCE stipulated these norms of behaviour, arguably to score ideological points in the Cold War struggle, but not exclusively for this reason. This practice became even more marked after the Cold War. The December 1991 EC document entitled 'Guidelines on the Recognition of New States in Eastern Europe and the Soviet Union' codified certain requirements for secessionist movements to fulfil. These included the 'rule of law, democracy and respect for human rights' and 'guarantees for the rights of ethnic and national groups and minorities in accordance with commitments subscribed in the framework of the CSCE'.[9] The EC, in particular, recommended that referendums take place in order to determine the extent of support for secession. In the same spirit, the Badinter Arbitration Commission was established as part of the EC Peace Conference on Yugoslavia to establish whether democratic practices and provisions had been undertaken by prospective states.

However, while the international community has paid lip-service to these normative concerns, their application has not been consistent. Especially during the Cold War, fair hearings on self-determination were rare and selective. As Misha Glenny has written, the West 'understood self-determination to mean the right of East European countries to leave the Soviet bloc (whereas there was much lobbying in favour of the independence of the GDR, Poland, Czechoslovakia or Hungary, supporters of self-determination for the Ukraine barely got a hearing from Western governments)'.[10] This selective approach by the West continued especially towards the end of the Cold War, when secessionist claims were ignored even if they clearly passed the democratic test.

In view of the failure of historical attempts to deal with the problems of minority rights and secessionism within the liberal theory of international society, it is not surprising that an unambiguous application of a democratic test of self-determination has not occurred in the post-Cold War era. It is not our intention to suggest that self-determination exercised in a democratic fashion, including provisions for minority rights, alone justifies or dictates international recognition. There are always other considerations that have to be taken into account. One reason is the contradictions in the application of the principle of self-determination itself and it is to that which we turn in the remainder of the chapter. We begin with the Baltic republics, particularly Lithuania, which had a democratic basis to its secessionist movement but failed to receive international recognition.

DEMOCRACY BUT NON-RECOGNITION

The Baltic Republics

The first major test of international response to national self-determination (as distinct from political self-determination, where recognised sovereign states sought to change only their political orientation rather than their state-membership) in the post-Cold War era occurred in the Baltic. The starting-point for the Baltic itself was Lithuania, for not only was it the first of the Soviet Republics to declare independence but arguably did so on behalf of the others. As Lithuanians said of Estonians, 'Estonians were willing to fight for Estonian independence down to the last Lithuanian'.[11]

The Democratic Basis of Lithuanian Self-Determination

Lithuania is the most homogeneous of the Baltic republics, with the titular nationality constituting approximately 80 per cent of the population, albeit with Russian and Polish minorities of about 8.9 and 7.0 per cent respectively.[12] The movement towards independence began in March 1989 when Sajudis candidates won 37 of the 42 Lithuanian seats in the elections to the Soviet Congress of People's Deputies and then, following the February 1990 elections, earned a majority in the Lithuanian Supreme Soviet. On 11 March, the Lithuanian Supreme Soviet undertook to achieve sovereignty, with Chairman Vytautas Landsbergis proclaiming:

> During the election on 24 February 1990 to the Lithuanian SSR Supreme Soviet the people of Lithuania, having the right of election, by their own will granted a mandate to the representatives of the people and obliged them to restore the Lithuanian state and to express the nation's sovereign will through this Supreme Soviet....[13]

This procedure was supported both firmly and broadly within the population. First Secretary of the Lithuanian Communist Party, Algirdas Brazauskas explained:

> The restoration of an independent Lithuania is the basic and most urgent task. This is recognized by the whole of Lithuania, this is recognized by all parties, including the Communist Party....[14]

He also recognised the need for democratic credentials to be explicit in the self-determination process. Speaking on 11 March 1990, he said:

> I understand that independence is not yet a democracy. Therefore, to my mind, the basis of sovereignty is the matter of sovereignty of each citizen, each Lithuanian. I think that this state sovereignty must be based on this human basis, on the sovereignty of our citizens.[15]

Even though the self-determination process was supported by democratic means, rather than offering recognition, the international community, notably Western states, encouraged Lithuania to come to an understanding with the Soviet Union. US President Bush even refused to visit the Baltic republics during the summer of 1991.[16]

Estonia and Latvia

While few would deny that Lithuania fulfilled the democratic requirement for secession, it is harder to assess in the cases of Estonia and Latvia. Although their governments claimed to have sought independence on democratic grounds, both have substantial Russian minorities that complicate any assessment of the extent of popular support for secession. In Estonia the Russians account for 30 per cent of the total population, and were outnumbered by Estonians only by two to one; in Latvia the Russians constitute more than a third of the population and the Latvians just over half, at 52.5 per cent. That said, there is some doubt as to how opposed to independence these minorities were, and to what extent they saw – or came to see – Russia as a spokesperson for their interests.[17] Even though Russian minorities in these republics seeking to maintain ties to the Russian Federation formed National Salvation Fronts, 40 per cent of Estonia's Russian minority voted for Estonian independence.[18]

The Estonian government maintained that its independence was democratically based. When Estonia declared independence in the wake of the August coup, Dr Marju Lauristin, Deputy Chairwoman of the Supreme

Council, emphasised that the independence decision had not been hastily reached but was firmly based on Estonian independence before 1940 and on the overwhelming vote for renewed independence in a referendum in March.[19]

Regardless of how these developments might be judged, it was clear that the international community was not willing to recognise them. This became conspicuous when the three Baltic republics were denied full seats at the 1990 Paris CSCE meeting which was considered the formal end of the Cold War. Non-recognition continued even in the face of the conclusion by the Russian Federation (which itself did not declare independence until after all other republics save Kazakhstan) of a treaty with Lithuania in which each recognised the other as 'sovereign states' and the treaty specifically referred to the Lithuanian declaration of independence.[20] More important to the issue of non-recognition was the fact that most Western states had continued *de jure* to recognise Baltic independence, having refused to recognise the Stalinist annexation.

Even the January 1991 attacks by the OMON, the notorious Ministry of Interior Black Berets, in Lithuania and Latvia failed to secure Western recognition. The fatal assaults in Lithuania saw '[s]upport for independence increased, even among non-Lithuanian residents', and '[t]he defence of the parliament building by many thousands of ordinary citizens convinced many in the West that Lithuania would not be subdued and that the international community would eventually have to recognise its independence'.[21] Nevertheless, recognition was not generally forthcoming. Only the August coup and Yeltsin's rise to power would result in recognition, which was probably made easier when the State Council of the USSR itself recognised Baltic independence on 4 September.[22] As a response to the August coup, recognition of the Baltic states came in waves at the end of August 1991, when most of these states recognised the Baltic republics not as new states but as 'states having restored their independence'. Even in this best-case scenario, where democratic credentials did underscore the drive to independence, the Baltic republics were not allowed full representation at the Paris Conference of 1990, because, as will be discussed below, Western powers subordinated those principles to the futile attempts to sustain the moribund USSR.

Slovenia

Slovenia's move to independence resembles that of Lithuania, in that the democratic credentials of national self-determination were also established. Even more than for Lithuania, a vote for secession could easily be considered legitimate because of the Republic's ethnic homogeneity. Slovenia's results were 'democratic enough because it was almost exclusively Slovenes who voted,'[23] and who also comprised the bulk of the Slovene Republic's population. Not only was the manner in which independence was pursued 'democratic', but the Draft Slovene Act of Autonomy and Independence, broadcast by Tanjug on 25 June 1991 contained provisions for minority protection. Its third part read:

> The Republic of Slovenia ensures the preservation of human rights and basic freedoms for all persons on the territory of the Republic of Slovenia regardless of their national affiliation and devoid of any discrimination, in keeping with the constitution of the republic of Slovenia and (currently) valid international treaties. All rights set out in the constitution of the republic of Slovenia and (currently) valid international treaties are ensured for the Italian and Hungarian communities in the Republic of Slovenia and for their members.[24]

The Badinter Commission concluded that Slovenia had met its requirements for recognition of democratic practice and minority protection.[25]

Georgia (Mark I)

Georgia presents a curious case. An argument could be made that Georgia was initially democratic and as such its move towards independence was also democratic and should consequently have received international recognition. However, Georgia entered a phase of domestic political turmoil, which included violence against political and ethnic minorities. It was these developments which the international community cited as reasons for withholding recognition. The first period, from the November 1989 declaration of independence to the end of 1991 will be called Georgia Mark I and is discussed in this section; the latter period is referred to as Georgia Mark II and is considered presently.

The elections of 14 November 1989 in Georgia generated a pro-independence parliament which, on 19 November 1989, pronounced the sovereignty of republican laws over Soviet central laws. The move to independence was reiterated and arguably further legitimated, when Georgians, rather than partake in the USSR-wide referendum of March 1991, voted almost unanimously for independence in their own referendum. On 9 April 1991, the Georgian parliament proclaimed the republic independent.

Thus, Georgia seemed to be approaching independence in a democratic manner. Not only had the population voted overwhelmingly for independence, 87 per cent had voted for president Zviad Gamsakhurdia. While Gamaskhurdia's rule was to become notorious, initially there was optimism abroad that this former political prisoner and academic, who had translated Shakespeare into Georgian, would lead the Georgians to liberal democracy. Support for Georgian independence was also generated in the West by the behaviour of the Soviet regime. A newspaper editorial is indicative:

> Few incidents in the recent history of the late Soviet Union so outraged opinion in the Western world as the brutal suppression by army units of a peaceful demonstration for independence in Tbilisi, the capital of Georgia, in April 1989. Using poison gas canisters and sharpened spades, the troops killed 20 participants, including women, and injured many more. The episode was a turning point for the independence movement, and gained it great sympathy abroad.[26]

However, Georgia's initial attempts at democracy and a democratically-based secession failed to secure international recognition. The chief reason for non-recognition was probably, as discussed below, the strategic imperative to support Gorbachev and the USSR against the forces of fragmentation.

Macedonia

The southern Yugoslav republic of Macedonia seemed intent on pursuing independence in a fashion tailored to Western, particularly EC, norms. It did not request but responded to the EC's proposal of recognition on a conditional basis and was deemed to have met the criteria. Leading political parties, such as the SK-PJ, acknowledged that secession had to occur according to certain principles, including a plebiscite: 'no political party in Macedonia has a blank mandate to speak on behalf of the Macedonian people because that is its exclusive, indivisible and sovereign right. Only the Macedonian people, through a referendum, can decide about the nature of the Yugoslav community'.[27]

This view was asserted in spite of, or because of, Macedonia's ethnic composition. Macedonian political leaders realised that the referendum would be a difficult matter because of the republic's ethnic composition. The Serb minority in Macedonia claims to number 300 000 and the Albanian minority constitutes a full quarter of the whole population of 2.25 million, and in fact Skopje, rather than Tirana, is the world's largest

Albanian city.[28] These factors were taken into consideration. For example, Belgrade radio observed of discussions in the Macedonian Assembly on 31 July 1991, part of a several-day debate, that there was '[a]n obvious fear of calling a referendum for the independence and autonomy of Macedonia was also present in the discussion because, as they say, it is unforeseeable what decision will be reached at the referendum by the Macedonian people'.[29] The decision to go to a referendum cannot therefore be seen as a political expediency.

Macedonians voted 'overwhelmingly' for independence in the referendum held on 8 September 1991. The Albanian minority, however, boycotted the referendum. Despite, or because of the Albanian boycott, the Macedonian government took a cautious approach to the referendum. Despite the Albanian boycott, only Macedonia's independence plebiscite, along with Slovenia's, satisfied the Badinter Commission's requirements. Macedonia also endeavoured to create exemplary domestic and foreign policies. Five cabinet posts, including Finance, were given to the Albanian minority and the Constitution not only provided universal citizenship but also, as the British MP Tony Worthington noted, 'civil rights denied to the citizens of Britain'.[30] In addition to this positive judgement, Macedonia negotiated a peaceful withdrawal of Federal Yugoslav forces and endeavoured to uphold UN sanctions against Yugoslavia enduring a significant drop in trade as a result.[31] However, as we shall see below, recognition was withheld for more than a year.

RECOGNITION WITHOUT DEMOCRACY

Having considered those cases where the democratic test could be said to have been fulfilled but international recognition denied, it is necessary to examine the opposite: cases where the democratic criterion was either absent or unobtainable but where international recognition was nevertheless granted.

Croatia

Leaving aside any question of provisions for minority protection, the democratic basis of Croatia's move towards independence is highly suspect. As one commentator observed on the Croatian election campaign in early 1990: 'Tudjman exploited Croatia's simmering ethnic tensions, even parading with Croatian flags through ethnic Serb areas. Opponents accused him of making racist remarks and, in some speeches, he appeared to lay claim to all, or parts of, Bosnia and Herzegovina'.[32] A referendum on independence was held on 19 May 1991, the results of which, however, presented a problem. A majority of the electorate supported independence, but the overall legitimacy of the vote was called into question because, as Misha Glenny quipped, 'Croats voted to take with them a large number of Serbs from Yugoslavia, who, as we later discovered, were not overjoyed about leaving.'[33]

Demand by the international community for minority protection can be said to have occurred in that recognition was of course delayed. Croatia's legislation of 4 December 1991 ensuring Serbian rights was seen as an attempt to win international recognition.[34] Nevertheless, if not overshadowed by the war, these steps were considered insufficient. Recognition, however, would be forthcoming.

Czechoslovakia

Slovak Prime Minister Ján Čarnogurský, acting in his capacity of head of the Slovak Christian Democratic Movement, sent congratulatory telegrams to Slovenia and Croatia following their declarations of independence. In so doing, he acknowledged that the declarations were the result of 'an expression of majority popular will in the republics as confirmed in referendums'.[35] The split of Czechoslovakia was a surprise to many both within and without. Yet the two constituent republics were recognised without any democratic procedure legitimising the separation.

Following the national elections of 5 and 6 June 1992, the Federal parliament resigned on 26 June and on 20 July Václav Havel resigned as Federal President. At the same time, Václav Klaus and Vladimir Mečiar, who each won a plurality but not a majority of votes in only their native Czech Lands and Slovakia, concurred in laying the groundwork for separation in principle. On 26 August they formally agreed that the Czechoslovak Federation would split into two parts on 1 January 1993.

Western observers were surprised, especially in light of Czechoslovakia's 1989 democratic 'Velvet Revolution', that the split could occur without a referendum.[36] Indeed, the possibility of a referendum was specifically blocked by Slovak deputies in the Federal Parliament. Even the Slovak press demonstrated concern that the international community would not be receptive to the division of Czechoslovakia were it to be the result only of undertakings by Slovak politicians.[37] Minorities in the country, particularly the large Hungarian constituency in Slovakia were alarmed at the prospect of division, particularly because nascent Slovakia did not seem intent on making provisions for minorities. The result in Czechoslovakia was that separation was a pact made 'from above' without endorsement from below. Once the separation seemed likely, however, the international community offered recognition without contest.

DEMOCRACY DEMANDED

Whereas in the cases of Croatia and Czechoslovakia recognition was made without specific reference to a democratic basis, in other instances the international community was explicit in its demands.

Bosnia-Hercegovina

Bosnia-Hercegovina provides a case where democratic procedures were demanded by some members of the international community as a precondition for recognition. This was formally specified by the Badinter Arbitration Commission which recommended in January 1992 that diplomatic recognition be made conditional on a referendum of all citizens of the republic.

The majority of voting Muslims and Croats elected for independence. The legitimacy of the referendum, as defined by the Badinter Commission's phrase of 'All the Citizens', was undermined because the Serbs, 34 per cent of the population of Bosnia-Hercegovina, boycotted it.[38] The Bosnian Constitution, as John Zametica contends, supports the Serbian position because 'not only were the Muslims, Serbs and Croats equal "nations" in the republic, but no far-reaching decisions affecting them all could be taken without consensus'.[39] This recognition, which is considered by many to have provoked the Serbs into war, occurred with the EC ignoring the internal constitution of Bosnia-Hercegovina.[40]

The Third Yugoslavia

A case of de-recognition almost occurred in the name of democracy and minority protection when rump Yugoslavia, consisting of Serbia and Montenegro sought to inherit the seat of the Federal Republic. The new Yugoslav state attempted to give itself legitimacy through democratic practices. On 27 April 1992 the parliaments of Serbia and Montenegro proclaimed a new, smaller Yugoslavia which was to be the successor to the SFRY. The newly adopted constitution called for parliamentary democracy and a market economy. Despite these provisions, 'main opposition parties in the two republics, as well as most Albanians, boycotted the ceremonies and oppose the new constitution'.[41] While it was unlikely for the country to be de-recognised, for some of the reasons considered below, it also showed that the Yugoslav regime acknowledged that it had at least to pay lip-service to certain principles.

The demands on the successor state to Yugoslavia were probably motivated to some extent by a general desire by the international community to see certain norms adhered to, especially in light of the violence in the former Yugoslav space. It could also be argued that the efforts to bar, or at least make difficult, the accession of the new Yugoslavia to the SFRY's UN seat was a type of punishment. Austria, which was chairing the UN Security Council at the time of the debate on Yugoslav succession, disregarded any legal basis for Belgrade to inherit the former Federal Yugoslav seat and said that the country would have to fulfil the Badinter Commission's requirements to gain recognition.[42]

Georgia (Mark II)

When the USSR disintegrated in December 1991, the US recognised Georgian statehood but made diplomatic relations conditional on 'Georgia's civil order and commitments to responsible security policies and respect for human rights'. Perhaps the international community had the good foresight not to recognise Georgia because of Gamaskhurdia's internal political practices. As a newspaper editorial indicated, 'The West has sensibly indicated that it will make no move towards recognising Georgia as an independent country until it has a stable and democratic government'.[43] After the violent ouster of Gamsakhurdia, Eduard Shevardnadze 'returned to Georgia, promising to lead the transition to civilian government. On 24 March 1992, the United States established diplomatic relations with Georgia in light of its commitment to conduct parliamentary elections and to restore civilian rule.'[44]

The EC also decided to recognise Georgia following the receipt of a message by Shevardnadze in which he pledged that Georgia would respect human and minority rights and democracy, as well as its existing borders and disarmament and nuclear non-proliferation.[45] While the US was considered particularly cautious, more so than the EC, for example,[46] in its decision to recognise fully and establish diplomatic relations with Georgia, Japan also did not recognise Georgia in any form until April 1992 because of the internal conflicts.[47] While democracy might not have been a criterion in the non-recognition of Georgia between November 1989 and 1989, it was certainly made an explicit condition for full recognition thereafter.

Central Asia

Another area where certain criteria were imposed, at least by some countries, notably the United States, before full diplomatic recognition would be extended, included several republics of former Soviet Central Asia. The US only fully recognised Kazakhstan because of its inherited nuclear arsenal, and Kyrgyzstan, because it was 'the republic ostensibly most committed to reform'. Otherwise, the US declared that it would withhold diplomatic recognition from the other three Central Asian Republics (as well as Azerbaijan) until human rights and democracy were ensured.[48] Nevertheless, the US extended full recognition to all of these republics by February 1992, in part to counter what were perceived as diplomatic successes in the region by Iran.[49]

SUB-FEDERAL UNITS AND DEMOCRACY

If a trend is detectable in recognition patterns it is that the international community has seemed willing to recognise pre-existing sub-federal units in Eastern Europe, namely all the constituent republics of the region's three federations. Several Soviet republics, however, were constituted on a basis similar to that of the USSR itself. Georgia and Moldova contained autonomous political units, composed and run ostensibly by the titular ethnic group. Russia, while more than 80 per cent Russian, is a Federation and consists of an extensive patchwork of autonomous republics and regions. While the international community has ultimately granted recognition to every federal unit in Eastern Europe that requested it, recognition has been strenuously denied to sub-federal units. It is to two of these cases that this section turns.

Before proceeding, it is beneficial to recall that the international community has also operated on the principle that a right to secession only exists with the consent of the centre. The recognition of Slovenia and Croatia, as well as the eventual recognition of the Baltic republics, however, provide a precedent to the contrary, and arguably, therefore, this precedent should be applicable to sub-federal units as well.

Abkhazia

Abkhazia is a fragment of territory which, under the Soviet system, was made an autonomous republic in the northwest of Georgia. According to the 1989 Soviet census, 17.8 per cent of Abkhazia's 500 000 inhabitants are

Abkhaz, while 46 per cent are Georgian. Since 1978 the Abkhaz have pressed regularly for independence from Georgia.[50] In July 1992, the Abkhazian parliament voted by a simple majority to restore a 1925 Constitution, which effectively announced Abkhazia to be independent. This decision was revoked in Tbilisi.[51] Whatever the democratic basis to Abkhaz secession, the international community was unwilling to contemplate, let alone extend recognition.

Tatarstan

Tatarstan, one of a number of titular Muslim autonomous republics along the Volga River in the Russian Federation, provides an example of the efforts by a sub-state group to seek a qualified form of independence and of the international response to that attempt. Tatarstan is at most 48.5 per cent Tatar,[52] giving it one of the highest concentrations of a nationality within the borders of its titular republic in the Russian Federation. At the same time, the Tatar diaspora is far greater than the number of Tatars residing in the republic. Tatarstan proclaimed itself an independent republic on 30 August 1991. The Republic's national assembly sought to give an air of tolerance to its domestic politics. On 2 February 1992, it adopted a Law on the Status of the Tatar Language which expanded the number of recognised languages from Russian and Tatar to all 'the other languages of nations living in the republic as official languages of Tatarstan' and condemned discrimination on the basis of language.[53] A referendum on independence was subsequently held on 21 March 1992 in which 61 per cent voted in favour.

In both the Abkhaz and Tatar cases, some form of democratic procedure could said to have occurred, but this is at best questionable. Even if they had such credentials, recognition of these entities almost certainly would almost certainly not have occurred, due to reasons discussed below.

To conclude this section, it is clear that several movements towards self-determination in Central and Southeastern Europe and the former Soviet Union have been undertaken on a democratic basis. These procedures have included a popular referendum or a vote by a democratically-elected assembly on the question of secession. Most expressions of self-determination have been accompanied by laws, constitutions and public pledges to adhere to international norms on human and minority rights. These provisions, however, even where the international community has asked for them in advance, appear insufficient to legitimate a secessionist claim. There have also been several cases where recognition occurred when the democratic credentials were weak or even absent. Other factors, therefore, must determine recognition and non-recognition. It is to these factors that we now turn.

OTHER CONDITIONS GOVERNING RECOGNITION

The Dynamic of Recognition: A Snowball Effect?

It is a tautology to say that when international recognition occurs, it occurs *en masse*. The US, a country to which nascent states obviously turn to for recognition, officially takes as one of its considerations of recognition 'whether the entity in question has attracted the recognition of the international community of states'.[54] If this is the case, one would expect that states either consult one another on recognition or that they instinctively extend recognition or watch each other and extend recognition almost in response. This is certainly meant to be the case in the European Union which, under the Maastricht Treaty, is meant to have a Common Foreign and Security Policy. The latter seems to be the norm in non-controversial cases of recognition.

However, universal recognition is not necessary either in theory or practice. Membership in an international organisation, foremost the United Nations, is generally taken as the hallmark of statehood. But according to international law, such membership is not synonymous with international recognition and technically represents no more than 'an acknowledgement of statehood for the purposes of the Organisation. It does not constitute recognition by the international community, or recognition of the entity by individual Member States of the United Nations'.[55] Of course, several states have managed not only to exist but also to conduct successful and vibrant domestic and foreign policies without full international recognition. Taiwan, recognised by a decreasing number of states, Israel, the two Koreas and, until the early 1970s, the two Germanies were among such examples. Nevertheless, a 'critical mass' of recognition could be said to be necessary. If more than a few countries had recognised Chechen independence, the Russian invasion could not so conveniently be treated for so long by the international community as an internal police matter rather than a foreign military intervention.

The foremost example of the 'snowball effect' of recognition resulting from the decision of a few states to recognise another is the EC's recognition of Slovenia and especially Croatia.[56] Despite not having the democratic guarantees and provisions for the protection of minorities that were expected, Croatia was recognised by Germany. Whether this act lessened or encouraged violence is not germane to the present enquiry. What it did mean was that because of the internal dynamics of the EC – the need to manufacture the idea of a common foreign and security policy – the other EC member-countries went along.

EC recognition was done contrary to the counsel of both US Secretary of State Baker and UN Secretary General Javier Pérez de Cuéllar. Germany was considered to have 'pressed' the EC into recognition of the two northern Yugoslav republics, something that 'was not an easy decision for many Community members, especially France and Britain, which together had helped to create Yugoslavia and preferred it to remain an entity'.[57] While Garton Ash attributes 'diplomatic finesse' to Germany he nevertheless writes of Bonn's approach to its EC allies that it

> therefore bounced them into it [recognition], by declaring that it would go ahead with the recognition itself anyway, and before Christmas. Having then secured a reluctant resolution of all the EC member states to extend recognition on 15 January 1992, provided certain conditions were met, it proceeded to do so itself, before Christmas, declaring that the conditions had already been satisfied.[58]

National Interest

To the extent, however, that snowballing helps to achieve a critical mass of recognition, then it is important to consider the issues which motivate some states, including influential regional states, to recognise others. These motivations come in different forms but can all be ascribed to national interest. Recognition occurs not so much for principles, as much as states may advocate them, but as a result of the pursuit of national interest. A leading example of the role of national interest was Greece's non-recognition of the Yugoslav republic of Macedonia. Even though Macedonia had fulfilled democratic requirements and had suffered severe economic consequences from upholding the economic sanctions on Serbia, its main trading partner (and in fact had sanctions applied against it by Greece), Skopje's requests for recognition went unanswered.

Opposition to recognition came not from the idea of the state but from its name. Greece viewed 'Macedonia' as national heritage which could not be misappropriated. Some have argued that Greece persuaded the EC to delay recognising Macedonia for over a year.[59] Greece almost certainly had an influence on the lack of recognition by the wider world,[60] and particularly by the UN. Greece was observed to be 'using all its leverage to have Macedonia's [UN] application rejected' and was lobbying Britain,

France and Spain to reject the UN Security Council vote on Macedonian membership.[61] It gained membership in the UN only on 9 April 1993.

Bulgaria seemed ready to recognise Macedonia and their mutual border – something akin to Germany recognising the Oder-Neisse line as its border with Poland. This makes Greece's intransigence on recognition all the more striking. Timothy Garton Ash muses that a plot may have been at work: 'Could it, just possibly, be a deal: Germany would not (yet) support the recognition of Macedonia if Greece did not oppose the recognition of Slovenia and Croatia? Oh, brave new world!'[62] Greek Prime Minister Andreas Papandreou 'threatened to retaliate against members of the European Union which established ties with Macedonia'.[63] Such an attitude led Danish Foreign Minister Uffe Ellemann-Jensen to say that he believed the other 11 EC states felt that Greece had held the EC hostage and that they were 'sick and tired' of the recognition issue and that Greece had 'not acted with community spirit'.[64] Thus, even though Macedonia finally gained recognition, it probably did so more as result of the fatigue Greece inflicted upon its allies than a conscious decision. Acknowledgement of Macedonian democracy and minority protection, as well as the 'good citizenship' of costly sanctions against Serbia, played no role in recognition.

Expression of Political Will

The first states to extend recognition to nascent states in Eastern Europe were often their neighbours. Several explanations, none of which are mutually exclusive, account for this. One consists of an expression of political will by states that have recovered their own ability to engage in independent diplomacy and were conceivably intoxicated by the idea of self-determination.

For example, the first countries to recognise independent Ukraine were Bulgaria, Czechoslovakia, Hungary, Poland and Canada.[65] While Canada's motivations are discussed elsewhere, it is striking that the other four were Ukraine's neighbours, three bordering directly. Arguably, these countries felt threatened by the USSR and acted out of national interest to abet its disintegration. At the same time, however, Czechoslovakia, Hungary and Poland, although less so for Bulgaria, were considered the most 'politically advanced' of the former Soviet bloc and all had proclaimed their support for national self-determination. Charter 77, the Czechoslovak dissident group which included leading post-communist officials including President Václav Havel and Foreign Minister Jiří Dienstbier codified such ideals in July 1991:

> The nations of Yugoslavia are striving to free themselves from totalitarian conditions. As the recent referendum shows, they are able to defend this will in a legal, democratic way. Charter 77 therefore appeals to politicians of countries with democratic traditions to properly assess the means they are using, since ignoring the free will of nations does not contribute to peace or stability in a region but slows down development, escalates tensions, and can lead to further cruelties.'[66]

Similarly, even before the EC made its controversial recognition of Slovenia and Croatia, Ukraine and the Baltic republics (in addition to Sweden), had extended recognition.

This is not to say that political morals predominate. The non-communist government in Poland provides an illustration. It maintained relations with the Soviet centre while nevertheless opening direct cultural, economic and political relations with the three Slavic and the three Baltic republics. While this practice enabled Poland to achieve the objective of bolstering national self-determination movements, it also advanced two other aims, setting 'the foundation for future regional cooperation; and at the same time it managed not to jeopardize its vital political and economic links with the Union'.[67]

Domestic Pressures

An additional 'national interest' which might be served is that of fulfilling domestic demands, particularly those of ethnic minorities. Canada became the first Western state to recognise Ukraine. The country of 26 million has a population of Ukrainian origin numbering more than a million. In addition, several leading Canadian political figures are of Ukrainian origin. The leading Canadian newspaper observed that the 'Prime Minister was under considerable pressure from his caucus to recognise Ukrainian independence'. It also noted the number of Canadians of Ukrainian origin and added that 'many of them live in ridings held by Conservative MPs in Western Canada'.[68] Alberta, for example, returned all of its 21 seats to the ailing Conservative government. Nevertheless, Canada also insisted on guarantees from Ukraine on human rights and the non-use of nuclear weapons.

In a similar vein, it has been suggested that a Croatian lobby contributed to the German decision to recognise Croatia. While not overemphasising the point, Garton Ash points to a speech by Genscher in which he referred to the Croatian constituency.[69] Whatever influence an ethnic lobby might have on a decision to recognise, the Central Asian republics, which faced among the firmest conditions from Washington for recognition, could have suffered from having 'no political constituency' in the US.[70]

Recognition Because the Centre is Dead

Another motivation behind recognition ensues from the inability of a state to achieve its objectives by dealing with the metropole. India, described as a dedicated ally of the Soviet Union, instituted direct relations with individual republics, 'increasing problems in mutual relations' with the USSR as a whole.[71] By early December 1991, before the establishment of the CIS or of the formal end of the USSR, Japan likewise acknowledged the impotence of the central authorities and began negotiations directly and exclusively with the Russian Federation over the disputed Kirile Islands.[72]

Strategic Considerations

If one factor above all determines recognition of secessionist movements, it is the cost and risk of so doing. The foremost concern of the West was to preserve the status quo in both Yugoslavia and the Soviet Union. Nations for which the West had expressed sympathy – and had *de jure* relations – such as the Baltic were clearly sacrificed to perceived regional or even global security concerns. Major states adopted a two-track policy towards the Soviet Union, recognising the instruments held by the centre but still cultivating the emerging power centres. For all of the US's efforts to shore up Gorbachev – a policy that has subsequently been accused of shortsightedness – Yeltsin was nevertheless 'received warmly by the White House and the Congress' on his June 1991 visit.[73]

Whatever democratic principles could be found in Abkhazia, the international community did not undertake to recognise it primarily because it was feared that such action would encourage conflict in the region to spread. As one commentator wrote, 'the Abkhaz were joined by volunteers from the North Caucasus, whose leaders perceived both a common bond with the Abkhazians, as well as the possibility of gaining their own independence, through destabilizing relations between Georgia and Russia'.[74] As the critics of the recognition of Croatia maintained, so too would sub-state recognition in the Caucasus have encouraged further violence.

Fragmentation has been considered the biggest threat to post-Soviet Russia.[75] Although this danger has receded since 1992, the need to maintain the status quo of the Russian Federation, like that of Yugoslavia and the USSR, has doubtless ensured that the international community has not extended recognition to the autonomous republics clustered on the Volga.

CONCLUSION

What general conclusions can be drawn from this review of diplomatic reactions to the collapse of communism in Eastern Europe and the disintegration of the former Soviet Union? In the sense that, at the time of writing, the redrawing of the political map in the former Yugoslavia and parts of the former Soviet Union is incomplete, it is clearly too early to say with any confidence what will be the final impact of these events on international society. However, two tentative observations may perhaps be offered.

The first is that after 1989, as after 1918 and 1945, the primary cause of the creation of new states has been the collapse of empire rather than popular nationalist revolt, let alone any widespread conversion to liberal principles of constitutional self-government. Now as then, the empire has more or less disintegrated into its constituent parts. In the end other states have found it easier to recognise existing entities, just as after 1945 they found it convenient to confine the right of self-determination to former colonies than to recognise the creation of entirely new nation-states. Now as then, the hard cases, some of which we have reviewed, are those where the ethnic or communal map is not merely at odds with the political map at various points – that, after all, is the norm in most countries – but is regarded by a sizeable minority of the population as fundamentally unjust.

The second observation is that, despite the continued predominance of power political over legal or ethical considerations, one cannot discount altogether the impact of liberal ideas of the state and international society. The positing of democratic criteria for self-determination is not just a rhetorical veneer masking the real interests of the powers. It also reflects the fact that there is no longer any alternative macro political and economic scheme which can legitimise the exercise of state power. To this extent the establishing of criteria for democratic statehood represents a genuine attempt to bring practice into line with the only available principle. The fact that recognition does not automatically follow when all the criteria have apparently been met, and that it frequently does occur when one or more of the criteria are absent suggests that recognition remains primarily a question of practical political judgement. It could hardly be otherwise. Democratic requirements, in so far as they constitute rules of entry into international society, are rules that will be adjusted to satisfy national interests. But this does not mean that the rules are unimportant or that they will not over time exercise an influence on the evolution of international society.

NOTES

The authors wish to acknowledge the valuable comments of Margot Light on this chapter.

1. See Rebecca M.M. Wallace, *International Law* (2nd edn), (London: Sweet & Maxwell, 1992), p. 79.
2. This distinction between an international society of shared values and an international system of regular interaction is derived from Hedley Bull, *The Anarchical Society: A Study of Order in World Politics* (London: Macmillan, 1977), pp. 7–10 and 13. It has been criticised as a distinction without a difference by Alan James in 'System or Society?', *Review of International Studies* (Vol. 19, No. 3, July 1993), pp. 269–88.
3. On Russia, see for example, Jessica Eva Stern, who contends that the Russian federation 'is not sustainable as a state.' *International Security* (Vol. 18, No. 4, Spring 1994), p. 40. For Ukraine, the 'looming economic catastrophe has raised doubts about whether the state can survive in any form.' Renée de Nevers, *Russia's Strategic Renovation*, Adelphi Paper 289 (London: IISS, 1994), p. 46.
4. For an overview of the role and success of international institutions in transforming domestic political practices predominantly in existing, rather than nascent states, see Jennone Walker, 'Regional Organizations and Ethnic Conflict', in Regina Cowen Karp (ed.), *Central and Eastern Europe: The Challenge of Transition* (New York: Oxford University Press, 1993), pp. 45–66; Marianne Hanson, 'Democratisation and Norm Creation in Europe', in *European Security after the Cold War. Part 1*, Adelphi Paper No. 284 (London: IISS, 1994, pp. 28–41; and Adrian G.V. Hyde-Price, 'Democratization in Eastern Europe: The External Dimension', in Geoffrey Pridham and Tatu Vanhanen (eds), *Democratization in Eastern Europe: Domestic and International Perspectives*(London and New York: Routledge, 1994), pp. 220–52.
5. For an overview of contemporary secessionist movements worldwide, see the useful appendix in Morton H. Halperin and David J. Scheefer with Patricia L. Small, *Self-Determination in the New World Order* (Washington, DC: Carnegie Endowment for International Peace, 1992).
6. Halperin *et al.*, *Self-Determination*, p. 47.
7. *Strategic Survey, 1992–1993* (London: International Institute for Strategic Studies, 1993), p. 16.
8. Ted Galen Carpenter, 'The New World Disorder', *Foreign Policy* No. 84 (Fall 1991), p. 26.

9. See Rein Müllerson, *International Law, Rights and Politics: Developments in Eastern Europe and the CIS* (London & New York: Routledge, 1994), p. 118.
10. Misha Glenny, *The Fall of Yugoslavia* (new edn) (Harmondsworth: Penguin, 1992).
11. Cited in Andres Kasekamp, 'Paths to Baltic Independence', paper presented at the School of Slavonic and East European Studies, University of London, 7 March 1992.
12. See, for example, De Nevers, *Russia's Strategic Renovation*, p. 29, although the figures are for 1992.
13. Vilnius Domestic Service, 11 March 1990, in *Foreign Broadcast Information Service. Daily Report. Soviet Union*, 12 March 1990, p. 80. Hereafter cited as *FBIS-SOV*.
14. Although, of course, one of the blows to the integrity of the USSR and a boast to the Lithuanian independence movement was the defection of the Lithuanian Communist Party from the Communist Party of the Soviet Union. Brazauskas was speaking when his party has declared itself independent.
15. Vilnius Domestic Service, 11 March 1990, *FBIS-SOV*, 12 March 1990, p. 83.
16. See Allen Lynch, *The Cold War is Over – Again* (Boulder, San Francisco and Oxford: Westview Press, 1992), p. 142.
17. See the findings in William Maley, 'Does Russia Speak for Baltic Russians?', *The World Today* (January 1995), pp. 4–6. At the same time, however, it is clear that Russian minorities oppose additional citizenship requirements and the requirement of learning the indigenous language as a condition of citizenship. See Graham Smith, Aadne Aasland and Richard Mole, 'Statehood, Ethnic Relations and Citizenship', in Graham Smith (ed.), *The Baltic States: The National Self-Determination of Estonia, Latvia and Lithuania* (London: Macmillan, 1994), esp. pp. 192–201.
18. Jonathan Steele, 'The Baltics at Breakdown: Barely a Year After Independence, Economic and Political Crises are Bringing the Republics to Their Knees', *The Guardian*, 20 November 1992.
19. Anatol Lieven, 'Estonia Reaffirms its Independence', *The Times*, 21 August 1991.
20. See Müllerson, *International Law*, p. 120.
21. Kestutis Girnius, 'Lithuania', *Eastern Europe and the Commonwealth of Independent States 1994* (London: Europa Publications), p. 418.
22. Ibid.
23. Glenny, *Fall of Yugoslavia*, p. 165.
24. Published in *Foreign Broadcast Information Service, Daily Service. East Europe*, 25 June 1991, p. 36.
25. Sarah Lambert, Marcus Tanner and Steve Crawshaw, 'Croatia and Slovenia are Recognised by the EC', *The Independent*, 16 January 1992.

26. 'Gamsakhurdia Must Resign', (editorial) *The Independent*, 23 September 1991.
27. Tanjug in Serbo-Croat, 27 February 1991, in *Summary of World Broadcasts*, 'SK-PJ opposes proposed resolution separation from Yugoslavia', 2 March 1991.
28. John Zametica, *The Yugoslav Conflict*, Adelphi Paper 270 (London: International Institute for Strategic Studies, 1992), p. 35.
29. Belgrade Home Service 1300 GMT 31 July 1991, reproduced as 'Yugoslavia: Tupurkovski Warns Of "All-Out War"', in BBC Summary of World Broadcasts, 2 August 1991.
30. Tony Worthington, 'Outsider: Macedonia: Suffering from Excess of History', *The Herald*, 21 January 1993.
31. Janusz Bugajski, *Nations in Turmoil: Conflict and Cooperation in Eastern Europe* (Boulder: Westview Press, 1993), p. 236.
32. Marcus Tanner, 'The Conflicts in the Former Yugoslavia', *Eastern Europe & the Commonwealth of Independent States 1994* (London: Europa Publications), p. 90.
33. Glenny, *Fall of Yugoslavia*, p. 165.
34. Associated Press, 'Croatia to Protect Serb Rights', *The Globe and Mail*, 5 December 1991.
35. As stated in broadcast by Prague ČTK, 27 June 1991.
36. See, for example: 'After 1989's "velvet revolution" established this [Czechoslovakia] as the most progressive and self-confident of the region's new democracies, the idea that Czech and Slovak leaders would dissolve their 74-year-old country without ever asking voters for their opinions seemed far-fetched.' Marc Fisher, 'Czech–Slovak Divorce Seen as a Splitting Headache', *Washington Post*, 31 December 1992.
37. *Narodná obroda*, 1 July 1991.
38. Zametica, *Yugoslav Conflict*, p. 39.
39. John Zametica, 'Squeezed off the Map: Bosnian Serbs Refuse to be Fobbed Off with a Settlement which Leaves Them Worse Off than Before', *The Guardian*, 11 May 1993.
40. Ibid.
41. See the weekly review in *RFE/RL Research Report*, Vol. 1, No. 19 (8 May 1992), p. 68.
42. See Yaroslav Trofimov, 'Inside Track: Belgrade Poses a Catch-22 Dilemma for UN', *The European*, 14 May 1992.
43. 'Gamsakhurdia Must Resign' (editorial), *The Independent*, 23 September 1991.
44. Halperin *et al.*, *Self-Determination*, pp. 150–1.
45. *Izvestia*, 25 March 1992.
46. See, for example, ibid.
47. ITAR-TASS, 3 April 1992, in *FBIS-SOV*, 3 April 1992, p. 71.

48. Summarised in James Rupert, 'Dateline Tashkent: Post-Soviet Central Asia', *Foreign Policy* No. 87 (Summer 1992), p. 177.
49. Ibid.
50. See Elizabeth Fuller, 'Abkhazia on the Brink of Civil War?', *RFE/RL Research Report* (Vol. 1, No. 35, 4 September 1992), p. 1.
51. John Wright, 'The Caucasus Region: An Overview', *Eastern Europe and the Commonwealth of Independent States 1994* (London: Europa Publications, 1994), p. 76.
52. See the statistical data for the Russian Federation published in ibid., p. 591.
53. Tass International Service, 2 February 1992, *FBIS-SOV*, 3 February 1992, p. 55.
54. Cited in Müllerson, *International Law*, p. 118.
55. Wallace, *International Law,* pp. 87-8.
56. EC and EU are used according to the time of events.
57. W.R. Smyser, *Germany and America: New Identities, Fateful Rift?* (Boulder: Westview Press, 1993), pp. 64–5.
58. Timothy Garton Ash, *In Europe's Name: Germany and the Divided Continent* (New York: Random House, 1993), p. 396.
59. For example, Eve-Ann Prentice, 'Greece Accused of Slav Rights Abuse', *The Times*, 22 August 1994.
60. See, for example, 'The Macedonians of Greece,' *The Times*, 22 August 1994. Macedonia succeeded, however, in being admitted to the UN before EC states established diplomatic relations with the republic.
61. Sarah Lambert, 'Greek Refusal to Recognise Macedonia Comes Under Fire', *The Independent*, 21 January 1993.
62. Garton Ash, *In Europe's Name*, p. 396.
63. 'Grow Up, Greece', *The Times*, 18 December 1993.
64. See Sarah Lambert, 'Greek Refusal to Recognise Macedonia Comes Under Fire', *The Independent*, 21 January 1993.
65. Libor Roucek, *After the Bloc: The New International Relations in Eastern Europe*, Discussion Paper 40 (London: R.I.I.A., 1992), p. 12.
66. As reported by Československý rozhlas radio, 2 July 1991, in JPRS-EER, 5 July 1991, p. 2. Charter 77 continued to issue statements after the Velvet Revolution of November 1989 but it was not a formal part of the government.
67. Roucek, *After the Bloc*, p. 10.
68. John Gray, 'Election Results a Blow for Soviets: Nationalist Wave Sweeps Republic', *The Globe and Mail*, 3 December 1991.
69. *Das Parlament*, cited in Garton Ash, *In Europe's Name*.
70. Rupert, 'Dateline Tashkent', p. 176.
71. Cited in John Lloyd, ' USSR RIP: Ukrainian Independence is the End for Gorbachev', *The Financial Times*, 4 December 1991.
72. Chrystia Freeland and John Lloyd, 'Ukraine Votes to Ignore Draft Union Treaty', *The Financial Times*, 7 December 1991.

73. William Green Miller, 'American Diplomacy and Soviet Disintegration', in Hans Binnenendijk and Mary Locke (eds), *The Diplomatic Record, 1991–1992* (Boulder: Westview Press, 1993), p. 13.
74. Wright, 'The Caucasus Region', in *Eastern Europe*, p. 75.
75. See, especially, Stern, 'Moscow Meltdown'.

10 Europe's Three Empires: A Watsonian Interpretation of Post-Wall European Security[1]

Ole Wæver

A reassessment of European security after the Cold War in terms of International Society can take two routes. The first is to focus on international society as an empirical phenomenon: to study international norms, institutions and culture and to identify this as international society. The second is to investigate the theoretical perspectives that emerged as a result of the development of the concept international society. This would necessarily entail some consideration of the close relationship between international society and the 'English School'. The advantage of reaffirming this link is that international society is neither isolated nor reified but understood as part of a wider re-conceptualisation of international relations. For, in adopting the concept International Society, other concepts like international system, balance of power, state and security will change their meaning accordingly. This is not to suggest that priority is necessarily given to international society, but that we should adopt a perspective which is able to theorise the possibility of international society.

As Martin Wight argued, the dominant realist and radical perspectives in the discipline do not logically allow for the possibility of international society existing as an important independent phenomenon.[2] Yet, to acknowledge that international society is an independent and significant category does not necessarily mean that international society is the most powerful dimension of international relations. Quite the contrary:

> Powers will continue to seek security without reference to justice, and to pursue their vital interests irrespective of common interests, but in the fraction that they may be deflected lies the difference between the jungle and the traditions of Europe.[3]

Consideration of security institutions in Europe since 1989 can accordingly be approached in two different ways. First, one can study the role played by norms, institutions and possibly culture in shaping European security after the Cold War. However, the danger of this approach, which would focus primarily on institutions with the aim of emphasising their importance, as contrasted with a 'state-centric' perspective, is of converting the English School into a variation of regime theory or neo-liberal institutionalism.[4] In this context it could be said that much American IR has spent several decades re-inventing the English School. Conversely, if the English School was tempted to meet the Americans half-way, the danger would be of diluting international society into another form of liberal IR theory, looking and hoping for progressive developments in the non-state field that would promise a softening of inter-state conduct. The most likely result of approaching the study of European security in this way would be a form of regime theory or neo-liberal institutionalism, seeking to identify the norms and institutions most likely to assist in stabilising Europe.

The alternative approach is to let international society modify one's outlook on international relations. This more theoretical approach is directed towards a general study of international political forms; a geopolitics freed from the limitations of sovereignty. The English School, by introducing the elements of time and meaning, thereby opens up analysis to more than just the mechanical laws governing relations between sovereign states. We still study 'power politics', but not in an abstract world of physical forces; it is re-inserted into a general history of human cultures and polities. This is the approach that will be adopted in this chapter. However, questions raised by the first approach concerning institutions in a narrow sense are not necessarily sacrificed by opting for the second one. Indeed, the penultimate section of the chapter directly addresses the question of security organisations from within this latter perspective.

The chapter begins with a discussion of the re-articulation of IR theory suggested by Wight and Watson; in particular, it is concerned with their claim that international systems need not be based on sovereign states. Their concept of 'degrees of empire' is used in the main sections of the chapter to present a reinterpretation of the way the EU functions as the core of a unipolar system of concentric circles and, accordingly, provides security in ways that cannot be grasped within the normal categories of security studies. After looking at the EU-based system in some detail, two other quasi-empires, centred on Moscow and Ankara, will be discussed. The potential relationship between the three empires will also be considered, asking whether they are indifferent to one another or are able to co-exist more successfully than states. The chapter then directly considers the European security institutions, and shows how the current, complex pattern of organisations can be explained by applying the empires model. The findings are then reconnected to the Watsonian framework, and some conceptual tasks for future work pointed out. Finally, and by way of conclusion, the chapter will briefly discuss whether it makes sense from a macro-historical perspective to imagine that empires will return after the era of nation-states is over, or whether for socio-economic reasons they belong to another age.

WATSON, INTERNATIONAL SOCIETY AND EMPIRES

The writings of Charles Manning aside, international society was launched as an academic concept by Martin Wight. Wight insisted that any international system should be viewed in its cultural, philosophical and religious context.[5] Wight's writings on Western values and on the origins of the principles shaping the European states system were linked to his interest in the historical variations of international systems.[6] Hedley Bull, by contrast, was more interested in developments within the modern European system and its worldwide extension, that is, with one specific system based on sovereignty, in order to assess the forces that strengthen and weaken international society.

This contrast between Wight and Bull has recently been emphasised by Barry Buzan.[7] His distinction between Wight's historical and Bull's structural explanation of the evolution of international society might, however, underestimate Wight's approach. It is not only the relative importance of unique historical factors versus a generalisable structural logic in explaining *how much* international society emerges in a system that is at stake. In Wight's work, the issue is *what* type of international society has evolved, measuring not only the degree of international society present in a particular international system, but also the peculiar form each international society takes. For Wight, broad cultural trends influence systems of states and shape their specific principles: different cultures produce different logics of international relations:

> Is there wide variation between the common code of one states-system and of another? Or do they all belong to the great pool or practices and platitudes, supposedly common to the human race, where men seek for Natural Law?[8]

Thus, while for Bull there can be a system without a society, but no society without a system – the image here is one of a system of states in the mechanical, ultra-realist sense, which can then be softened by a gradually refined society of states – in a Wightian world, there is no 'neutral' system of states. Every system of states is embedded in a specific cultural and historical context.

Although most of the recent writings by or on the English School have *de facto* taken Bull as their main inspiration, Adam Watson's book *The Evolution of International Society* clearly stands in the Wightian tradition.[9] Watson builds on Wight's concern to broaden our perspective on states-systems by rejecting a narrow conception of states-systems as premised on sovereign equality, and by embracing one that includes systems based on suzerainty. Such suzerain systems involve an accepted, or at least institutionalised, relationship of supremacy and subordination, though not one that reaches the point of direct rule (empire):

> Here there is indeed a group of states having relations more or less permanent with one another, but one among them asserts unique claims which the others formally or tacitly accept....We might distinguish these from international states-systems by calling them *suzerain* state-systems (in the first phrase the word 'state' should be in the plural, but in the second in the singular). And we may note that, while the fundamental political principle of the first will be to maintain a balance of power, for the second it will be *divide et impera.*[10]

A significant part of the history of international relations is thus rendered invisible if we insist on studying only those systems based on sovereign states.[11] Wight adds suzerain systems, and Watson later replaces Wight's dichotomy between international states-systems and suzerain systems, with a spectrum which ranges from absolute independence to absolute empire and incorporates hegemony, suzerainty and dominion along the way.[12] For Watson, the extremes, which are generally unstable, are rare and there is always a centrifugal pull towards the middle.[13] However, this middle way, although the historical norm, has often been hidden behind the rhetoric of rulers who have tended to present things as being closer to either extreme. Furthermore, in Europe, empires have had bad press during the last 300 years, due mainly to the fact that Europe prides itself on being the one region that has broken with the imperial model. Europeans have claimed that by keeping the continent divided into independent and equal states, centralisation has been avoided, cultural diversity ensured and personal liberty guaranteed. This state of affairs has often been contrasted to other regions which, Europeans have readily pointed out, have either failed to create states or created grand and repressive empires. Thus 'empire' was considered to be bad because Europe defined itself as the anti-imperial continent.[14]

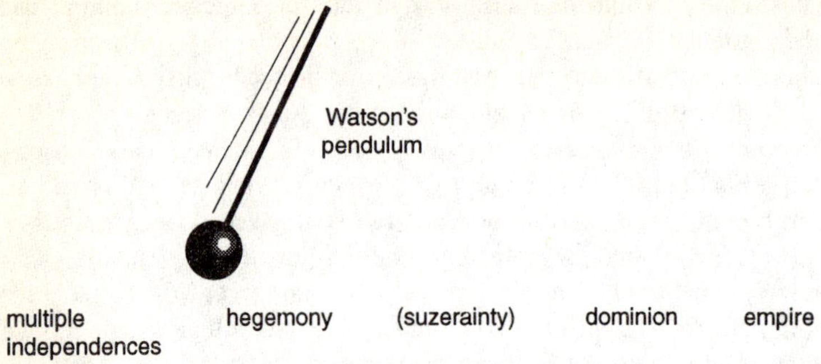

Figure 10.1 A Spectrum of International Systems

However, despite the European denigration of 'empires' *per se*, in reality empires have not always been unpopular and imposed upon subject populations. Commercial and business concerns have usually benefited as empires establish zones of peace, thereby enhancing trade and generating wealth. Political units also have not always resisted inclusion into empires. Inclusion could have beneficial effects, not least of all the enhanced prospects for peace, as long as the centre understood the principle of subsidiarity, which, Watson concludes, most empires of the last 5000 years have. Indeed, despite the popular (mis)representation of empires as repressive, imposed and inherently unstable entities, they have proven track-records as peace systems.

This spectrum, from direct rule to multiple independent political units exists not only in time, but also in space. Not only does a system move back and forth between the various forms (Fig. 10.1) but a single system can combine the forms in a distinct pattern (Fig. 10.2). Imperial and quasi-imperial systems are usually organised in a pattern of concentric circles.[15] Within the first inner circle, direct authority over and administration of a heartland is exercised. In the second circle there is a periphery of locally autonomous rulers who recognise overlordship and pay tribute – some also tolerate infringements of their domestic as well as their external independence. The third incorporates units which possess almost full domestic independence, but who have their foreign policy circumscribed not least because their ability to wage war is ruled out – a key feature of empires. Finally, in the outer circle are located units which although recognised as being independent are not equal to the central power – they all recognise that the suzerain is of a different order. If we approach international relations from a broad historical perspective, spanning 5000 instead of the usual 300 years and incorporating different regions and civilisations other than those of Europe, the normal pattern that emerges is one of such mixed constellations; neither multiple independencies nor tight empire, but the concentric circle patterns of gradated empires.

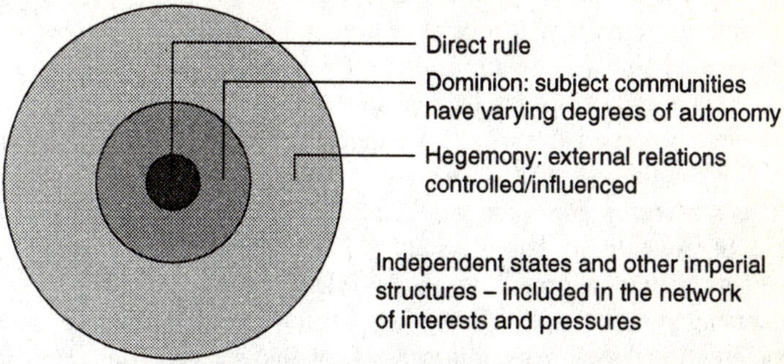

Figure 10.2 The Structure of Imperially-Organised Systems

However, in the following presentation of Europe's three empires, I have not used Watsonian terminology to the full. I have chosen to approach the matter in a more narrative manner because it is not possible to argue logically for an interpretation of Europe exclusively from a perspective than either through a perspective that emphasises 'sovereign equality' or one that advocates 'concentric circles'. The reality we are presented with is like a picture puzzle: it can be seen through different perspectives, employing different terminologies. Yet I do suggest that it is extremely illuminating to try to interpret Europe in terms of centres and concentric circles rather than sovereign states. In my account of contemporary Europe, I make vague references to the 'imperial side' of the axis (the mid-to-right side in Fig. 10.1). Rather imprecisely, I talk about three 'empires', although they are not exactly empires in Watson's sense. However, these new political formations are far from being equal sovereign units in a system of multiple independencies. Indeed, they resemble empires far more than is usually recognised. However, to be more precise, I would suggest that they, like many formal empires, come somewhere in the complex mid-zone where the pendulum spends most of its time.

General definitional problems concerning the term 'empire' suggest another reason for not applying the terms along the spectrum too rigidly and for employing the term 'empire' metaphorically. One of the most quoted definitions of empires is Michael Doyle's, for whom '[e]mpires are relationships of political control imposed by some political societies over the effective sovereignty of other political societies'.[16] In this definition, 'societies' are taken as given and constant units. This is problematic, however, because when one moves towards the imperial end, it is *the empire as such* that becomes a political unit with a centre and to varying degrees rules this larger space, and acts as a unit towards the external world.[17] It is a mode of political organisation extending over an area which combines a particular mix of central authority and local powers. To define it as the (unequal) relationship between central and peripheral units is to interpret empires through the lens of sovereign equality; as a deviation from some privileged norm.[18] It is important to stop using terms like 'empire', 'dominion' and 'sovereignty-based system' as normative distinctions wherein 'dominion' and 'empire' are treated as deviations from the norm of 'sovereignty-based systems'. These terms should rather be used to designate different forms that whole orders can take, as different ways of organising political space.[19] Mogens Trolle Larsen defines an empire as 'a supernational system of political control, and such a system may have either a city state or a territorial state as its center'.[20] As Watson points out, the opposite of this are sovereignty-based systems, that are *international* rather than *supernational*. This definition emphasises one distinctive feature of empires: they are radially managed; they take the form of concentric circles.[21] Empires are about radial not territorial power; the former are differentiated, the latter homogenous.

Yet, while emphasising one element of Watson's analysis – the concentric circles pattern – it is possible to question another, that is, the distinctions between independence, hegemony, dominion and empire. Most political orders *combine* these as layers of different intensity within themselves and the main noticeable feature becomes the concentric circles. There is then a case for not making the distinctions of the spectrum too rigid and returning to Wight's concept of suzerainty as that which is too centred to be identified as a system of sovereign states.

POWER AND PATTERNS: EUROPEAN SECURITY AFTER THE COLD WAR

What use is this perspective if our task is to understand European security during the last five years? For one thing, it ensures that we avoid analysing the contemporary constellation of power in terms of the straitjacket imposed by assumptions of sovereign equality, a move which would seriously compromise our ability to understand the emergent political pattern. Before proceeding, it is worthwhile emphasising what did *not* happen after 1989. The normal pattern of European international interaction since the emergence of the states system has been one of great power rivalry based on a number of centres, such as France, Germany, England, Russia, Turkey and Austria, with small states forced to manoeuvre within the confines of the system. However, despite the prophecies of the 'Back to the Future' brand of Neo-realists, this has not been the pattern of politics since 1989.[22] Instead, European politics is unfolding not between centres but around one centre.

It is worth considering the experience of a country like Sweden which has been challenged by the changed circumstances. Swedish foreign-policy makers have been forced to slaughter many sacred cows including neutrality, the commitment to non-membership of the EU, and the Swedish model. However, the panic that has precipitated this has not arisen from concerns about emerging relationships between the surrounding powers – Britain, Germany and Russia – but from a general fear that Sweden has landed too far out in the circles; from a fear of becoming peripheral in the new politico-economic geography of Europe.[23] Conversely, Denmark's 1992 'No' to Maastricht was driven by a fear of coming too *close* to the centre. Indeed, a large number of European controversies of the last few years can be directly traced to concerns regarding centre-periphery, distance, and the dilemma between 'getting in' in order to achieve influence as against 'keeping distance' for the sake of independence. The overall picture is of one centre and concentric circles – a completely different mental geography from the traditional view of several competing great powers.

In this context, the EU is now also the most important security 'institution'. It will determine which of the two European patterns will unfold: integration or fragmentation.[24] At present, the concept of security is used in two different ways. On the one hand, there is the move to embrace, at least rhetorically, a 'wider' concept of security that emphasises environment, economy and identity. On the other, there is, in the light of the former Yugoslavia, renewed interest in classical military concerns about intervention and the ability of institutions to muster the necessary military muscle for such actions. There is still a strong tendency to talk about the appropriate means for ensuring security in Europe in terms of military-related institutions (i.e. NATO, WEU and possibly a reformed OSCE). These two perspectives on security are rarely combined. If the security agenda is to be enlarged this will necessitate not only a redefinition of the concept of security by which it comes to refer to a completely new set of questions, but also a willingness to handle the classical questions of violence, sovereignty and survival in terms of the new contexts.

An important part of the security agenda lies in-between these two poles of the debate, that is, the political dimension concerning the structure of the region. A crucial question for European security concerns the fate of

European integration – not in terms of EU 'foreign and security policy' or the West European Union (an unfortunate self-limiting discussion of specifically security-related institutions), but the issue of integration generally: the political-economic reshaping of Western Europe. This is about identity and organisation, about politics. The European continent will operate very differently depending on whether or not there is a strong pole of integration at its centre.

The importance of the EU for European security can be grasped if we locate it within a framework based on the pattern of the circles. Here it is necessary to take into account three levels. The EU has:

1. A primary responsibility towards itself. It must keep the core intact to ensure that there *is* one centre rather than several in Western Europe.
2. A stabilising leverage over 'the Near Abroad'; this process is already at work in East-Central Europe.
3. A potential role as a direct intervener in specific conflicts.

In the light of our Watsonian framework, this list of the EU's three most important security functions is especially interesting in so far as they accord with the quasi-geographical distribution of the concentric circles. The first is about the core itself, the second pertains to close outsiders, and the third refers to those peripheral actors that circle around this centre.[25]

Keeping the Core Intact

The first function, that of keeping the core intact, is the most important for the EU. Even if this self-centred task can, at times, lead to dubious policies (for instance when Balkan policies are determined mainly by concern for their intra-EU effects), it would not be in the interest of East-Central or Southeastern Europe to have competitive interventions from the Western powers. This would transform the peripheral areas into arenas for competition in power-struggles which would remain non-military at the centre, but could easily develop into wars at the periphery. If this scenario sounds over-blown, one should study French and German politics in the summer of 1991, when the Yugoslav crisis first erupted. They supported opposite sides in the conflict – Germany on the side of Croatia and Slovenia, while France held out for Yugoslav unity with Belgrade. This situation was not as different from that of 1914 as we would like to think.

According to the logic of the 'normal' development of such events, the likely outcome would have been a situation where those two, together with other major powers, were pulled increasingly towards active partisan support for the warring parties. Although it is not really possible to imagine France and Germany at war with each other, one can imagine them supporting opposite sides in a war in Europe. This would have coloured all aspects of their relationship and reversed European integration. Indeed, some indications of a slide in this direction could be detected in the recriminations in both the French and German press as to the other's intentions.[26] Ultimately though, this scenario did not come to pass because neither France nor Germany was prepared to sacrifice Maastricht for Yugoslavia. The most critical phase of the recognition issue coincided with the final phase of negotiating Maastricht. They spent half a year negotiating a joint position, which although it was of dubious value in relation to the conflict, nevertheless succeeded in containing it within the borders of former Yugoslavia.[27]

The primary relevance of the European Community as regards security is not then its expression in narrowly-defined security structures like the WEU or the Eurocorps, but the general political and symbolic importance of the Community as such, the strength of the process of integration. This is, however, rarely made evident. French and German leaders are disinclined to discuss how strained their relationship is and how important the EU is in preventing its break-down. Officially they love each other, so the EU is not needed to repair that which is not broken. Yet, this is the most important security function of the EU, and a precondition for all the others in so far as all discussions about what 'we' should do in the East are premised on the assumption that there is a 'we' in the first place.

Discreet Disciplining

The second security role of the EU is in exercising 'power' over the East through discreet disciplining or indirect influence. As Robert Keohane has acknowledged, one possible strategy to combat the 'hyper-nationalism' in Eastern Europe could be:

> to use the economic and technological dependence of Eastern European societies on Western Europe as a source of leverage.... Some combination of EC as magnet and CSCE as an encompassing framework of rules would seem to be the proper institutional antidote to the danger of hypernationalism in Eastern Europe.[28]

Certainly, the most western part of Eastern Europe (Poland, Hungary and former Czechoslovakia) have been strongly influenced – and 'disciplined' of their close proximity to the EU. Here the 'magnet' clearly impact on foreign as well as domestic policies: politicians in ries have been well aware that the EU's eyes are on them, and aware of what is considered to be appropriate behaviour as mocracy, minorities, privatisation and sub-regional relations. also entertained expectations of gradually moving closer to, and entually joining the EU. Even today, decisions taken in Brussels ortant to the Polish economy as are decisions taken in Warsaw. ırket access and the agricultural policy of the EU are decisive those countries in Western Europe's 'near abroad'. In the long sue for these countries is EU membership. This, of course, gives ı enormous leverage which is operative both when consciously and when not. The Eastern neighbours operate in the shadow of The attractiveness of EU membership has led to a *good-will on* among EFTA countries as well as those East European which have a realistic chance of joining. As Hans Mouritzen has n a Europe of concentric circles, the 'would-be insiders' have a margin for manoeuvre than those either in the EU or those ıny chance of joining.[29]

ıechanism is not and should not be visible. Therefore, the EU does redit for its operation – the mechanism is not acknowledged – but sible and polite 'disciplining' is no less important for that. One ıstration of its operation was provided by the Czech and Slovak In reading the divorce papers, one notices the curious presence of layer in these proceedings: the EU. Both parties were concerned to that the divorce was carried out not only in a way which was civilised by the West but which also allowed both of the new states nue their existing arrangements with the EU.[30]

French idea for a 'stability pact', the so-called Balladur plan d by the EU in May 1994 and signed in April 1995, is an attempt ıalise this role – to use the political and economic leverage of the secure a stabilisation of borders, minority rights and related issues. oblematic in that it singles out East-Central Europe for particular ent – it is hard to imagine Western European countries accepting international obligations regarding minority protection. However, the asset of the Balladur plan is that it reflects a reality: East-Central e *is* stabilised through an unbalanced relationship to Western Europe. is 'pact' is only the most explicit expression of a function which the ıs anyway and which has several institutional expressions, including BRD and the various agreements between the EU and East-Central ean countries, especially the 'Europe agreements'. The Europe

agreements represent the attractiveness of the EU, thereby tying the East Europeans into a system of concentric circles. It is a system which demands much from the EU system because ultimately it can only function if the promise of eventual membership is kept alive. This security function only works when new members move towards the EU at a pace that is neither too fast nor too slow. One might almost say, *they have to move closer as slowly as possible*: they have to move – the process must never stop, for if the promise disappears the Eastern countries will fall off the magnet – but if they enter too fast, the EU loses its coherence and thus its ability to function as a magnet at all.

Direct Intervention

The third level of security is that of direct intervention. When a conflict is of a military character, the EU will not, in the foreseeable future, be very well equipped to deal with it. It is, however, at this level of European security that the EU's security structures and institutions are judged. Despite all the claims to the contrary, public, political and academic debate is still caught up in the assumption that military capability is *the* test. This is, however, simply a restatement of the classical prejudice that war is the true 'rite of passage' for an international subject. Yet, as already indicated, the EU is important in the realms of security and stability in two other ways – stabilising the core and disciplining its own 'near abroad' – that should not be underestimated.

This is especially so since the abilities of *anyone* to handle military conflict seem severely circumscribed. Pierre Hassner has argued that the anti-militaristic – in a positive sense 'decadent' – West is unable to act militarily unless the action is extremely well-legitimised and carried out with overwhelming superiority, thereby guaranteeing minimal human cost to Western troops. Intervention is most likely to take the form of a joint venture involving more or less all the relevant international organisations. Thus, questions as to whether a particular organisation is or is not able to handle intervention are therefore misdirected as no single organisation is well enough equipped for this and many actors will be party to any operation.[31]

The root cause of this weakness is not institutional but social. The strengthening of society in relation to the state in the West has resulted in the predominance of attitudes and priorities that place a high price on individual life.[32] Thus while media pictures of conflicts can force us to 'do something', the media can equally rapidly create a political crisis which halts our actions. The problem is not only one of military casualties, the use

of military force *per se* is problematic for our societies. The pressure for military operations to be undertaken with overwhelming force and be swift and clinical as in the Gulf War, creates a tendency for military operations to be either absent or enormous. Furthermore there is pressure for military operations to be secured through political agreement between as many relevant organisations as possible.

During the tragedies in the former Yugoslavia, a favourite pastime of the media, assisted by 30-second security experts, has been to condemn the performances of NATO, the EU, OSCE and the UN in turn as failures. Far-reaching conclusions have been drawn about the possibilities of a future Europe without one or all of these organisations: 'now that in Yugoslavia, we see that NATO (alternatively OSCE, EU or any other organisation) has failed in respect to its stated purpose of keeping the peace in Europe, so we can conclude that this organisation is dead for European security'. This unproductive approach is related to the popular view that it is the very nature of the security architecture, the multiplicity of organisations, that has prevented earlier and more rational action over Yugoslavia. In fact there is no basis for the claim that rivalry among institutions prevented the right one from getting to the table. Yugoslavia started on the agenda of the OSCE, which passed it on to the EU, which handed it over to the UN, which commissioned NATO. They have all had their chance, which they have failed to use. The failure to intervene in Yugoslavia is not to be explained in terms of an overcrowded club of institutions, but by the lack of political will in key countries.

In this particular case, intervention has not been forthcoming because of a combination of concerns about 'the nature of the case' – the assumption that Yugoslavia is not necessarily peaceable – and restraint by the main powers – the US, Britain, France and Russia have all taken turns to oppose intervention and then to favour it when another power opposed it. There is strong opposition in Western societies to interventions unless they promise to be simple and swift. Still, the process of integration in the EU is the main force determining whether or not we are sliding into a Balkan war with Europe-wide implications. Thus, if one shifts the perspective slightly from a focus on the specific horrors of Yugoslavia to look at stability in Europe generally, it becomes clear that the general direction of developments in ex-Yugoslavia will depend primarily on the fate of integration in Western Europe. At the same time, it is clear that the military component has a special status and is not easily integrated into the emerging quasi-empire. Factors relating to general societal development – post-military societies[33] – or to the character of European integration could explain this resistance to an easy inclusion of military force into the new

polity. A subsequent section will examine this aspect of the EU's relationship to other European institutions.

'WELCOME BACK TO THE EMPIRE OF THE TSARS...'

Before discussing the institutional arrangements of a unipolar EU-based security order operating through concentric circles, we must address the possibility that the European continent will not become purely uni-centric because two other centres are emerging in the East: Russia and Turkey.

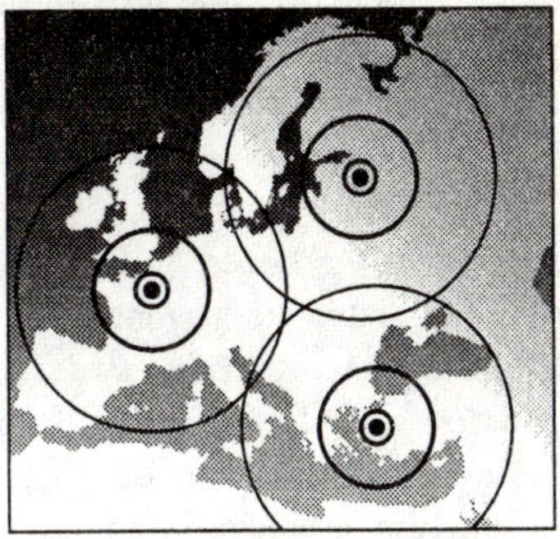

Figure. 10.3 The Three Empires of Europe

As regards an integrating Europe, Russia has three options:

1. Opt for a subservient position in this arrangement by acknowledging that it is located in the outer periphery. This would contribute to the full integration scenario whereby all of Europe becomes ordered around one centre.
2. Insist on an equal role. The implication of this is that 'the other side' could not be the EU, which would mean inequality for Russia, but would have to be other individual great powers. Here, Russia would attempt to revive great power politics within Europe by sabotaging EU integration and forcing France and Germany back into a balance-of-power-based mode of existence.[34]
3. Divide Europe once again. The EU would get its sphere of influence, and Russia would take its – more or less equivalent to either the CIS or the former Soviet Union.

The third option is certainly not the most unlikely outcome. If Western Europe integrates in the direction of a uni-centred structure a significant part of Europe will take the form of concentric circles centred on Brussels.

However, the structure centred on Moscow also has strong concentric circles features. Yeltsin clearly does not rule the 17 million square kilometres that are the Russian Federation. Some might claim that, at best, he rules Moscow and thirty kilometres out, after which he needs to negotiate with local mafia bosses and war-lords.[35] Certainly, Moscow does not rule in a manner characteristic of an ordinary state, but more according to the divide-and-rule principle that corresponds to suzerainty systems, weak empires and systems of dominion. Several entities within Russia are semi-independent and only really bow to Moscow over foreign policy. The centre cannot just make 'rules' and 'laws' and expect that they function in North Caucasus! Instead, it can support and play off competing power groups against one another. This is a mode of governance far removed from the modern rule-governed state, but one associated with imperial rule.

This gradual fading-out of power from the centre continues beyond the borders of Russia. This is reflected in the concept of the 'Near Abroad' which, having progressed from the status of a right-wing oppositional slogan to being the new consensus, has gained a strong following in Moscow since 1993.[36] For Moscow, the former Soviet republics come neither under the remit of foreign policy nor domestic affairs but somewhere in between. This situation is exemplified by the numerous statements issuing from Russia on the prerogatives that it demands in relation to peacekeeping and supervision of minority rights, not just on the territory of the CIS but over the whole of the former Soviet Union including the Baltic States.[37]

In the Western media, it often appears as if the behaviour of Russia is just getting 'worse' with both its 'Near Abroad' policy and great power politics in Bosnia seen as symptomatic of the same general malaise. While this is in some respects true, it is also true that the two policies are contradictory and one can compensate for the other. It is important for Russian self-esteem that it is seen to be one of the global great powers. A formal or informal great power concert, handling global crises and conflicts could give Russia this position. Alternatively, Russia could unilaterally press for what it can get – either through action in the 'Near Abroad' or elsewhere by obstruction and individual manoeuvring as in Bosnia in early 1994.

The Russian leadership needs to show that it is capable of conducting its own foreign policy, rather than simply following American whims, as Kozyrev was accused of during the first two years of independence.[38] Thus, there is a certain trade-off between concert and neo-imperialism. This was visible, for instance, in February 1994 after the diplomatic triumph resulting from Russia's successful brokering of a deal over Sarajevo, which not only provided the Bosnian Serbs with a face-saving story and relieved the West of the need to bomb the Serbs, but also placed Russia in a central role. Following this achievement, the pressure on the government in Moscow weakened – the opposition in Parliament backed the foreign-policy leadership and especially the President in their pursuit of a great power role. However, if Russia wishes to be part of a concert, tensions will arise between that privilege and any desires to undertake unilateral actions in the 'Near Abroad'. Russia's demands for participation in the general supervision of NATO operations in Bosnia carries with it the implication that Russian 'peacekeeping' in the CIS area should also be subject to UN supervision and mandating.[39]

This can be conceptualised as the logic of international society operating at two levels. The literature on international society is not clear as to whether there can be several international societies super-imposed on each other. It is, however, acknowledged that there can be patterns of differentiated density within international societies, i.e. there are 'insiders' with more fully-developed norms, and a continuum towards peripheral members, who are only covered by the most basic norms such as, for instance, mutual recognition.[40] But what if there is a general system of minimum norms and within this several nodal points of more developed sets of norms and institutions? While systems with one inner core have been discussed in this literature, as Watson has noted, one potential prospect is

> that the worldwide society established by the Europeans, which separated politically into some 160 nominal sovereignties, may perhaps reintegrate into a number of distinct *grandes républiques*. The regional societies would still be bound to each other by the interests and pressures of a global system, which they would manage by means of a developed version of the arrangement between Europe and the Ottomans: that is, with regulatory rules and operational practices, including legitimacies, but with few or no common values or codes of conduct.[41]

Seen from this perspective, it is likely that Russian policy will evolve as a mixture of participation in general agreements and cooperation in the UN, together with separate arrangements for the region. This would necessitate two things. First, the development of an international society and institutions at the global level of a far higher degree than was characteristic of the Cold War period. Second, distinct sets of codes, including, for example, one set for the Eurasian complex around Russia, and others for the OECD-elite, East-Asia and Africa, each with separate declarations of human rights, different rules for intervention and different ideas about stability and legitimacy. This implies that the best to be hoped for regarding global conflict management after the Cold War is not the kind of 'New World Order' vision modelled on the Gulf war, but regional peacekeeping constrained by the need to obtain a UN mandate – what Charles William Maynes has dubbed 'benign realpolitik'.[42] Rather than the UN acting a regional power or power collection in some regional organisation will assume the role of 'peacemaker'. Because 'the peacemaker' or great power, will seek the legitimacy that comes from global mandating, the operation will only be manipulated minimally in order to serve the peacekeeper's own ends. However, because the peacekeeper will be able to manipulate the operation to some extent to suit its own ends, it ensures that it will be carried out.

As regards Russia, it is, at present, not clear to what extent it will seek to cooperate within a concert system and how much it will rely on its own spheres of interest. But it is almost certain that it is too late for the West to prevent some element of a Russian sphere developing. The Grand Bargain of 1990 has been mismanaged. At the time there was a real possibility that Russia – then the Soviet Union – could be kept within a pan-European system. Russia was given compensatory gains in return for German unification and East European liberation.[43] Just as France obtained accelerated EC integration to compensate for German unification and thereby secured a meaningful vision of France's place in Europe which made sense to French political thinking, Russia was to be given access to European structures primarily in the form of the CSCE.[44] This was meant to reassure Russia that it was neither excluded from Europe nor that Western Europe was ganging up against it. However, the CSCE largely failed in this respect and no new structures were created to ensure that Europe would appear to the Russians as containing a promise and a place for Russia. Russia has been given no 'vision of itself', and thus the nascent new order was unstable from the outset.[45] Domestically, it is uncertain to Russians what Russia is (to be), but this is not a purely domestic problem; a great power's vision of itself is an international question – it views itself in the world. Thus the world influences its choice of self through the international roles offered to it.

So far Russia has – in contrast to the expectations of the 1990s and the 'grand bargain' – had little stake in the Europe that eventually evolved. Russian identity cannot be realised within a European process centred solely on Western Europe. Russian self-esteem will be realised partly by more involvement in global politics and partly by Russia shaping a region with Moscow as the centre.

'...AND OF THE OTTOMANS?'

Having seen the potential for the emergence of two empire-like structures, a Turkish formation centred on Ankara could generate a third. The post-Cold War world presents Turkey with new challenges and opportunities. Its membership of 'the West', based on geostrategic importance, was temporarily questioned as Western Europe's new-found affection for Eastern Europe increased the distance between Brussels and Ankara. Simultaneously the disintegration of the Soviet Union begot five new Turkish-speaking republics (four in Central Asia and Azerbaijan). Turkey, therefore, has been and is in the process of redefining its foreign policy orientation. This process even entails a re-evaluation of the meanings of state and nation for 'Turkey'. The new 'Turkish Republics' in particular have questioned the relationship between state and nation. Seen from Turkey, the nation stretches further than the borders of 'Turkey'. However, the Turkish authorities have not reacted by adopting a radical pan-Turkism, that seeks to extend the state's borders to match language borders. Rather, it has attempted to combine traditional cautious Kemalism with a soft pan-Turkism, where the state still ends at the established borders, but a larger nation is 'imagined' in the form of a family of consanguineous states.[46] The long-term aim then is not for a 'greater Turkey' – as in a 'greater Serbia' or 'greater Bulgaria' – but for a family of states in which Turkey is first among equals. This would constitute less than suzerainty – perhaps a hegemony. However, it is not clear to what extent Turkey will succeed in this project – its rivalries with Iran, China and especially Russia in Central Asia will all play a decisive role in determining the eventual outcome. Yet it is clear that this project has already had a decisive impact on Turkey's own self-perception and the profile Turkey will have in the future. For Europe, a different Turkey is thus a reality, even if the Central Asian project remains largely in the realm of fantasy.

In accordance with traditional European prejudices, the more Turkey is seen to turn towards the East, the less it will be deemed 'European' – as if being 'European' can only be done in Europe. In practice, however there is a compelling argument that Turkey might become *more* European by orienting itself towards the East. Turkey's comparative advantage in the competition against Russia and Iran is precisely in its self-promotion as European, Western and modern: Turkey as the only truly secular Muslim state and a member of Western institutions. The Central Asians are neither very keen on Iranian-style fundamentalism, nor on returning to the Russian fold. Turkey has a cultural appeal based on language and race and is also able to present itself as the gateway to the West. Thus, it has an interest in emphasising its Western and European profile. The US, and to a lesser extent some of the West European powers, have noted the Western interest in strengthening Turkey in this competition and thus are attempting to supply Turkey with additional financial assistance in order to enhance the cultural capital supplied from Turkey.[47] It is therefore not too far-fetched to imagine that whatever form the Turkish empire eventually takes, it is likely to become the third *European* empire. This stands in contrast to a widespread image in Western Europe that the neighbouring power-centre to the South-East is 'the fundamentalist Middle East'. This exaggerated perception of a Muslim threat to 'Europe', would be countered by a clearer understanding of imperial geopolitics where 'our' sphere does not meet some Middle Eastern power centre, but a Turkic one which, although Muslim, is basically a secular Western state and certainly operates as a centre of power between Brussels, Moscow and the Middle East.[48]

It should be noted that the three-empires perspective neither claims that the three empires are organised in a similar way, nor that they are equally powerful. It is perfectly possible to talk of 2½ empires, or of one strong and two weak ones. However, what is important is not that they are equally powerful but that they succeed in forming a centre of gravity, a self-conception as a centre, which pulls other states into their orbit and within which they behave differently than if they were just periphery to the one 'European' society.

Accordingly, it is necessary to study the domestic debates in the new centres. In Turkey, the opening of Central Asia has radically transformed political discourse, even to the extent that 'Turkey' itself has achieved a different meaning. Thus, one cannot conclude, as have many Western observers, that since Turkey has had less success than expected in Central Asia this project will soon be given up. When the identity factor is taken into account, one can see why the reorientation of Turkish self-conception is likely to be stable, even if the 'pay-offs' in a material sense might be ambiguous. The identity gained from redefinition as part of a larger Turkish nation is immediate and definitely preferable to constantly banging on a shut EU door.[49] With the increased 'weight' Turkey gains from its new role as the mainly self-appointed spokesman of a larger group, it is natural for it to demand more of a say in other arenas such as the Balkans. Thus, Turkey acts like the centre of a separate solar system, even if this system is smaller than the neighbouring systems, or itself rotates around a bigger star.

BLOC CONFRONTATION OR HAPPY INDIFFERENCE?

To an ear tuned to the Cold War all this sounds like a new form of 'bloc politics', and one ripe for confrontation. Johan Galtung has warned of the possible dangers of this three centred development in so far as the divisions follow the boundaries of religions: the EU is Catholic-Protestant, Moscow's empire is Orthodox and Ankara's Muslim. Due to religion, deep historical and cultural patterns could reassert themselves. According to Galtung the logic of this conflict can be observed where these three religions meet in Yugoslavia; the ultimate microcosm being Bosnia-Hercegovina.[50] However, I think that taking Bosnia as a prognosis for Europe is wrong. Scale does makes a difference: Europe is not Bosnia. The division of Europe into large, radial empires with the centres far apart has less potential for conflict than the traditional territorial division into nation-states. In the latter case each state meets its neighbour at the border – they rub against each other and easily create conflicts. The three empires are not about clear borders. They have a relatively clear identity at the centre, but towards the periphery their character and expressions of power fade away and one zone shades into the next. In some places the grey zones will be conflictual, but the empires will not rub against each other in the way nation-states do.

While power in an empire dissipates towards the borders, a state, in theory, exercises control evenly over its territory. In the Cold War not only did states stand full-force at their borders but power was also directed outwards, through the iron curtain and into the other side. However, a new dotted line is now being drawn across the European continent, a new division is envisioned, and many actors are already manoeuvring in anticipation of the day when the line is fully drawn. This new situation – so far most vividly captured by Yeltsin as 'cold peace' – *is* different from the Cold War. It is not an iron curtain, but rather an 'iron veil'. It is not characterised by the mutual build-up of pressure against a defined line, but rather by fragmentation into separate worlds. Each side takes what it can get, but is not so concerned with the other centres. It is not a single security complex defined by one overarching conflict constellation but rather separate security complexes, each of which is established around its own security concerns. On neither side is there a drive for confrontation. In contrast to nation states and ideological blocs, separate empires can have blurred and 'low-intensity' borders where they both fade out. The primary concerns of these empires will not be each other. The main concern of the EU will be neither Moscow nor Ankara but Washington and Tokyo, i.e to secure its position in the world economic order in relation to these other two. Ankara's main rivals are most likely to be in the Middle East, while

Moscow's main conflicts will, for many decades, be situated within the empire. At present, strategic planners in Russia claim that the main threats come from the South.[51]

As Yugoslavia has shown, the contemporary logic within the EU tends towards 'under' rather than 'over' involvement in peripheral European affairs. Perhaps if the EU collapsed some of the likely emergent great powers – Germany France and Italy – would be inclined to intervene in the Balkans because for individual powers of this size there are identifiable and significant gains to be accrued from such action. However, for an actor of the scale of the EU, such concerns would only constitute a distraction from the primary arena of competition. The EU political unit is constituted at a higher level; as a global actor competing with Japan and the US in the techno-economic sphere. Thus, it will be inclined to turn its back on old-fashioned, unpromising sub-regional struggles among smaller units.[52]

In order to understand the nature of the relations between the centres it must be stressed that they are *not* sovereign states. Instead of envisioning a world of geographic states, borders, and expanses of pink, green and yellow on a map, we have to think in terms of spots, degrees of control, and subordinate centres at lower levels, which can accommodate each other without demanding 'equality' and without recognising any 'sovereign' authority. Within each of these centres, politics will still follow the logic of concentric circles and therefore in the case of Western Europe materialise in the 'integration' model I have outlined above. For those in the outer circles, however, the 'three empires' scenario is radically different. A country like Ukraine is not first and foremost defined by its location outside the EU, but rather from its position within the Russian zone. Similarly, for Lithuania the main issue will not be its distance from Brussels, but the possibilities for balancing between Brussels and Moscow.[53]

It is now possible to take stock of the EU as a security project: the first circle is basically stable as long as the integration project continues – the main worry being the gradual weakening of the French pillar in the sense that, for France, the choice of a European over a national-geopolitical strategy is now much less definite than it was five years ago, and certainly much less solid than it is in Germany.[54] As regards the second circle, the centre will most likely be able to prevent conflict, but should it break out, the centre will feel obliged to carry the burdens – moral, refugees, etc. – so strongly that it *will have* to be solved. The EU would be forced to act in the case of, for instance, a conflict between Hungary and Slovakia. In the third, outer circle, by contrast, the centre will not always intervene unless it is easy. If it is not easily manageable, the centre will try to pass the conflict on to the global level and the UN. In some cases, the outer circle of one system will also be the outer circle of another and therefore the source of potential rivalry.

One advantage of adopting the 'empires map' is that it avoids embracing a clichéd image of 'Eastern Europe' as an undifferentiated unity. There is currently a danger that the West re-establishes the categories of Eastern and Western Europe that became 'politically incorrect' in 1989–91. The popular media image of Eastern Europe as one large Yugoslavia just waiting to erupt into multiple ethnic conflicts would contribute to a militarisation of politics – we should just prepare for the wars instead of envisaging these areas as successful societies. With the 'empires' image, we see instead a zone of stability *that grows* and promises to import gradually East-Central European nations into this zone; only some specific areas at the margins would be difficult to discipline – typically mountainous areas at the periphery of empires: the Balkans, Caucasia and Transcaucasia. Finally, an explanation of conflict prevention and interventions in *different zones* as determined by their location in the pattern of concentric circles would identify the most likely serious conflict areas, such as the Baltic states, which besides 'internal' reasons for conflict are located where the circles cross.

INTERNATIONAL ORGANISATIONS FOR EUROPEAN SECURITY

It is often said that the pattern of competing European security institutions is illogical and the result of institutional inertia. In fact the pattern is extremely logical. It is a triangle: military affairs are concentrated in NATO, legitimisation and norm formulation are produced by the OSCE, and the EU produces the basic economic–political shape. The triangle has, however, been overlooked by many analysts because they underestimate the security importance of the EC/EU and assume that in matters of *security*, the EU should be 'represented' by either its military arm (WEU) or its Foreign Policy Cooperation (EPC/CSFP).

It has been argued in this chapter that European integration is *the* central process which produces the basic underlying political–economic direction for the continent. Furthermore, it must be acknowledged that this is a *process* and may be unstable if left in *status quo*. One cannot just say: 'NATO works, don't duplicate it', because NATO in itself does not keep countries together; the EU does, and the EU only works as a security mechanism when it is a *process* of integration which is able to uphold visions for future integration. Therefore, plans for involvement in the military sphere are unavoidable, as some development in this direction is necessary for the stability of the integration project. However, giving the EU exclusive responsibility for military affairs is an unattractive option with few advocates; it would not only create tensions within the EU but also antagonise the US and everyone feels more secure having the Americans involved in European defence.

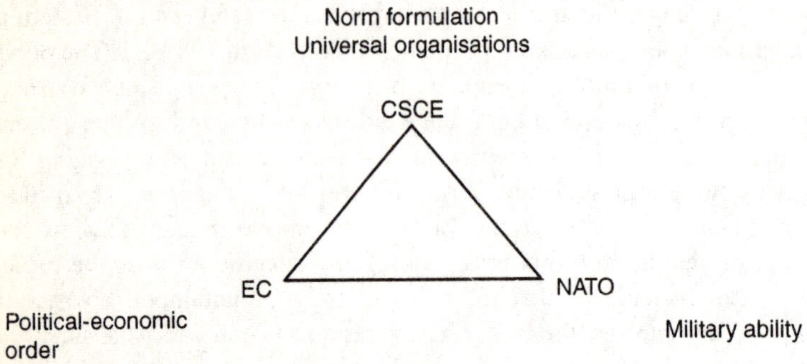

Figure 10.4 The European Security Triangle

Thus, it is preferable to have military capacity located in a separate specialised institution: NATO. Any friction between the EU and NATO can be handled by the WEU, an arrangement which has been on the cards since the Rome summit of NATO in November 1991, but which only became evident to the wider public during the January 1994 summit. Bush's replacement by Clinton has certainly helped the compromise along. Clinton's Presidency has a strong orientation towards domestic affairs and is generally well-disposed towards West European defence cooperation, feeling that burden-sharing will easily outweigh concerns about the loss of American influence. Furthermore, as the spectre of American 'dominance' has faded, the French have moved closer to NATO and eventually struck a Franco-American deal whereby the WEU abstained from duplicating NATO structures, while NATO opened up for WEU use of NATO infrastructure and facilities. The WEU has thus assumed a new role as a bridge between NATO and EU while retaining its traditional role as a potential West-European replacement for NATO, should NATO suddenly disintegrate. Short of this, the WEU functions as a way of avoiding clear-cut answers to questions about the military dimension of the European Union. The WEU means both 'yes and no' – the EU has a *link* to military means, but is basically located in the non-military field.

As regards the Eastern circles, the EU has power but not legitimacy. The EU is a *de facto* stabilising force in the East, but it cannot make decisions that have formal legitimacy 'for Europe', that is, in the name of those not taking part in decisions. A process is needed for the formulation of norms and rules whereby those who are subject to the rules have participated in their creation. The OSCE can produce rules that have legitimacy because all states have been party to their formulation, but it lacks the power to enforce these rules. The EU and OSCE are thus complementary. The EU is an actor, the OSCE an arena. The EU can accumulate power, the OSCE can provide legitimacy. As argued above, there are layers of legitimacy and layers of international society. There is a global international society and the global universal organisation for norm formulation is, of course, the United Nations. Even in Europe, the UN often appears as the most important universal organisation, and one might therefore add in the triangle (Fig. 10.4), UN/OSCE in the universal corner.

The three sides of this triangular structure are more revealing than the corners, for it is along these sides that the new institutional activities can be located. The stabilising role of the EU for wider Europe has taken the form of the Balladur plan. This connects the EU and the OSCE, since the task is all-European and some agreement has to be reached in wider Europe, but the force and solidity comes from the EU core. The NATO–OSCE axis faces the challenge of extending military security outwards from the NATO core. This was first tried in the format of the North Atlantic Cooperation Council (NACC). Then in 1994, Partnership for Peace was added as a structure which in principle contains much the same as NACC, but does so in a different form. Whereas East European members of NACC all had to do the same at the same speed, PfP is an elimination race, where it is left to the partners in the East to take initiatives and prove their ability to cooperate, and thus move closer to the core according to their own performance. Finally, the EU–NATO axis needed, as argued above, the WEU as buffer or bridge.

This pattern is logical, but often overlooked because of the prevalent concepts of security and security systems. Between 1989 and 1991 the desire for a coherent and 'logical' 'security system' often produced visions of the CSCE as the over-arching institution which would gradually arrange the others as sub-ordinate sections. This is because the CSCE had, in principle, activities in all three corners, although primarily in the areas of norm-formulation and soft conflict management. More recently, NATO is often – especially by Americans – advanced as the key institution. Looked at in this way, the multitude of organisations may appear confusing and untidy. The temptation in acknowledging all three sides of stabilisation and particularly the key role of the EU could be to understand this perspective as another variant of the 'one super-organisation approach'. However due to the reasons presented above, the three are not integrated into one institution, but find their individual institutional expressions. None of them commands the other, but they all relate to each other. With three separate institutions we get a need for mediation (on each axis), thus the three-plus-three pattern.

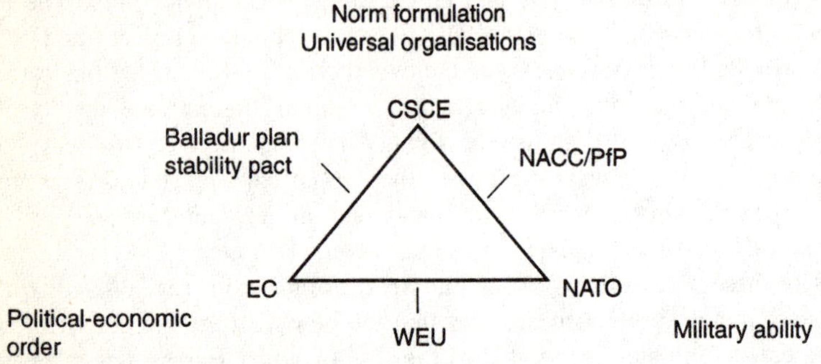

Figure 10.5 The Refined Triangle

This pattern is so logical, obvious and functional that one has to ask why the figure of the triangle is not the common approach; why, to my knowledge, it has never previously been suggested. The answer is that the word 'security' tends to triggers responses in terms of military institutions and organisations for inclusive cooperation – the 'congresses' of previous days. In a 'states as sovereign equals' perspective, this is logical – states can both make alliances against each other and they can set up cooperative structures. If patterns of power and thus structures of stabilisation are included, we recognise the third component, which is incompatible with the 'states as sovereign equals' perspective and are thus able to capture the logic of contemporary European security. Paradoxically, in order to understand the forces at play in Europe at the end of the twentieth century, it is most helpful to consider the lessons of several millennia of international relations such as, for example, those of Mesopotamia, India and China. The form of political organisation based on concentric circles, characteristic of the ancient empires, is the lens through which Europe should be viewed.

A whole language based on 'sovereign equality' operates as the dominant code in international law, in the UN and in cultivated behaviour among states. This is important to remember, for it is the grammar of the dialogue among states and the guiding fiction. Thus, while it is important to investigate the evolution of concepts such as intervention and recognition, such investigations should not be conducted under the illusion that this is the pattern of *power*. In power terms, the configurations are, as has been common throughout history, somewhere in between empires and sovereign equality. By adopting the concentric-circles perspective, we can see not only the patterns that explain what is going on in and among the three empires of Europe, but we may also be able to begin constructing institutions for European security that are relevant to the basic patterns of power.

FEDERATIONS OR EMPIRES?

We are now in a position to assess where the three empires can be located on the spectrum; and to identify their degree of 'imperialness'. According to Watson's distinction, all three would be closest to the categories of 'hegemony' and 'dominion'. Empires involve direct administration of different communities from the centre. In a hegemony the power is able to 'lay down the law' regarding the operation of the system and to dominate the external relations of the subordinate units while allowing them relative independence as regards their domestic affairs. In a dominion, 'an imperial authority to some extent determines the internal government of other communities, but they nevertheless retain their identity as separate states and some control over their own affairs'.[55]

The Watsonian approach, however, assumes that imperial structures will always be more intrusive in foreign policy than in domestic politics. However, in the EU the centre is active in all sorts of 'domestic' affairs but relatively weak in foreign affairs. It has a structural effect in the form of 'the King's peace' but this is minimal compared to the numerous ways by which it can influence the (formerly) domestic affairs of its member states. Turkey, too, is most active in low politics *vis-à-vis* the new Turkic states. Turkey has realised that when it comes to confrontational high politics, the military-political power is still Russia. Turkey seems to be playing a game similar to that of the West during the Cold War: penetrating societies from below with the low politics of economy, media and culture, while Moscow penetrates from above with the high politics of military security.[56] The Russian case probably accords most to the model. Perhaps then a rethinking of the original Watsonian argument might be appropriate. One possible revision would be to re-conceptualise a part of the 'foreign affairs' of the units as the emerging 'domestic' sphere of the new 'centre'.[57]

One obvious way to compare the three 'empires' would be to determine to what extent they are considered to be either 'voluntary' or 'imposed'. Buzan and Little have highlighted the importance of the distinction between imposed and voluntary supranational formations. They take Watson's empires as examples of the imposed variant and Dan Deudney's US

'Philadelphian system' as illustrative of a voluntary formation – into which category the EU should be placed.[58] Yet this distinction is not convincing for several reasons. First, 'voluntary' and 'imposed' are problematic categories because something that we might view today as 'voluntary' – for example most 'nation-states' – were imposed through violent means at the time of their formation.[59] Second, the categorisation of 'voluntary' *vs* 'imposed' easily becomes a tautological confirmation of that which survives – today Ukraine is considered voluntary and the Soviet Union imposed; by tomorrow this might have changed. Finally, empires and Federations have similar external manifestations, share the same position on the different axes. Watson does not just emphasise the imposed nature of empires, but stresses the importance of *legitimacy*, namely, how power and legitimacy mix in different cases.

Although the different routes taken to the same location should normally be of little interest to a conceptual category, there might be a case for 'path dependence' if it can be proven that specific internal, structural differences do stem from different formative routes.[60] Different histories can make for differences in the nature of the eventual form a unit takes. The main cause of difference results from whether the federation or empire in question is constructed by and around one centre or by a number of units *constructing* a new 'artificial' centre – as in the case of both the US and the EU.[61] When the centre is a social construction it will usually be constructed in a way that ensures that its power is limited. It will also be seen differently by the individual units – it will not be clearly identifiable with specific interests (as with Prussia's motivations for German unification), but rather as another, larger 'we'. In addition to being of different European states and nations, we now also construct a Europe, a Union, which is also us. This is an independent distinction separate from the contrast between territorial and radial power: both classical empires and some modern federations like the EU take the radial, concentric circles form, while both centralised nation-states and some federations (the USA, Germany) are territorial and homogeneous power units.

The concentric-circles features of the three contemporary power centres of Europe are therefore better visualised through the lens of 'empires' than federations. The EU is a 'social construction' in which there can hardly be said to be a city-state or territorial state at the centre. The EU is built around a socially constructed centre which emerges from the political will to have a centre. Like Sumer, there has to be a centre because there has to be a centre, not because a centre is strong enough to impose itself. This would also seem to have been the case originally in the US. Characteristic of the EU today is, however, the fact that its power takes the form of concentric circles in a unipolarised region. There is an imperial quality to the way authority is extended and distributed across a large area, even when the centre of this power is arrived at voluntarily.

AFTER THE NEW MIDDLE AGES: MACROHISTORY AND METAPHORS

One possible objection to the present analysis could be that it is ahistorical to apply premodern imperial and suzerain models to a contemporary world in which the socio-economic conditions make them very unlikely competitors to the all-dominant sovereign nation-state. They were viable under very different economic conditions – today only the nation-state can organise society and economy.

Charles Tilly, however, has shown that the route to the 'national state' was far less unilinear than is usually assumed. For several centuries, both city-states and empires competed very well with the nation-state, and only recently did political forms converge on the latter. The nation-state is not as evidently superior as is often assumed.[62] Its weaknesses include the high costs of administration and service that a state incurs *vis-à-vis* its subjects. In the late twentieth century the state is becoming an obstacle to economic competitiveness in the global political economy. Throughout the 1980s, the order of the day has been deregulation, flexibilisation and privatisation. In the private sphere, firms have undertaken divisionalisation, decentralisation and franchising. These trends suggest that future political organisations will need to emphasise indirect rather than direct rule in order to rid themselves of responsibility. During the modern era of the history of the international political economy, the most competitive form was one that could mobilise and commit its members maximally by taking on ever-increasing responsibility for their total life-situation. But maybe when the parameters of competition, due to technological developments, change again, it might become more rational to use indirect means of control and thereby take less responsibility for everything in society. Tilly writes about another age:

> On a national scale, in fact, no European state (except, perhaps, Sweden) made a serious attempt to institute direct rule from top to bottom until the era of the French Revolution. Before then all but the smallest states relied on some version of indirect rule, and thus ran serious risks of disloyalty, dissimulation, corruption, and rebellion. But indirect rule made it possible to govern without erecting, financing, and feeding a bulky administrative apparatus.[63]

Unless one assumes a unilinear relationship between techno-economic development and political forms, we have to take seriously the possibility that the relative rationality and efficiency of different forms of political–economic organisation can change again, not only by moving 'back down' towards lower technological levels, but also by moving 'up' to higher levels of what Buzan *et al.* call 'interaction capacity'.[64] Structural trends in political economy could make suzerainty and soft empires possible options, although not necessarily *the* models to be emulated around the world, nor options inherently inferior to centralised national states.[65] To this economic factor, which at least does not close off the option that empires may replace nation-states as the most viable political forms, should be added what is probably the more decisive pressure in this direction: security and politics.

Since the Second World War, the nation-state in Europe has lost some of its legitimacy as a security structure.[66] This has led to security-driven pressure for the creation of a 'centre'. There is increased legitimacy for the construction of an order that has a centre and where security concerns will be based less and less on decentralised balance of power logic. Centralisation should therefore not be viewed through the image of empire-building as conquest: a major driving force is the *legitimacy* of a centre. As Watson showed in the classical Sumerian case, there was a strong idea that there had to be *some* centre which could be based on different city-states dependent on particular power relations. What carried legitimacy was not so much a particular city as the idea that *something* had to assume the role of centre. In postwar Europe there has been a similar idea that multipolar power rivalry has to be avoided and a therefore a power-pole constructed. While, during the period of Cold War security structures, this pole was maintained merely in the form of a moderate ambition, once exposed to the unconstrained pulls of international politics following the withdrawal of the superpowers, Europe has faced a clear choice between a reversal into mutual power balancing and pole construction.[67] In this way, the construction of the centre carries higher legitimacy than a complete 'multiple independence' swing of the pendulum. This is not, in itself, enough to guarantee its success, but it has resulted in an attempt to challenge the dominant principles of recent centuries: sovereignty and balance of power.[68] Europe is marked in this period by a will to centre.

One historical irony is that at the time of European expansion, when the globe began to become one, the regional European 'world system' was the only one that was anti-hegemonic; the flood-tide and subsequent ebb of European expansion transformed the world into a global, international society based on the European principle of sovereign equality with its implicit rejection of hegemony.[69] However, suzerainty-like logics have been reintroduced into the system. First, by the West at the inter-regional level through a concentric-circles-shaped ordering of the international system with the West as a core and with degrees of sovereignty accorded to non-Western states. This process can be seen both in the period of 'standards of civilisation' and mandated areas[70] and in the post-Cold War period.[71] Now, and somewhat ironically, it is also possibly becoming the organising principle for Europe, the region where the anti-suzerain, anti-empire ideal was born.

There is no uniform global trend either towards or away from the imperial end of the spectrum. Current trends towards regionalisation seem to imply that different pendula swing according to independent rhythms. Southern Africa is one place where concentric circles seem to have formed around South Africa as a new pole of attraction and as a motor of regional development. Similarly, the different circles of regional cooperation in Latin America with smaller and larger groups within each other might be read as an attempt to achieve an integrationist dynamism similar to that in Europe. East Asia and the Middle East are the strongest examples of the opposite logic, where trends towards the acceptance of sovereignty are the best hopes for security and stability. East Asia is one of the regions with the clearest historical ties to empires and suzerainty and is not well accustomed to mutual recognition and equality. As argued by Buzan and Segal, one of the reasons to fear future rivalry and instability in post-Cold War Asia is the tendency for China and Japan to act and to expect the other to act according to imperial rather than equality logic.[72] In the Middle East, constant references to 'pan' formations (pan-Arabic or pan-Islamic) as competing with or complementing states have contributed to constant rivalry and instability, whereas the current trend towards a more clearcut system of sovereign statehood and equality might contain the promise of a more stable system of regional security.[73] In Europe, however, the pendulum is travelling in the opposite direction at present: security hopes are attached not to decentralisation and sovereign equality, but to centredness.

The European construction will not necessarily be either a bigger and better state or a sovereign entity. The driving logic behind the European polity is the emergence of a pole in the international system – as both a global competitor and a barrier against intra-European rivalry. But a pole is not necessarily a state; it can be a socially constituted pole that operates as a centralising force in complex multi-layered European politics.[74] It can even be argued that European unification is actually impossible if attempted in the format of the sovereign state. A strong reason for this is to be found in the area of *societal security*: nations have and will defend themselves against perceived threats to their identity from Europeanisation.[75] Nations will strike back – as the Eurocrats possibly learned during 1992 – and thus the European construct must be of a kind that does not threaten nations on their most sensitive issues. Thus it must not be a greater nation-state, but a unit with a more limited political identity. This creates pressure in the direction of a construct that could be labelled neo-medieval.[76] The emerging political structures can be seen as 'neo-medieval' in the sense that in Western Europe political organisation no longer fits into the format of territorial sovereignty and exclusivity. The nation-states are not sovereign, but nor is the EU a sovereign state. This is a construction unseen so far in the history of modernity, and the easiest way to enable contemporary understanding of it might be to make parallels to the period immediately preceding that of the modern state, i.e. the Middle Ages. The medieval is, however, not the only non-sovereignty-based system. A post-sovereign system can find analogies from all kinds of suzerain systems, and the security-based argument about 'the need for integration in order to avoid fragmentation' points to the importance of making parallels with a *centred* region. Thus while the medieval metaphor is appropriate for provoking the necessary rethinking regarding the concept of sovereignty,[77] it is less appropriate as an indication of the centredness of the new order. Martin Wight describes Medieval Europe, as 'a uniquely complicated dualistic or double-headed suzerain state-system'.[78] However, perhaps 'ordinary' suzerainty exposes the centred-ness better. Possibly, the best metaphor in the end is not that of new middle ages, but rather something approximating a soft empire or hegemony as articulated by the English School writers Martin Wight and Adam Watson. Maybe Europe is rather *neo-Sumerian*.

NOTES

1. Thanks for helpful criticism and suggestions to Barry Buzan, Lene Hansen, Jaap de Wilde, Peter V. Jacobsen, Tonny Brems Knudsen, Ola Tunander, Iver B. Neumann, Bjørn Møller, Heikki Patomäki, Susan Strange, Philippe C. Schmitter, Adam Watson and the editors: Jeremy Larkins and Rick Fawn. Also audiences in Åarhus, Oslo, Hørsholm, Florence and Stanford who responded to oral versions of the article were most helpful.
2. This is a constant theme in Wight's writings, but is probably most clearly expressed in 'Western Values in International Relations' in Herbert Butterfield & Martin Wight (eds), *Diplomatic Investigations: Essays in the Theory of International Politics* (London: George Allen & Unwin, 1966), pp. 89–131; and in Martin Wight, *International Theory: The Three Traditions*, Gabriele Wight and Brian Porter (eds), (Leicester & London: Leicester

University Press, 1991). See also Hedley Bull, *The Anarchical Society: A Study of Order in World Politics* (London: Macmillan, 1977), ch. 2.

3. Martin Wight, *Power Politics* (1st edn), Looking Forward Pamphlet No. 8, Royal Institute of International Affairs 1946, p. 66; quoted by Bull in his 'Introduction' to Wight, *Systems of States* (Leicester: Leicester University Press, 1977), p. 10.

4. See Tony Evans and Peter Wilson, 'Regime Theory and the English School of International Relations: A Comparison', *Millennium* (Vol. 21, No. 3, Winter 1992), pp. 329–52; Tonny Brems Knudsen, *Det Nye Europa: Orden eller Kaos?*, MA thesis, University of Åarhus, 1994; Andrew Hurrell, 'International Society and the Study of Regimes: A Reflective Approach', in Volker Rittberger (ed.), *Regime Theory and International Relations* (Oxford: Clarendon Press, 1993), pp. 49–72; and Barry Buzan, 'From International System to International Society: Structural Realism and Regime Theory Meet the English School', *International Organization* (Vol. 47, No. 3, 1993), pp. 327–51.

5. This correlates with the emphasis placed by Herbert Butterfield on the importance of thinking and ideas within power politics. Butterfield has shown, not least in two elegant, brief pieces, how – despite the fact that relations among powers has been self-serving and ruthless all along – we should not use terms like *raison d'état* and 'balance of power' as timeless laws, but seek to understand how these *ideas* were produced and started to function in the conceptual apparatus of the actors. See Herbert Butterfield, 'The Balance of Power' in *Diplomatic Investigations*, pp. 132–48; and Butterfield, *Raison d'état: The Relations Between Morality and Government*, The First Martin Wight Memorial Lecture, delivered at the University of Sussex, 23 April 1975.

6. In the preface to *Systems of States*, Hedley Bull writes of Wight's approach 'that by contrast with those studies of states-systems which view them as determined purely by mechanical factors such as the number of states in the system, their relative size, the political configuration in which they stand, the state of military technology, he places emphasis on the norms and values that animate the system, and the institutions in which they are expressed. A states-system, in Wight's view, presupposes a common culture', p. 17. For a clear statement of the contrast between mechanics and beliefs of international relations, see Wight, *Power Politics* (2nd edn), (Harmondsworth: Pelican, 1979), p. 81.

7. Buzan, 'From International System to International Society'. The argument is briefly repeated in Buzan's chapter, 'International Society and International Security', in the present volume.

8. Wight, *Systems of States*, p. 34.

9. Watson's book is important for two reasons. First, in the midst of a revival of interest in the school among younger scholars, Watson, a long-established member, published his major work which acted as a bridge between two of

the most creative periods of the English School. Second, and more importantly, the book widens the historical outlook of IR thinking. No previous book has made an equally serious attempt to map 5000 years of international relations from a global perspective with an eye to the diversity of 'systems'. The only other possible candidate here is Adda Bozeman's impressive but less comprehensive *Politics and Culture in International History* (Princeton, NJ: Princeton University Press, 1960).

10. Wight, *Systems of States*, pp. 23–4.
11. Watson astutely notices how Wight's protest against the parochial tendency to view the European states system as the only international system links up to his famous analysis of lack of any coherent IR theory. Wight argued that the poverty of international theory is 'due first to the intellectual prejudice imposed by the sovereign state, and secondly to the belief in progress'. Martin Wight, 'Why is There No International Theory?', in Butterfield and Wight, *Diplomatic Investigations*, p. 20. See also Adam Watson, *The Evolution of International Society* (London: Routledge, 1992), p. 4.
12. Watson eventually discards suzerainty as too vague a term, and therefore operates with only four points along the spectrum. I retain it here precisely because it does cover the vaguely defined mid-zone of the spectrum.
13. Watson, *Evolution of International Society*, pp. 17, 22, 136, 228, 252, 254f, and especially 122–5.
14. See, for example, Pim den Boer, 'Europe to 1914: The Making of an Idea', in Pim den Boer *et al.*, *The History of the Idea of Europe* (Milton Keynes: Open University Press, 1993), especially pp. 41–4. Martin Wight also harboured a similar suspicion: 'For what reasons are we inclined (as I think we probably are) to judge a states-system as *per se* more desirable than the alternatives, whatever those may be?', Wight, *Systems of States*, p. 44. Of course, European states were far from anti-imperial in their relations with other parts of the world, but these European empires were not meant to be(come) universal empires. It was seen as a positive value that Europe/the World was pluralist, divided among a number of (European) powers. What was castigated as repulsive and repressive was centralisation under one overarching authority.
15. Wight, *Systems of States*, pp. xx and 23f; Hedley Bull & Adam Watson (eds), *The Expansion of International Society* (Oxford: Oxford University Press, 1983), p. 3; Watson, *The Evolution of InternationaL Society*, pp. 16, 38, 115 and 124ff. See also in Mogens Trolle Larsen (ed.), *Power and Propaganda: A Symposium on Ancient Empires* (Mesopotamia 7), (Copenhagen: Akademisk Forlag, 1979), the chapters by Trolle Larsen, Steiner, Gurney and Frandsen.
16. Michael W. Doyle, *Empires* (Ithaca, NY: Cornell University Press, 1986) p. 19. An almost identical definition is to be found on p. 30.

17. Another problem with the approach which views peripheral units as 'repressed' versions of what ought to be sovereign states, is that it is difficult to distinguish among the subject cities and countries within an imperial system which are units and which are not, as there are numerous different degrees of independence. This problem is illustrated if, for example, one asks of the British Empire how many political units it contained. See Martin Wight, *British Colonial Constitutions 1947* (Oxford: Clarendon Press, 1952), p. 1. It might be interesting to speculate about the ways in which Wight's early work on British colonial constitutions influenced his attentiveness towards forms other than straightforward sovereign states.
18. See Wight's discussion in *Systems of States*. The discipline of IR is caught in ways of thinking which constantly project backwards into history a set of categories which are particular to our modern states-system and which prevent us from understanding other systems on their own terms. Beyond the problem of fixing sovereign equality as the 'natural' order, this approach has the problem of knowing in advance *which units* are predestined to become independent.
19. This problem is even more noticeable in much of the literature on 'informal empires' and 'spheres of interest'; see, for example, Alexander Wendt and Michael Barnett, 'Dependent State Formation and Third World Militarization', *Review of International Studies* (Vol. 19, No. 4, Oct. 1993), pp. 321–40. This literature is either concerned with particular ways of being dominated (i.e., as experienced from the periphery) or, more rarely, with particular strategies chosen by great powers. Thus, the separate existence of the component units are presupposed, whereas the Watsonian perspective opens up the possibility of conceiving of empires, dominion, hegemony and independencies as distinct modes of organising political space.
20. Mogens Trolle Larsen, 'The Tradition of Empire in Mesopotamia', in Trolle Larsen (ed.), *Power and Propaganda*, pp. 75–105, quotation p. 91.
21. Watson, *Evolution of International Society*, p. 127f.
22. John Mearsheimer, 'Back to the Future: Instability in Europe after the Cold War', *International Security* (Vol. 15, No. 1, 1990), pp. 5–56.
23. See, for example, Ole Wæver, 'Nordic Nostalgia: Northern Europe after the Cold War', *International Affairs* (Vol. 68, No. 1, Jan. 1992), pp. 77–102; and Hans Mouritzen, 'The Nordic Model as a Foreign Policy Instrument: Its Rise and Fall', *Journal of Peace Research*, (Vol. 32, No. 1, Feb. 1995), pp. 9–21.
24. These two options are singled out as the relevant ones for post-Cold War Europe by the theory of security complexes. This is demonstrated with most empirical detail in Buzan *et al.*, *The European Security Order Recast: Scenarios for Post-Cold War Europe* (London: Pinter, 1990); with more theoretical elaboration in Ole Wæver, 'Europe: Stability and Responsibility' in *Internationales Umfeld, Sicherheitsinteressenund Nationale Planung der*

Bundesrepublik. Teil C: Unterstützende Einzelanalysen. Band 5 (Ebenhausen: Stiftung Wissenschaft und Politik, SWP – S 383/5, February 1993), pp. 31–72; and with the most up-to-date empirical sources in Buzan's Chapter 1 and the concluding Chapter 10 in Wæver, Buzan *et al.*, *Identity, Migration and the New Security Agenda in Europe* (London: Pinter, 1993).

25. Phillippe Schmitter has correctly pointed out to me that in terms of European geography there should really be four levels of security here. Between the first and, what is here, the second levels should be interposed a security community. The first concerns the *core* members, basically France and Germany and their choice of internal versus external balance of power. The second in my scheme concerns the near non-members and their disciplining through asymmetrical dependence. Between these two are the outer layers of *members* whose 'peacefulness' is secured through a security community of a Deutschean type of which the EU is the core. Thus, their security is also to some extent secured through the EU. However, this seems to me the least problematic and the most stable part of the security map and therefore does not need to be included in the present discussion.

26. Peter V. Jakobsen, *EC Great Power Disagreement over Policy vis-à-vis the Wars in Croatia and Slovenia: Causes and Implications for the Future Stability in CSCE-Europe*, MA thesis, Institute of Political Science, University of Åarhus, Denmark 1993; Carsten Giersch & Daniel Eisermann 'Die Westliche Politik und der Kroatienkrieg 1991–92', *Südosteuropa: Zeitschrift für Gegenwartsforschung*, (Vol. 43, No. 3–4, 1994), pp. 91–125, esp. pp. 103–5; and Martin Rosefeldt, 'Deutschlands und Frankreichs Jugoslawienpolitik im Rahmen der Europäischen Gemeinschaft (1991-1993)' *Südosteuropa: Zeitschrift für Gegenwartsforschung* (Vol. 42, No. 11–12, 1993), pp. 621–53.

27. Contrary to widespread accusations, it has not, since then, primarily been intra-EU conflict that has blocked Western intervention. However, the Franco-German disagreement did have a decisive and probably negative impact on Western policy in the crucial, early period of the Yugoslav crisis; see references in above note.

28. Robert O. Keohane, 'Le Istituzioni Internazionali del Mondo Nuovo' in *Relazioni Internazionali* (Dicembre 1990), pp. 3–17, quote p. 10f.

29. Hans Mouritzen, 'The Two Musterknaben and the Naughty Boy: Sweden, Finland and Denmark in the Process of European Integration' in *Cooperation and Conflict* (Vol. 28, No. 4, 1994), pp. 373–402; and Mouritzen, Wæver and Wiberg, *European Integration and National Adaptations*, forthcoming (New York, NY: Nova).

30. Jiri Pehe, 'Czechs and Slovaks Define Postdivorce Relations', *Radio Free Europe/Radio Liberty Research Report* (Vol. 1, No. 45, 13 November 1992), pp. 7–11.

31. Pierre Hassner, 'Beyond Nationalism and Internationalism: Ethnicity and World Order' *Survival* (Vol. 35, No. 2, Summer 1993), pp. 49–65; reprinted in Michael E. Brown (ed.), *Ethnic Conflict and International Security* (Princeton, NJ: Princeton University Press, 1993), pp. 125–42.
32. Edward N. Luttwak adds to this the sociological factor that the West has become a 2.2-children-per-family society. Families with one or two children are less likely to risk their children in war than families with five or eight children. Luttwak, 'Where Are the Great Powers? At Home with the Kids', *Foreign Affairs* (Vol. 73, No. 4, July/August 1994) pp. 23–8. The use of force is ultimately constrained by the *mammismo* of modern, post-industrial societies.
33. See Martin Shaw, *Post-Military Society: Militarism, Demilitarization and War at the End of the Twentieth Century* (Cambridge: Polity Press, 1991); Michael Howard, *The Causes of War and Other Essays* (London: Maurice Temple Smith, 1983); John Mueller, *Retreat from Doomsday: The Obsolescence of Major War* (New York, NY: Basic Books, 1989; Carl Kaysen, 'Is War Obsolete? A Review Essay', *International Security* (Vol. 14, No. 4, 1990), pp. 42–64; and Robert Jervis, 'The Future of World Politics: Will it Resemble the Past?', *International Organization* (Vol. 16, No. 3, 1991), pp. 39–73.
34. This strategy of playing off national interests within the EU is more of a logical possibility than an actual policy so far. Potentially, it could be combined with some elements of the third option, that is, Russia attempting to reconstitute an empire of its own in the Near Abroad.
35. Jessica Eve Stern, 'Moscow Meltdown: Can Russia Survive?', *International Security* (Vol. 18, No. 4, Spring 1994), pp. 40–65.
36. See Andranik Migranjan, 'Russia and the Near Abroad: the Shaping of the New Foreign Policy Line of the Russian Federation', *Nesavisimaia Gazeta*, 12 and 18 January 1994 (Danish translation by Lars P. Poulsen-Hansen). Vitalii Portnikov has pointed out how the near abroad policy become the new official line as the Russian government used the threat of the rise of Zhirinovsky as an excuse to pursue a more radical policy of its own while appearing as 'doves'. 'Thus, there will be a Zhirinovsky regime without Zhirinovsky. Or: if Vladimir Volfoviti ascends to power, he does not need to change anything. Nor to replace the minister of foreign affairs.' *Nesavisimaia Gazeta*, 20 January 1994.
37. Maxim Shashenkov, 'Russian Peacekeeping in the "Near Abroad",' and John W.R. Lepingwell, 'The Russian Military and Security in the "Near Abroad"', both in *Survival* (Vol. 36, No. 3, Autumn 1994); John W.R. Lepingwell, 'The Soviet Legacy and Russian Foreign Relations', *RFE/RL Research Report* (Vol. 3, No. 23, 10 June 1994), pp. 1–8; John Lough, 'The Place of the 'Near Abroad' in Russia's Foreign Policy', *RFE/RL Research Report* (Vol. 2, No. 11, 12 March 1993) pp. 21–39; Zbigniew Brzezinski, 'The Premature Partnership', *Foreign Affairs* (Vol. 73, No. 2, 1994), pp. 67–82;

and probably most clearly: Migranjan, 'Russia and the Near Abroad'. For an early statement of the need for an 'active post-imperial role' that includes a position in the Baltic states, see excerpts from a seminar organised by the Moscow Institute for International Politics: 'Problems of Russia's Foreign Political Strategy Regarding the 'Close Foreign Countries'', summarised by Sergei Karaganov, published in *Diplomaticheski Vestnik*, 22 December 1992, trans. in *The Baltic Independent*, 5–11 March 1993, p. 9.

38. Alexei G. Arbatov, 'Russia's Foreign Policy Alternatives', *International Security* (Vol. 18, No. 2, Fall 1993), pp. 5–43.
39. The Haiti/Georgia deal of September 1994 indicates a trend towards an American–Russian bilateral system of mutual recognition of each other's spheres of interest. After Chechnia (Winter 1994–95), suspicion in the West as to Russia's intentions penetrated government circles too much for such an easy solution. Russian unilateralism is therefore likely to be effected only at the cost of Western good will and therefore as a careful balancing of contradictory aims at the global and the regional levels.
40. See Watson, *Evolution of International Society*; and Buzan, 'From International System', and Buzan's chapter in this edited collection.
41. Watson, *Evolution of International Society*, pp. 307–8.
42. Charles William Maynes, 'Toward Spheres of Influence, Plus International Rules', in *International Herald Tribune*, 23 December 1993; and 'A Workable Clinton Doctrine', *Foreign Policy* (No. 93, Winter 1993–94), pp. 3–20.
43. See Ole Wæver, 'Three Competing Europes: German, French, Russian', *International Affairs* (Vol. 66, No. 3, 1990), pp. 477–93.
44. Ibid.
45. 'Vision of itself' is a concept adapted from Henry A. Kissinger, *A World Restored* (Boston, MA: Houghton Mifflin, 1957) and elaborated in my 'Power, Principles and Perspectivism: Peaceful Change in Post-Cold War Europe', in Heikki Patomäki (ed.), *Peaceful Change in World Politics* (forthcoming).
46. Işıl Kazan *Omvendt Osmannisme og Khanaternes Kemalisme: Tyrkiets Udenrigspolitik med særligt henblik på 'det nye Europa', EF, og de Central-asiatiske republikker efter opløsningen af Sovjetunionen*, MA thesis, Institute for Political Science, University of Copenhagen, April 1994; Işıl Kazan and Ole Wæver, 'Tyrkiet mellem Europa og Europæisering', *Internasjonal Politikk* (Oslo), (Vol. 52, No. 2, June 1994), pp. 139–76, English translation in preparation.
47. See, for example, Graham E. Fuller & Ian O. Lesser (eds), *Turkey's New*

48. Barry Buzan and B. A. Roberson, 'Europe and the Middle East: Drifting Towards Societal Cold War', in Wæver *et al.*, *Identity, Migration*, pp. 131–47.
49. The very act of re-orientating itself towards Central Asia gives Turkey a more attractive vision of itself. This relates to Hermann Broch's insight into the nature of collective identities: identities are chosen not only because either one 'has to' (I *am* this), or as a rational strategy for fulfilling long-term aims; often immediate gratification seems to be more important. By identifying with some grand past and future, one attains immediate 'ego growth'. Hermann Broch, *Massenwahntheorie: Beiträge zu einer Psychologie der Politik* [1939-48] (Frankfurt: Suhrkamp, 1979); and 'Politik: Ein Kondensat (Fragment)', in Broch, *Erkennen und Handeln: Essays Band II* (Zürich: Rhein Verlag, 1955), pp. 203–55. See also Isaiah Berlin's perceptive arguments about the way national identification grew from the function it performed in relation to mental wounds which might have been filled by other identities, but which nationalism was best able to compensate. Isaiah Berlin, 'Nationalism: Past Neglect and Present Power', *Partisan Review* (Vol. 45, 1978), reprinted in Berlin, *Against the Current* (Hogarth Press, 1979), pp. 333–55.
50. Johan Galtung, lecture, 'Geopolitical Tensions Around Europe' given at the Centre for Peace and Conflict Research, Copenhagen on 4 May 1993. For similar arguments, see Samuel Huntington, 'Clash of Civilizations' *Foreign Affairs* (Vol. 72, No. 3, Summer 1993); see also the responses in *Foreign Affairs* (Vol. 72, No. 4, Sept./Oct. 1993), pp. 2–26 and Huntington's reply in *Foreign Affairs* (Vol. 72, No. 5, Nov./Dec. 1993), pp. 186–94, and the interview with Huntington in *Moscow News*, 11–17 March 1994.
51. For example, the speech by military historian and adviser to Yeltsin, Colonel-General Dmitrii Volkogonov, 'Russia's Security Policy and the International Situation', given at the Commission for Security and Disarmament in Copenhagen, 18 May 1993. Coalition theory would predict a Russian–Muslim alliance, but although a programme for this – *Euroasianism* – is gaining some ground in Moscow (Karla Hielscher, 'Der Eurasismus', *Die Neue Gesellschaft/FrankfurterHefte* (Vol. 40, No. 5, May 1993), pp. 465–9), this marriage seems unlikely. Between the three centres, the most dangerous relationship is likely to be the Turko-Russian one. Some of the domestic problems in Russia arise from secessionist *Turkish* peoples within the Federation, and Russia could well define its own situation as a general struggle with 'the Turks'. Zhirinovsky is a Turkist by training. From the Turkish side, Russia is likely to be seen as the main obstacle in Central Asia, and a historical threat. Turkish policy-makers seem particularly interested at present in cultivating relations with Russia's significant neighbours: Poland, Ukraine, etc. (I owe this information to Işil Kazan.)

52. This is the context for defining Europe without the Balkans, i.e. for defining 'the Balkans' as non-European. Events in former Yugoslavia are portrayed as 'typically Balkan behaviour' and 'incomprehensible' to European rationality. The concept of 'Balkanization' has thus been re-activated. However, this strategy seems to have had limited success. The media attention in the West to the war in Yugoslavia seems to have been motivated by a sense of responsibility, precisely because it has happened *in Europe*. The outrage over Bosnia as compared with the neglect of the Armenian-Azerbadjian war for example, seems to be related to the fact that the former is seen to be 'in Europe', while the latter is not. While there may be geopolitical, geoeconomic or even cultural interests for Europeans to define the Balkans as outsiders, and despite the availability of a conceptual apparatus for this purpose, there are indications that this is difficult; these areas are within the circles of Europe. On Balkanisation as a concept and its application in recent years, see James Der Derian, 'S/N: International Theory, Balkanisation and the New World Order', *Millennium* (Vol. 20, No. 3, Winter 1991), pp. 485–506; Milica Bakic-Hayden and Robert M. Hayden, 'Orientalist Variations on the Theme of 'Balkans': Symbolic Geography in Recent Yugoslav Cultural Politics', *Slavic Review* (Vol. 51, No. 1, 1992), pp. 1–15; and Lene Hansen, 'Slovenian Identity: State Building on the Balkan Border', forthcoming (draft available as Working Paper no. 1993/14 from the Centre for Peace and Conflict Research, Copenhagen).
53. See Mouritzen *et al.*, *European Integration.*
54. Comparatively Germany is much more stable; developments are generally much more promising to Germany and a German 'vision of itself'. Therefore, Europe probably has more of a 'French problem' than a 'German problem'. Ulla Holm, *Det Franske Europa* (Århus: Århus University Press, 1993); Ole Wæver, 'Power, Principles and Perspectivism'; and Ole Wæver, Ulla Holm and Henrik Larsen, *The Struggle for 'Europe': French and German Concepts of State, Nation and European Union* (forthcoming).
55. Watson, *Evolution of International Society,* p. 15.
56. See Ole Wæver, 'Conflicts of Vision – Visions of Conflict', in Ole Wæver, Pierre Lemaitre and Elzbieta Tromer (eds), *European Polyphony: Beyond East-West Confrontation* (London: Macmillan, 1989), pp. 283–325, especially pp. 301–5.
57. Private correspondence with Adam Watson.
58. Barry Buzan and Richard Little, 'Reconceptualising the International System and Neorealism: The Need to Accommodate Structural and Functional Differentiation of Units', paper presented to the BISA Conference, York, December 1994; and Daniel Deudney, 'The Philadelphian System: Sovereignty, Arms Control and Balance of Power in the American States-union, ca. 1787–1861', *International Organization* (Vol. 49, No. 2, Spring 1995), pp. 191–228.

59. See, for example, Eugen Weber, *Peasants into Frenchmen: The Modernization of Rural France, 1870–1914* (Stanford, CA: Stanford University Press, 1976). The formation of a 'voluntary' nation state depends on the process of forgetting such formative violence and original diversity: 'Forgetting, I would go so far as to say historical error, is a crucial factor in the creation of a nation.... Yet, the essence of a nation is that all individuals have many things in common, and also that they have forgotten many things', says Ernest Renan in 'What is a Nation?' (1882); reprinted in Homi K. Bhaba (ed.), *Nation and Narration* (London: Routledge, 1990), pp. 8–22, quotes on p. 11.
60. Paul David, 'Clio and the Economics of QWERTY', *American Economic Review* (Vol. 75, 1985), pp. 332–7; Douglas C. North, *Institutions, Institutional Change and Economic Performance* (Cambridge: Cambridge University Press, 1990), ch. 11; Daniel J. Elazar in *Exploring Federalism* (Tuscaloosa and London: University of Alabama Press, 1987), pp. 2-4, argues that polities can come into existence in three ways: conquest, organic development and covenant (choice). 'Conquest tends to produce hierarchically organized regimes ruled in an authoritarian manner.' Organic evolution refers to an improvised process with only a minimum of deliberate constitutional choice. Most of political philosophy has dealt with this second type. 'Covenantal foundings emphasize the deliberate coming together of humans to establish bodies politic in such a way that reaffirm their fundamental equality and retain their basic rights.' These are essentially federal in character, because the separate polities retain their integrity. They are republican and power is shared.
61. Therefore, the metonymic use of 'Brussels' for the EU is really problematic. The EU is not held together – or drawn together – from Brussels, but rather through a *will to centre*.
62. 'The long survival and coexistence of all three types tells against any notion of European state formation as a single, unilinear process, or of the national state – which did, indeed, eventually prevail – as an inherently superior form of government.' Charles Tilly, *Coercion, Capital, and European States: AD 990–1992* (Oxford: Blackwell, 1990), p. 21.
63. Ibid., p. 25.
64. Barry Buzan, Richard Little and Charles Jones, *The Logic of Anarchy: Neorealism to Structural Realism* (New York, NY: Columbia University Press, 1993).
65. Wæver *et al.*, *Identity*, pp. 86–9.
66. Den Boer *et al.*, *The History of the European Idea*, esp. pp. 86ff and 151–3.
67. See the references in note 23.
68. Ole Wæver, 'Identity, Integration and Security: Solving the Sovereignty Puzzle in E.U. Studies', *Journal of International Affairs* (Vol. 48, No. 2, Winter 1995), pp. 389–431; and 'A Security Reading of Political Identifications', *Journal of Common Market Studies* (forthcoming).

69. Bull & Watson (eds), *Expansion*, p. 3.
70. Gerrit W. Gong, *The Standard of 'Civilization' in International Society* (Oxford: Clarendon Press, 1984).
71. Barry Buzan, 'New Patterns of Global Security in the Twenty-First Century', *International Affairs* (Vol. 67, No. 3, 1991), pp. 431–51.
72. Barry Buzan & Gerald Segal, 'Rethinking East Asian Security', *Survival* (Vol. 36, No. 2, Summer 1994), pp. 3–21.
73. For this I am indebted to a private conversation with Michael Barnett.
74. For the argument that a pole is not necessarily a state, see Barry Buzan, Morten Kelstrup, Pierre Lemaitre, Elzbieta Tromer and Ole Wæver, *The European Security Order Recast: Scenarios for the Post-Cold War Era* (London: Pinter, 1990), ch. 10; for the complex multilayered character of the security constellation see Wæver *et al.*, *Identity, Migration*, ch. 4.
75. Wæver *et al.*, *Identity, Migration*, esp. ch. 4.
76. On 'new middle ages' in international relations see, Hedley Bull, *The Anarchical Society*, pp. 254f, 264ff, 285f and 291ff; James Der Derian, *On Diplomacy: A Genealogy of Western Estrangement* (Oxford: Blackwell, 1987), pp. 70 and 79ff; Timothy W. Luke, 'The Discipline of Security Studies and the Codes of Containment: Learning from Kuwait', *Alternatives* (Vol. 16, No. 3, Summer 1991), pp. 315–344, esp. pp. 340f; Ole Wæver, 'Territory, Authority and Identity: The late 20th Century Emergence of Neo-Medieval Political Structures in Europe', paper for the First conference of EUPRA, European Peace Research Association, Florence 8–10 November 1991, 'Identity, Integration'; and John G. Ruggie, 'Territoriality and Beyond: Problematizing Modernity in International Relations', *International Organization* (Vol. 47, No. 1, Winter 1993), pp. 139–74.
77. The advantage of the medieval metaphor is its 'liberating' effect for non-sovereignty based political thinking. Our concepts are *so* marked by the understanding of a system based on state sovereignty, inside/outside and the distinction between domestic and international that it is difficult for us to imagine a system based on a different organization of political space and time. R.B.J. Walker, *Inside/Outside* (Cambridge: Cambridge University Press, 1993). A post-modern 'international' system will most likely be as different from the medieval as from the modern, but since our main intention is to de-modernise our concepts we can use the neo-medieval analogy for the time being.
78. Martin Wight, *Systems of States*, p. 29.

11 International Society and International Security

Barry Buzan

INTRODUCTION

The purpose of this chapter is to take a broad look at the relationship between international society and security.[1] I see security as the interplay between threats and vulnerabilities, and the attempts by a variety of actors to position themselves in this interplay to their best advantage given the circumstances in which they find themselves. In this sense, the logic of security is found in sociopolitical, economic and environmental relations, as well as in military ones.[2] For international society, I start with the classic distinction by Hedley Bull and Adam Watson between international system and international society.[3] By international society we mean a group of states (or, more generally, a group of independent political communities) which not merely form a system, in the sense that the behaviour of each is a necessary factor in the calculations of others, but also have established by dialogue and consent common rules and institutions for the conduct of their relations, and recognise their common interest in maintaining these arrangements.

I have added two refinements to the Bull and Watson position.[4] The first is to establish firm criteria for distinguishing between an international system with, and one without, an international society. As Little points out,[5] the English School's position is that international system, international society and world society all coexist, the question being how strong they are in relation to each other. Broadly speaking, these terms are understood as follows: international system is about power politics among states; international society is about the institutionalisation of shared identity among states; while world society takes individuals, non-state organisations and ultimately the global population as a whole as the focus of global societal identities and arrangements. My position gives ontological priority to the international system, and then defines terms for when a fully-fledged international society can be said to exist. The essential boundary between weak precursors of international society (where the logic of international system is still dominant), and a fully functioning international society (when the logic of international system begins to be significantly moderated) is when the units not only recognise each other as being the same type of entity, but also are prepared to accord each other legally equal status on that basis. Mutual recognition and legal equality signify not only a turning-point in the development of rules and institutions, but also acceptance of a shared identity. This act denies the possibility of suzerain, dominion and imperial relations (though not hegemonic ones), establishes the basis for international law and diplomacy, and sets the minimum conditions for societal relations among culturally diverse units. As Wight puts it: '[i]t would be impossible to have a society of sovereign states unless each state while claiming sovereignty for itself, recognised that every other state had the right to claim and enjoy its own sovereignty as well'.[6] The claim for '*every* other state' is too strong. International society, like the international system, is largely defined by the great powers. It was quite possible for an international society to exist among the (European) great powers that sometimes extinguished states within its compass (Poland), and frequently did not recognise the rights of states outside it in Asia and Africa. This power aspect of international society is one of the keys to understanding its implications for international security.

The second refinement is to deploy Tönnies's sociological distinction between *gemeinschaft* and *gesellschaft* conceptions of society to international society.[7] A *gemeinschaft* society is something organic and traditional, involving bonds of common sentiment, experience and identity. It is an essentially historical conception: societies grow rather than being made. A *gesellschaft* society is contractual and constructed rather than sentimental and traditional. It is more consciously organisational: societies can be made by acts of will. This distinction enables one to move out of the largely historical (*gemeinschaft*) approach of the English School, and to begin thinking in terms of an abstract model about how international societies form, develop, and (possibly) decay.

From this revised position it becomes possible to link thinking about international society to structural realist thinking about the logic of anarchy. In particular, it builds on Kenneth Waltz's idea that where military and economic contact between units is highly developed, the powerful tendency of socialisation (copying behaviour that is successful, or that generates power) and competition (coerced adaptation imposed by the strong on the weak) under anarchy, systematically encourages the development of 'like units'.[8] As the logic of socialisation and competition makes states more alike, it makes the formation of an international society of mutually recognising legal equals easier. This idea identifies the process by which the natural dynamics of anarchic international relations create the conditions for a *gesellschaft* international society to develop. In theoretical terms, it establishes international society on a par with the balance of power as a natural and expected outcome of international relations in anarchic systems in which the states are in close economic and strategic contact with one another. Once it is established that international society can develop along the self-consciously constructed *gesellschaft* route, and that there is a minimal condition for it (mutual recognition as legal equals), then it becomes possible to think about the logic of potential degrees and developments of international society that fill the space between this bottom line, and the point at which the units within the society become effectively federated. At that point they cease to be both an anarchy (i.e. an international system) and an international society. This space is large in terms of the spectrum of possible developments that it contains. The European Union (EU), for example, represents a very fully developed international society, with large numbers of shared norms, rules and institutions coordinating, constraining and facilitating the relationships among its members. Since nearly all existing states accord each other diplomatic recognition, there is a minimal international society embracing virtually the whole of the contemporary international system. Many of its members, however, are not much engaged beyond the minimal requirement.

It is within this space between minimal and highly developed international societies that I want to consider the relationship between international society and security. How does the existence of international society affect the interplay of threats and vulnerabilities? How does it interact with the logic of the balance of power? Before one can address these questions, it is necessary to establish four further general characteristics of international society. The first is that the existence of a *gemeinschaft* international society (a historically given shared culture) is a huge comparative advantage. *De facto*, the development of contemporary international society has been led by Europe, whose own local international society grew out of a shared cultural legacy from classical Hellenistic and Roman civilisations. *Gesellschaft* logic becomes relevant when this regional international society spreads beyond its historical cultural base, becoming the foundation for a wider and more multicultural international society.

The second point is that the development of international society towards its higher levels requires parallel developments in world society. Whereas international society is about common norms, rules, institutions and identities among states, world society would rest on common norms, rules, institutions and identities held by individuals across a whole system. The relationship between international and world society is complex, and arguably contradictory. Towards the minimal end of the international society spectrum there is no necessary relationship between the two. But as one tries to think through the middle and higher levels of international society, it is clear that extensive and deep-running international societies such as that in the EU simply cannot develop without parallel developments in world society.[9] In other words, modern states (ones in which sovereignty is lodged in the population), cannot follow a logic of convergence very far without taking their populations with them.

The third point about international society is that it it does not necessarily, or even probably, develop evenly. Like international systems, and like capitalist economies, and for much the same reasons, international societies are dominated by a logic of uneven development.[10] In practice, this can mean a variety of things. It may mean that some parts of the system are covered by an international society and others not, or that a system contains more than one international society, as during classical times when several independent international systems/societies coexisted on the planet.[11] Even if an international society becomes coterminous with the international system, as has been the case for several decades, it is highly probable that within such a society, states will differ markedly in both the general degree and the specific character of the norms, rules, identities and institutions that they share with others. Some states will form the core of society, sharing many things deeply. Others will form a periphery, perhaps sharing little more than the commitment to mutual recognition as legal equals. In between will lie a range of commitments, with some states leaning towards the centre on some issues and towards the periphery on others. One can view this construction as a formation of rough concentric circles, in which states place themselves at varying degrees of removal from the dense core in terms of the number and degree of their commitments to the norms, rules, identities and institutions that compose international society. The dynamics of uneven development are clearly illustrated by the recurrent debates in Europe about opt-outs from, and multiple-speed variants of integration. A variant on this structure is when two (or more) cores compete, placing themselves within the general framework of mutual recognition, but pursuing different value systems for the higher levels of development of international society. The Cold War can be seen in these terms.

This uneven quality of international society, even when the society is coterminous with the system, is a crucial factor in considering its security implications. At its most extreme, it creates insiders and outsiders, and suggests that they will experience quite different security environments. It can also be expressed as competing groups of insiders seeking to dominate the same outsider periphery. Even within a single global international society, the construction of concentric circles perpetuates an insider-outside logic, albeit of a more relative and complex kind. On this basis, and with due apology to Rob Walker for misappropriating his now fashionable concept of 'inside/outside', I plan to survey the security effects of international society in terms of its impact on both insiders and outsiders.[12] The general distinction between self and other is of course fundamental to international relations generally, and especially so for international security.[13]

The fourth point is that there is no apparent set sequence of development crossing the space between minimal and maximal international societies. Neither in the *gemeinschaft* nor *gesellschaft* perspective is there any reason to think that international society has a fixed pattern of development. Once the mutual-recognition boundary is crossed, it is in principle possible for development to take any one of innumerable paths (or conceivably, to remain static or to decay back to an international system without a fully fledged international society). Assuming that the same structural, *gesellschaft* logic (i.e. socialisation and competition) that pushes states into forming a minimal international society also tends to push them into further development of it, how is one to deal analytically with the fundamental indeterminacy of this developmental process? Recalling that Bull posits three elementary goals as basic to any society: (1) some limits on the use of force, (2) some provision for the sanctity of contracts, and (3) some arrangement for the assignment of property rights, one answer is to divide the possibilities into sectors: military, sociopolitical, and economic (one could also consider an environmental sector, but limits of space forbid exploring this here).[14] Sectors are understood here to represent views of the whole seen through a lens that filters for certain types of actors and activities. Sectors are not portions of a pie that can be cut out from the whole or treated as functionally independent from the whole.[15] However, each sector can be discussed coherently in terms of the logic of its own possible development between minimal and maximal models of international society. Doing so enables one to expose the security agenda more clearly, and this is the approach that will be taken below. Before tackling the security question, it is useful to clarify the possible range of international society developments within these three sectors.

INTERNATIONAL SOCIETY BY SECTOR

Sociopolitical

The first sector covers the shared sociopolitical identity that allows an international society to come into being with the mutual exchange of recognitions of sovereign equality. That exchange forms the minimal end of the spectrum. The maximal end would be confederation, in which a group of states have become sufficiently similar in structure, ideology, outlook, identity and policy that they can share some functions of government. Beyond confederation lies federalism, which, like empire, dissolves anarchy into hierarchy and eliminates both international system and international society. Between mutual recognition and confederation lies a range of possibilities for extending the similarities of units. Do the states share defining principles for political legitimacy, as opposed merely to acquiescing in the power realities of each other's existence? Do they share a political ideology and a form of political organisation (i.e. are they all absolute monarchies or all democracies)? Do they share common legal norms and rules about the relationship between government and society, and society and individual?

In other words, how 'alike' are the 'like-units' that compose an international society? At the bottom line of mutual recognition, they may share only the characteristic of being independent territorial entities, though history may have bequeathed them elements of shared culture or religion. International society can only develop by the expansion of shared norms, and the rules and institutions that rest on them. Such norms can only develop beyond a very basic level if the states themselves become more alike internally, i.c. if the elements that constitute their shared identity expand and thicken. In principle, a set of very unlike states could form a basic international society, though they are more likely to do so if they already constitute a civilisation, that is, if they share some significant elements of culture. The sense that states form a civilisation or a community (European or Western civilisation; the Atlantic or the Arab community) differentiates them from being a mere international system, or even a basic international society. Union (as in the EU) suggests an even higher level of sociopolitical cohesion, and thus domestic similarity. Confederation is unimaginable among units that do not share many important political characteristics in their domestic structures and values.

In one sense, of course, international society is at its strongest precisely when it is able to contain very different states within an agreed system of order. Indeed, some people will see this as its ideal form. Such an arrangement gives a high value to international pluralism in terms of states with diverse sociopolitical systems: literally an 'anarchical society'. Its key rule is live and let live within the single, simple framework of agreement about sovereignty. But although strong in this specific sense of being able to combine order and diversity, such an international society has almost by definition little scope for development or deepening in the sense sketched above, which requires that units become more alike. It is also vulnerable to a kind of spillover logic in which the achievement of a given level of order both lays the foundations, and creates the demand, for further developments of rules, norms and institutions, so putting pressure on the maintenance of domestic diversity.

Military

The second sector comes directly from Bull's point about the need for limits on the use of force. As discussed above, the institution of sovereign equality does pose some (not much) constraint on the resort to force. But implicit in even a very basic international society is a potential contradiction. The mutual acceptance of sovereignty points strongly to a principle of non-intervention in relations between states, but an international society can only transcend the insecurity of a system without society if that mutual recognition also implies the principle that 'no state has a right to establish a form of government which is built upon professed principles of hostility to the government of other nations'.[16] In other words, international society requires that states accept international sociopolitical pluralism: each must be prepared to tolerate the domestic governmental and cultural practices of the others. Failure to do so can be taken as a threat to international society, and thus open an exception to the general rule of non-intervention.

The international order that stems from these ideas does restrain the ways in which force may legitimately be used. But since an international order may require defending, such principles can also justify or provoke the use of force. Restraints of this kind define the minimal end of the spectrum. The maximal end is a pluralist security community in which the members of a group of states neither expect nor prepare to use force in their relationships with each other.[17] In between lies a range of laws of war, arms control agreements, a managed balance of power, confidence-building measures, and suchlike. All of these can be seen as elements of what Robert Jervis has labelled a 'security regime', where states seek to construct reciprocal assurances about their behaviour in order to reduce the impact of the security dilemma and lower the probability of a resort to war.[18] Multilateral alliances may also be important here, especially where, like NATO, they involve voluntary integration of command structures.

As international society develops in the sociopolitical and economic sectors, the values of peace and order become more strongly established both in fact and as a goal. This means that aggressive behaviour becomes less acceptable, which is by no means the same thing as saying that war is ruled out. The random, self-serving aggression that is quite normal in unmediated international systems, and even in ones with basic international societies (eighteenth-century Europe), becomes increasingly unacceptable, and international society begins to claim the right to intervene against states that threaten to disturb the peace. The First World War, and even more so, the Second, raised the idea that particular types of government might in and of themselves be unacceptable (absolute monarchies, fascist states), creating an acute contradiction between non-intervention and international society. Fascism, with its glorification of war, and its extreme manifestation of xenophobic, expansionist, aggressive nationalism provided a clear justification for overriding the rule of non-intervention. The occupation and political reconstruction of Germany, Italy and Japan after 1945 went a considerable distance towards narrowing the acceptable range of ideology in the international system. Diversity was acceptable, but the right of self-determination no longer carried the right to have governments that threatened aggressive attack on the international order. The ending of the Cold War can be seen as having narrowed the range of acceptability even further by having largely eliminated communist states. The curious episode of the second Gulf War in 1990–1 can also be seen in this way. Internal nastiness is broadly acceptable given the still-important general principle of non-intervention, but external aggression, especially the annexation of another country, is not. The military sector is thus linked to developments in the other sectors. As international society develops across the sectors, non-intervention norms may be increasingly overridden by the desire to defend a more complex and homogenous international order.

Economic

The third sector combines aspects of Bull's points about property and contracts, and concerns the willingness of states to open themselves sufficiently to become economically interdependent. Looked at from a different direction, this might also be seen as the willingness of states (albeit sometimes under very powerful external pressure, viz. Japan and China in the middle of the nineteenth century) to allow the development of an international economy among them. The minimal end of the spectrum in this sector requires that states accept/and or develop the basic conditions for international trade: some common units of value and account, and laws that allow goods to cross borders in both directions. The spectrum rises through a sequence of stages, each building on the one before it: most-favoured nation agreements (MFN) (in which parties to a trade agreement extend the agreed tariff concession to others participating in the reciprocal system); free trade areas (where quota restrictions and tariff barriers between participating countries are removed, but each keeps its own restrictive arrangements against the rest of the world); customs unions (where a common external tariff is maintained against non-members); common markets (where members abolish restrictions on the movement of goods, capital, services and labour among them). The maximal end is an economic union, in which the members also harmonise their economic and social policies. An economic union effectively creates a single 'national' economy, and beyond it lies full political federation. Movement upwards through this spectrum implies not only increasing openness among the states and societies involved (i.e. increasing the permeability of their boundaries), but also increasing harmonisation of their domestic legal and administrative rules and structures. The debate about the 'democratic deficit' in the EU provides an illustration of the linkage between economic and political integration, or at least of the difficulty of allowing too big a gap to open up between the two sectors.

In parallel with the view that international society might prefer sociopolitical diversity to homogeneous development, it is theoretically possible that an international society could develop on mercantilist principles, rather than the liberal ones just outlined. Such an arrangement would be based on a substantial degree of economic and social closure as a shared value among the states concerned. It would seek to avoid the competitive, zero-sum attitudes associated with classical mercantilism, and focus on managed trade. Such an arrangement would also by definition have little scope for development. It would be aimed at preserving the autarchy and independence of the individual national political economies. Compromise, middle-ground, positions are also possible, such as that which emerged with the Bretton Woods regime after the Second World War, which Ruggie has labelled 'embedded liberalism'.[19]

The possibilities for development in these three sectors can be summarised as in Table 11.1. Separating these sectors analytically does not mean that they are independent of each other. It could be the case that all three sectors advance together, and it is difficult to imagine very high levels of economic integration without accompanying developments in the sociopolitical sector. But separate development is possible, and there is no iron law that suggests that any one sector has to take the lead. For example, one would normally expect international societies that were well developed in the sociopolitical sector to be equally far along in the military sector, though the converse is not necessarily true. Even states in a rather basic sociopolitical international society might be able to agree on quite sophisticated war-avoidance regimes.

Table 11.1 Possibilities for development in international society by sector

Levels of Development	Sociolpol. sector	Military sector	Economic sector
Maximal	Confederation	Security Community	Economic union
Middling	Political union	Security Regimes	Common market
Minimal	Mutual Dipl. recognition	Mutual Dipl. recognition	MFN agreements

The strategy in what follows will be to look at both insiders and outsiders, and the spectrum between them, in terms of these three sectors, keeping an open attitude towards the possible range of development of international society within each sector. The aim is to develop an overall sense of the security agenda that international society raises for insiders and outsiders, and to see what the security issues, and their advantages and disadvantages, are from both perspectives.

THE SECURITY EFFECTS OF INTERNATIONAL SOCIETY ON INSIDERS AND OUTSIDERS

International society easily creates insiders and outsiders. When an international system is only partly covered by an international society (or there is more than one international society in existence), then there are absolute insiders and outsiders by definition. In historical perspective, this has been the normal case. The ancient Greek, the modern European and the classical Chinese international societies have all seen outsiders as barbarians. When the whole of the international system is covered by an international society, as in recent decades, then the picture is more complicated. Such an international society will almost certainly be internally differentiated by uneven development. Insiders and outsiders then becomes not an all-or-nothing distinction, but a question of how states are positioned in relation to the most developed core of international society. States can be relative insiders and outsiders to the extent that they do not share some of the values, or participate in some of the regimes, generated by the core. These positions are summarised in Table 11.2.

A rather large analytical framework is opened up by the interplay between the spectrum of insiders and outsiders on the one hand, and the three sectoral spectrums of degrees of development of international society

Table 11.2 Insiders and outsiders in international society

Position in International Society		
Absolute Insiders		*Absolute Outsiders*
Inner circles (Core)	Outer circles (Periphery)	Non-members Members of other international societies
	Relative insiders or outsiders	

on the other. It is not feasible in the space available to discuss all of the security possibilities within this framework. The aim in what follows will simply be to suggest how international society affects the interplay of threats and vulnerabilities, and consequently what range and type of security and insecurity issues it raises.

Sociopolitical

The most obvious security consequences in this sector hinge on recognition. For insiders, the status of sovereign equality gives even less powerful units some protection against elimination. The formal mutual recognitions required under sovereign equality serve to institutionalise the external status of sovereignty. Without an international society, units can only assert their claim to autonomy, and establish it by sustained and successful defence against challengers. With an international society, units can have their claims validated by the recognition of others. This validation gives them standing as sovereign members of a community of like units, and reinforces, though as the Poles know by no means guarantees, their right to exist as an independent entity. As the Japanese understood very quickly after the imposition of Western power on them in the middle of the nineteenth century, the right to exist adds importantly to the security of units by defining the boundaries of legitimacy and order within which they function.[20] In contemporary international society, legal equality has been the basis for the delegitimisation of many threats of intervention, annexation, secession and coercion that were earlier seen as part of the natural behaviour of states in an anarchic system.[21] In extreme cases, as demonstrated in recent times by cases such as Somalia, Lebanon, Cambodia, Bosnia and Chad, external sovereignty can even keep in existence states whose internal sovereignty is very weak. External recognition of secessions, as in the cases of Bangladesh, Yugoslavia and the Soviet Union, seals the internal demise of larger units. The absence of diplomatic recognition between states creates the possibility of legitimate annexation, as in relations between the two Koreas and the two Chinas. For Taiwan, the struggle to sustain some international diplomatic recognition in its zero-sum game with mainland China is an essential part of its security policy.

For outsiders, non-recognition raises the threat of exposure to a range of unequal treatments at the hands of insiders. At best, this involves the imposition of a 'standard of civilisation' on relations between insiders and outsiders. Outsiders find themselves subjected to unequal treaties that privilege the nationals of insiders in various ways (e.g. extraterritoriality), and restrict the exercise of sovereignty. Relations between Europe and much of Asia had this quality during the nineteenth century, a story excellently told by Gong.[22] Elements of this 'standard of civilisation' approach reappeared recently in Europe, when some of the post-Cold War successor states were confronted with conditions regarding democracy, human rights and economic law before being accorded recognition.

At worst, non-recognition means that outsiders are not recognised at all by insiders. Their sociopolitical institutions are not considered to embody legitimacy, and their territory is considered to be politically empty and available for occupation. They may not even be recognised as fully human, so facing the risk of being treated either like beasts of burden, and so enslaved, or like vermin, and so eradicated. Some parts of the European expansion into the Americas, Africa and Australia approached this extreme. Between the exterminations in Tasmania and parts of Africa and the Americas, and the unequal treaties between Europe and such Asian countries as Japan, China, Siam and Turkey, lay a whole range of degrees of unequal treatment. Treaties were made with chiefs, princes and kings in India, the Middle East and Africa that subordinated their polities in varying degrees to European colonisation.

This threat to outsiders of course presupposes that insiders are stronger, and able to impose their will. This is not always the case. The Ottoman and Chinese empires, for example, as well as Japan, were for hundreds of years strong enough to impose their own conditions on contact with Europeans, only succumbing to European power during the nineteenth century. These cultures considered themselves to be the insiders of their own international societies, and treated the Europeans as barbarian outsiders.

Beyond simple recognition, which lies at the border between international systems with and without international society, lies the sociopolitical spectrum of development within international society. This too has security implications for both insiders and outsiders. For insiders, the development of international society in terms of thickening layers of sociopolitical norms, rules and institutions has some very significant security benefits. Most obviously, such development must almost automatically be accompanied by progressive reductions of military threat among the participants. As ideological, legal and institutional differences narrow, and as habits of cooperation, transparency, familiarity and shared sense of community grow, the resort to force diminishes as a viable or acceptable instrument of policy. This process is illustrated by the growth of a sense of political community in Europe, and across the North Atlantic, since 1945, and to a lesser extent by the development of ASEAN since 1967.

This benefit may well be offset by the rise of threats in the societal sector to states participating in advanced forms of sociopolitical international society. Here the defining case is the EU, which is well within the upper realms of possible development in this sector. For the members of the EU, borders have begun to dissolve for many purposes, and sovereignty is already significantly divided between the state and union levels. This development has begun to create a sense of threat to societal identity in many of the participating and prospective member countries.[23] It has proved difficult to find the foundations for any collective sense of European identity that is anything like as strong as existing national identities.[24] This failure at the union level is matched by concern in many of the European countries, especially those such as Denmark, Norway and France, in which state and society are closely linked, that the weakening of the state will lead to the undermining of society, and a breakdown of the ability of national identity to reproduce itself. These societies risk losing their state shell, and being cast into the wider European Union political pool to compete naked with others. Some doubt that under these circumstances they could maintain many aspects of language and culture that are part of their national traditions. One fear is of population-mixing and migration. Another is economic and cultural homogenisation by wider market forces unrestrained by a protective state to which I shall return. This threat to societal security marks a disjuncture between international and world society, where development at the state level has outrun that at the individual level. In the European case, as illustrated by the problems over Maastricht, it may pose a more dangerous threat to the further integration of the EU than resistance from political elites.[25] Further development of international society could actually stimulate nationalist reactions.

For outsiders, the existence of a dominant international society can also pose societal and political threats, especially when that society embodies a hegemonic centre of power. Imperial Europe, and today the West, provide examples of this type of threat, and classical China another. In both cases, these powerful societies posed not only politico-military threats to those around them (the issue of recognition discussed above), but also sociopolitical ones. In the modern era, cultural westernisation has been as big a threat to some societies as direct Western domination. For large parts of the Islamic world, and also for much of East and South Asia, the individualistic, secular and material values of the West, not to mention many aspects of its lifestyle, are direct and serious assaults on indigenous cultural traditions. A dominant international society cannot help but project its culture and values abroad. The bigger and more powerful it is, the more likely that its culture and values will take on at least some of the appearance of a universal norm. Threats do of course operate the other way, as witness current concerns in the West about Islam, but these are relatively minor compared to those going in the opposite direction.[26]

These threats are all the more insidious because the dominant culture will be welcomed by some sections within outsider societies as a liberating force, as is the case with Western culture in the Islamic world and Asia, and so not be seen as a threat at all. One aspect of this threat is that westernisation undermines the ability of other cultures to reproduce themselves. It changes language, values and styles in ways that transform, or even extinguish, indigenous cultural patterns. Another aspect is more directly political. Contact with a hegemonic international society can easily threaten the legitimacy of indigenous political frameworks. Few places, for example, have succeeded in sustaining absolute monarchical rule in the face of a dominant Western international society that projects norms of popular sovereignty. It could now be argued that the same has happened with totalitarian communism, leaving Cuba, China and one or two other Asian states hanging on to an ideology and a form of government that is widely seen as delegitimised. Countries outside international society – most notably revolutionary states – or only sharing the basics of mutual recognition, thus come under intense political pressure even though there may be no threat to their political independence as such.[27] One could trace a similar pattern in the relationship between the core and the periphery of classical Chinese civilisation.

In contemporary international relations, the tension over human rights is perhaps the clearest example of this type of threat. Western notions of human rights represent a major intellectual and political tradition projected by a powerful group of states lying at the core of international society. But the notions of individualism, equality of the sexes, equality of the races, and suchlike that are part of this package are not shared by some other cultures. To the extent that these notions take on the quality of universal values within international society they threaten even peripheral members or outsiders. The Islamic world and China are currently the most noticeable victims of this homogenising and delegitimising threat.

It is also possible to read the whole story of the anti-apartheid campaign against South Africa in this way. One could argue that South Africa was a peculiarly-placed country in relation to decolonisation.[28] It occupied a boundary position on the spectrum of European colonisations in that its white population was too small to overwhelm or obliterate the native peoples (as was done in the Americas and Australia) and too big and too long established to pull up stakes and return to Europe (as in the rest of Africa and Asia). This dilemma made the decolonisation era extremely difficult for South Africa. Its domestic response of apartheid triggered a widespread international rejection of the state's external sovereignty, effectively casting it out of international society. This was in spite of the fact that it was virtually the only state in sub-Saharan Africa with a plausible claim to internal sovereignty, and that its domestic political affairs, should, in principle, have been subject to the rule of non-intervention. This principle was, however, overridden by widespread repugnance against such an explicitly racist political policy, and by the contradiction between South Africa's constitution and the newly-independent black-ruled states to the north of it that decolonisation had brought into international society. Regardless of one's moral stand on the question of apartheid, it is a very clear case of a wider international society imposing its values on the domestic political life of a peripheral state.

Cases of this sort raise the thorny question of intervention as a security issue in international society. Defining intervention is notoriously tricky: is all interaction intervention? Perceptions of what is and is not intervention vary sharply according to whether states are open or closed. Closed states see as threatening many aspects of economic and societal interaction that are seen as normal behaviour between open states. In the Soviet Union, for example, blue jeans and rock music were (rightly) seen as threats to the cultural and political project of the Soviet state. The most important sense of intervention is explicit, focused, coercive action against a state aimed at overriding its sovereignty in order to change a particular aspect of its behaviour. As argued above, the foundational principle of international society is non-intervention. The key purpose of exchanging mutual recognitions of sovereignty is to stabilise a pluralist political order on the basis of mutual acceptance. Even in its most basic form, however, international society legitimises intervention against regimes that threaten its established order. The question of intervention becomes more complicated as international society develops and differentiates into concentric circles. In reality, the arrangement of 'concentric circles' will be messy. There may, as during the Cold War, be more than one core of international society. Concentric circles will not be neatly distinct and symmetrical, but overlapping and irregular in shape. One could perhaps try to draw a picture of it in terms of state membership in the numerous regimes that make up the fabric of international society. Some states (those at the core) would be members of large numbers of regimes. A few (at the periphery) would only be members in the sense of exchanging diplomatic recognition and having a seat in the UN General Assembly. The rest would be distributed between these two extremes, being members of some regimes, but not others. Different mixtures of membership (for example, GATT but not the NPT, the EU but not the Exchange Rate Mechanism [ERM]) in this intermediate group produce the messy concentric circles. In order to think about the issue of intervention we can simplify this complexity into three classes of states: firstly, core members, belonging to most regimes (absolute insiders); secondly, peripheral members, belonging to some regimes but not others, and minimal members, basically sharing little more than diplomatic recognition (both relative insiders, and therefore for some purposes outsiders). Thirdly are non-member pariah states outside even the outer circle of diplomatic recognition (absolute outsiders) – see Table 11.2 above.

One way of understanding most regimes is that they constitute agreed, or at least accepted, forms of intervention. Most regimes involve states harmonising their behaviour in some way, and so also contain provisions for checking on compliance, and some mechanisms for resolving disputes. Many aspects of the nuclear non-proliferation regime, for example, require states to put their nuclear facilities under IAEA safeguards. This involves, *inter alia*, providing accounts and allowing in teams of IAEA inspectors. Among consenting states, regimes thus formalise patterns of intervention in agreed areas and under agreed terms and conditions. But as already noted, a dominant international society projects its values well beyond its core members whether it wants to or not. Simply by representing a large group of powerful states, such an international society endows its values with a quasi-universal quality. For the core members, such regimes enhance security. They make for reassurance about each other's behaviour, allow increased interaction along agreed lines, and replace potential bilateral frictions and interventions with generalised rules and procedures.

The security problem arises in relations between the core members on the one hand, and peripheral and minimal members on the other. Do core members have the right to intervene to uphold their values even against states that are not parties to the particular regime concerned? In other words, do the values of the core international society actually acquire universal standing, regardless of whether individual states choose to adhere to them or not? One example of this question is the Nuclear Non-Proliferation Treaty (NPT). When members such as Iraq and North Korea break the rules, intervention is clearly legitimised, even though it may not be explicitly authorised in the treaty. But what if non-members, now a rather small minority, break the rules? If India or Pakistan acquire nuclear weapons, does the international community have the right to intervene against them (a question distinct from, though related to, whether they have the power to do so)? Similar questions could be asked with respect to human rights regimes. The rules of basic international society suggest that the answer must be no. Sovereign states cannot be bound by what they have not explicitly agreed to. But higher levels of development in the core of international society mean that states agree to constrain and coordinate their behaviour for all sorts of purposes. If those core developments do have some universal status, then they threaten peripheral and minimal members with intervention. This threat might be viewed as simply imperial – the core of international society taking on the traditional prerogative of great powers to impose order on the international system, pretending that their own values are universal ones.[29] It might also be seen as more legitimate to the extent that the values of the core really had acquired universal standing. Either way, for the relative insider members of the wider international society, this tendency, for higher level developments in the core to be projected over the whole, constitutes a serious threat. In a multi-level international society security issues arise in the tensions between the levels, with higher-level developments tending to undermine the fundamental idea of sovereignty/non-intervention for those members not in the core.

MILITARY

In the military sector, the great benefit to insiders from the development of international society is a progressive reduction of the security dilemma. This effect begins even with a very basic international society, and gets stronger if the society develops military security regimes. When a group of states becomes a pluralist security community, military threat in relations among them is eliminated by definition.

When a basic international society is formed, much in the military sector remains the same. In particular, the anarchic system features of balance of power and war carry over as before. As witness the history of Europe during the eighteenth century, states in such an international society still need to seek security by adjusting to shifts in the distribution of power and status, and war and alliance remain legitimate instruments of policy.[30] But one major change that comes with the advent of even a rather basic international society is that political order and the balance of power become explicit foreign policy goals for many, though not necessarily all, states. In his analysis of early modern Europe, Holsti puts much emphasis on the development of anti-hegemonic goals as a driving force in the negotiations that produced major war-termination agreements at Westphalia (1648) and Vienna (1814–15).[31] Most of the major powers were actively concerned to take measures that would prevent any one state, or any one dynasty, from dominating Europe. This goal reflected a passionate concern to protect the system of independent sovereign states. Adam Watson has called this feature of international society *raison de système*: the legitimation of anarchy as defined by international society.[32]

Once the balance of power is recognised as a possible basis for international order, then the great powers can, if they agree, consciously manage their relations to preserve a balance.[33] In the nineteenth century this was done by agreements over allocation of territory and colonies. During the Cold War it was achieved by superpower agreements on levels of nuclear armament. In this way the principle of balance can become a means of reducing conflict among the great powers, and of moderating the security dilemma among them. It also gives great powers some security, but not a guarantee, against elimination from the system. Conscious pursuit of the balance of power as an ordering principle of great power relations reinforces the right of great powers to exist, and institutionalises an oligopolistic view of international order. In basic international societies, a development along these lines may, as is well established, increase threats to minor powers or units outside, or sometimes, as in the case of Poland, inside, the society, who can find themselves being used as resources for adjustments by the great powers.

Between the rather marginal security improvements of mutual recognition and a managed balance of power, and the virtual cessation of the security dilemma in a fully-fledged security community, lies a whole spectrum of possibilities within the idea of security regimes. In general, these are designed to, and do, reduce the level or the significance of military threats that states within international society perceive from each other. They reflect the development of norms and rules about war-prevention as a shared goal. There are many possibilities, all quite well understood in both theory and practice. States can reduce either or both of their levels of armament or military mobilisation. They can agree to ban or restrict types of weapons seen as especially threatening. They can manage their relations so that each remains vulnerable to the threats of the other, as in the 'mutually assured destruction' (MAD) formula of Golden Age deterrence theory. They can alter their modes of military deployment so as to reduce the immediacy of threat (non-offensive defence). They can increase the transparency of their military activities so that other states are better able to judge the level, quality, and readiness of their forces relative to their own. Improved transparency can also involve notifications of military exercises, and allowing in outside observers, so as to ameliorate fears of surprise attack. States can even integrate their command, training and logistical structures in such a way as to reduce both the psychological and the physical independence required for war.

Security regimes along these lines generally reduce perceptions of threat and so enhance the security of those that participate in them. They may lead to changing perceptions of the whole enmity relationship, and a shift towards security community, as happened in Europe during the late 1980s. There may, however, be back-eddies in this general current that actually reduce the military security of participants in security regimes. These mostly involve cheating by one or more participants, who use the regime to increase the vulnerability, or reduce the strength, of other actors, while secretly maintaining their own. The cultivation of nuclear weapons options by Iraq and North Korea while remaining members of the NPT are classic examples. Mutual fears of cheating during the long history of the Strategic Arms Limitation Treaty (SALT) talks between the United States and the Soviet Union are another example. As is well recognised, the rewards for cheating in disarmament agreements rise sharply as the level of forces allowed drops towards zero. Perfect inspection is impossible, and any state that succeeded in retaining even a handful of nuclear weapons would have a considerable advantage. A variant on this theme is the abuse of transparency arrangements to gather data for strategic targeting in a surprise attack. Open-skies-type arrangements, in which states seek to reassure each other about their military intentions by allowing regular photographic reconnaissance of each other's military facilities, are vulnerable to this type of abuse.

Some security-decreasing dangers are inherent to anarchical societies, whereas others may come from badly designed, or badly implemented security regimes. Some people in the United States (and probably also in the Soviet Union), felt less secure as a result of the SALT treaties than they did with open-ended arms racing. They felt that the risk of cheating within arms-control arrangements was greater than the costs and risks of unrestrained military competition. There is also the possibility that security regimes involving substantial measures of disarmament, or restraints on weapons, though successfully reducing the security dilemma among the participating states, increase it between them and outsiders. Outsiders may gain in relative military strength, as China has done because of the SALT, INF and START agreements between the Soviet Union (and its successors) and the Western powers. A variant on this logic is that the core members of international society lose their military inclinations because of their very success in reducing the security dilemma among themselves. If outsiders remain militarily hard, then insiders could be storing up serious threats for the longer term.

This line of reasoning suggests a possible security benefit for outsiders (in this case, the relative insiders who are not part of the specific military security regimes, though they may well be part of the wider, lower-level, international society), who become relatively stronger as the insiders weaken themselves. There are however two significant sources of threat to these outsiders, and even more so to absolute outsiders. The first is that the security arrangements in the core may enable its members to operate militarily with more effect against outsiders. If the core members are not threatening each other militarily, this can make them stronger against outsiders even if they do not constitute an alliance for this purpose. One example of this is the European powers during the nineteenth century. Although the European powers could, and occasionally did, make war against each other during this period, the Concert of Europe functioned quite effectively as a security regime.[34] It not only reduced the resort to war within Europe, but enabled the European powers to coordinate their external expansion. China and Japan both came under coordinated European military pressure, and at the Berlin Conference of 1884, Africa was partitioned by an agreement that reflected calculations about the European balance of power. The security regime within Europe thus worked to the disadvantage of outsiders. Indeed, it could be argued that external expansion was necessary to the stability of the security regime in Europe.

A somewhat different example of the same phenomenon is the contest between the West and the Soviet Union during the Cold War. This event can be seen simply as a standard alliance in which the United States combined its power with Western Europe and Japan to contain the Soviet Union. But it could be argued that underlying this was a more important and durable phenomenon: the emergence of a security community among the major centres of capitalist power. In the long run, it was more important that the United States, Western Europe and Japan had eliminated military rivalry from their own relations, than that they had agreed to stand together against Soviet power. The security community among them meant that they stood, in effect, back to back in military terms. Even if their alliance was militarily inconsequential, as in the case of the US and Japan, where Japan contributed very little additional military strength, the point was that these three centres of power did not have to worry about each other in military terms. This enabled them both to focus their military strength on the Soviet Union, and to play more effectively in the longer-run economic game. It was the combined economic growth of the Western powers and Japan that eventually defeated the Soviet challenge. The continuation of this Western security community in the post-Cold War era continues to give the Western powers a massive advantage against any potential military challengers.

The second significant source of military threat to outsiders arises from the use of force or coercion by the inner circle(s) of international society to project core values onto outsiders. These values may be derived either from the military sector (for example, arms control, non-proliferation, war prevention) or from other sectors (most notably human rights). This is the question about the legitimacy or not of intervention discussed above. The legitimacy of intervention is clearer when a state is found to be violating the rules of a regime to which it has subscribed, than when it is in violation of norms promoted by the core, but not specifically accepted by the state in question. As members of the NPT, Iraq and North Korea can expect to have action taken against them if they break the rules, though even here large questions arise about what level of intervention is justified. Does infringement by a member state of the NPT rules justify the bombing of its nuclear facilities? The question is more difficult as regards non-members. India and Pakistan are not members of the NPT, but the NPT represents a nearly global non-proliferation regime. Does international society have any right to act against these states if they act to acquire nuclear weapons? The legal and political arguments may or may not give a clear answer to this question, but such states have to take a calculated risk that international society will seek to impose its own norms upon them by citing those norms as a universal standard. Outsiders face risks of this sort on chemical and biological weapons, and ballistic missiles, as well as on nuclear weapons. At a lower level, outsiders may simply face the attempts of the core to impose its own standards on them by measures to restrict supply. The London Club of nuclear suppliers, the Missile Technology Control Regime and (the recently defunct) CoCom all have or had this function.

One should not lose sight of the fact that most of the framework of the contemporary international system was created by precisely such an imperial imposition of values. The European powers reshaped the whole world into their own political image. Decolonisation left behind a system of sovereign states, and an international society, modelled on the European experience. Many of these states were badly made, and yet organisation into a sovereign-state form remains essential to achieving political recognition. For many of the peoples involved, this legacy merely trades the insecurity of being an absolute outsider for the insecurity of being pawns in a long and often violent process of state-making. The newness and instability of many of its members poses an awkward dilemma for international society. The international society itself rests upon, and has to support, the process of state formation. It also supports non-intervention, and values international peace and order. But the process of state formation is itself violent and disorderly, often spilling over borders and/or violating norms. The violence of state-making is an old story.[35] Massacres in Rwanda and Cambodia are not dissimilar from those in Europe during the Thirty Years War. Ethnic cleansing in Yugoslavia and Iraq has parallels in the expulsions of Jews from Spain and Huguenots from France centuries ago. The irony is that for many individual human beings, the greatest insecurity comes from the very process by which international society has been, and is being, created.

Economic

The question of economic security is at the best of times fraught with logical complexities.[36] Capitalism as an economic system requires the individuals, firms and states participating in it to endure a high degree of insecurity as a necessary condition of participation. Without such insecurity, the system cannot work. In this sense, the core question for international political economy is how to find the best tradeoff between economic efficiency, with its associated insecurity, on the one hand, and the level of security necessary to sustain societal and political order, on which the functioning of the market ultimately depends, on the other. Within this general problematic lie a number of characteristic economic security issues for both insiders and outsiders.

For insiders, the main threats result from being caught up in liberal economic regimes. Participation in such regimes requires states to open their economies, and thus their societies, to penetration and competition from outside. In return they get the right to compete in the markets of others. This fundamentally simple arrangement quickly becomes extremely complex as powerful independent actors (multinational firms, banks, criminal organisations) occupy the economic space opened up by states, and as intricate regimes covering trade and finance develop. In the economic sector, international society can quite quickly develop to the point at which the fundamental political framework of the international system begins to be called into question.[37] Within this framework, insiders face two sorts of threats, first that the system itself will become unstable, and second that the operation of the system will destabilise their domestic life.

The causes of system instability are complex and contested, and need not concern us in detail here. Perhaps because of weakening leadership, perhaps because of conflicts over leadership, perhaps because of collapse of the supply of credit due to overextension of liability, or perhaps because of nationalist reaction against trade competition, liberal international economic orders are vulnerable to collapse. When they do crash, as in the late 1920s, they inflict huge welfare losses on the states that had been participating in them. Foreign markets close, trade and credit shrink, and economies that had adapted themselves to an open system have to make massive adjustments. This threat is a background risk for all participants in liberal economic regimes.

Even when such regimes are functioning effectively, they still pose threats to insiders. The most obvious threat is of losing in the economic competition. As industrialisation spreads, and as more countries participate in the liberal international economy, competition intensifies. As there are more suppliers of goods and services, so competition increases. As competition increases, states and societies have to adapt themselves ever more frequently and deeply in order to remain competitive. Unless the overall size of the market expands more quickly than the number of suppliers, the number of losers will increase. The domestic consequences of losing mean the closure of whole industries with consequent rises in unemployment and social dislocation. Even winners may have to abandon older industrial or agricultural activities in which they can no longer compete, while attempting to move up-market to higher-tech areas in which they can still construct a comparative advantage.

These processes pose threats of social homogenisation even for winners. The cost of broad spectrum openness (i.e. in both trade and finance) is loss of ability to defend cultural distinctiveness, and exposure to powerful forces of internationalisation that compete with local traditions. The demand for level playing-fields in economic relations rapidly has consequences for society and culture. To the extent that cultural distinctiveness is valued, economic liberalisation is a threat. For losers, there is in addition the threat of social and political instability arising from failure to reap the rewards of the global market. The most obvious cases here are Third World countries crushed by debt burdens, and squeezed between IMF pressures for structural adjustment programmes, and rioting by the poor who can no longer afford the basic necessities of subsistence. Many of the successor states to the ex-Soviet Union also illustrate the costs of losing (albeit not by the usual route), with whole industrial sectors wiped out and large sections of the population facing impoverishment. To the extent that the ultimate end of liberal economic regimes is to free capital from its dependence on labour (by pursuing efficiency through automation, and by escaping from national regulation by internationalising markets), the entire system contains a sociopolitical time-bomb of rising unemployment. Such circumstances create the conditions for nationalist reactions against the whole regime.[38]

For outsiders, the main threat is of stagnation and relative decline in power. For all of its problems, the liberal economic regime is relatively successful in encouraging economic growth. Indeed, the history of the twentieth century can be read as the triumph of liberalism as a system for generating power. Liberal regimes triumphed in severe tests of war, both hot and cold, to prove themselves against autocratic, fascist and communist challengers. As the communist states discovered to their cost, a regime of economic closure cannot in the long run compete with one that is open. Closure restricts economies of scale and stifles incentives for innovation. It allows either preservation of a local culture (Bhutan, up to a point Japan, China, India), the preservation of a self-interested political order (Argentina, Brazil, Burma), or the conducting of major sociopolitical experiments (Soviet Union, China, Iran), but only (with the notable exception of Japan) at the cost of relative impoverishment and long-term decline in power. Outsiders lose access to markets and finance. They may also find themselves exposed to pressure from international society in the form of political or military conditions in return for aid, transfer of technology or access to markets. American pressure on China over human rights, and on Pakistan over nuclear weapons illustrates the point.

In the economic sector, one is hard put to make judgments about which arrangements produce more security, and which less. The choices on offer seem to be about different types and mixtures of security and insecurity, which come in exceptionally complex packages.

CONCLUSIONS: INTERNATIONAL SOCIETY AND INTERNATIONAL SECURITY

Disaggregating international society into sectors as I have done here produces a rather complicated picture of the relationship between international society and international security. The most obvious conclusion is that there *is* a relationship, and an important one, between the two. The existence (or not) of a fully-fledged international society affects security relations between states in a wide variety of ways. The second conclusion is that international society is not an unmixed blessing in security terms for states. On balance, it is a security benefit for insiders. But as revolutionary states and pariahs quickly discover, being an absolute outsider is extremely dangerous, so there are big advantages even to minimal membership. But international society does generate security problems for insiders. The most obvious of these is societal, where the growth of internationalism undermines the ability of local cultures to maintain and reproduce themselves. The development of international society in the economic sector is a major element in generating these societal threats, and also carries serious potential economic security risks for losers. International society generally exacerbates the security problems of outsiders by confronting them with the risk that outside values will be imposed upon them. Absolute outsiders are at serious risk across the board when international society is powerful. Even relative insiders, who are outsiders for specific regimes, face the risk of intervention from the core.

Although it produces a rather complicated picture, there would seem to be merit in trying to blend international society with security analysis. One gain is that the idea of insiders and outsiders generates useful insights into the dynamics of security relations. Another is that international society provides a necessary holistic backdrop against which to consider the difficult question of the rights and legitimacies of intervention. A third is that security analysis raises some interesting questions about international society, linking it squarely into mainstream Realist and International Political Economy thinking about the international system.

NOTES

I would like to thank David Armstrong, Lene Hansen, Richard Little, Ole Wæver and Jaap de Wilde for comments on an earlier draft of this chapter.

1. The chapter can be read as a direct follow-on from my 'From International System to International Society: Structural Realism and Regime Theory Meet the English School', *International Organization*, (Vol. 47, No. 3, 1993), pp. 327-52.
2. Barry Buzan, *People, States and Fear: An Agenda for International Security Studies in the Post-Cold War Era* (Hemel Hempstead: Harvester-Wheatsheaf, 1991).
3. Hedley Bull and Adam Watson (eds), *The Expansion of International Society* (Oxford: Oxford University Press, 1984), p. 1.
4. Buzan, 'From International System'.
5. Richard Little, 'Neorealism and the English School: A Methodological, Ontological and Theoretical Reassessment' (unpublished manuscript, 1994).

6. Martin Wight, *Systems of States* (Leicester: Leicester University Press, 1977), p. 135.
7. F. Tönnies, *Gemeinschaft und Gesellschaft* (Leipzig: Fues's Verlag, 1887).
8. Kenneth N. Waltz, *Theory of International Politics* (Reading MA: Addison-Wesley, 1979), pp. 74–7 and 128–9.
9. Buzan, 'From International System'.
10. Barry Buzan and Richard Little, 'The Idea of International System: Theory Meets History', *International Political Science Review* (Vol. 15, No. 3, 1994), pp. 231–56.
11. Ibid.
12. R.B.J. Walker, *Inside/Outside: International Relations as Political Theory* (Cambridge, Cambridge University Press, 1993).
13. Iver Neumann and Jennifer Welsh, 'The Other in European Self–Definition: An Addendum to the Literature on International Society', *Review of International Studies*, (Vol. 17, No. 4 1991), pp. 327-48.
14. Hedley Bull, *The Anarchical Society: A Study of Order in World Politics* (London: Macmillan, 1977), pp. 4–5.
15. Barry Buzan, Charles Jones and Richard Little, *The Logic of Anarchy: Neorealism to Structural Realism* (New York, Columbia University Press, 1992), pp. 30–3.
16. Martin Wight, 'Western Values in International Relations', in Herbert Butterfield and Martin Wight (eds), *Diplomatic Investigations* (London: Allen and Unwin, 1966), p. 99.
17. Karl Deutsch *et al.*, *Political Community and the North Atlantic Area* (Princeton, NJ: Princeton University Press, 1957), pp. 1-4.
18. Robert Jervis, 'Security Regimes', *International Organization*, (Vol. 36, No. 2, 1982), pp. 357–78; and 'From Balance to Concert: A Study of International Security', *World Politics* (Vol. 38, No. 1, 1985), pp. 58–79.
19. John G. Ruggie, 'International Regimes, Transactions, and Change: Embedded Liberalism in the Postwar Economic Order', *International Organization*, (Vol. 36, No. 2, 1982), pp. 379–415.
20. Gerrit W. Gong, *The Standard of 'Civilisation' in International Society* (Oxford: Clarendon Press, 1984), esp. ch. 6.
21. Alan James, 'The Equality of States: Contemporary Manifestations of an Ancient Doctrine', *Review of International Studies*, (Vol. 18, No. 4, 1992), pp. 377–92.
22. Gong, *The Standard of 'Civilisation'*.
23. Ole Wæver, Barry Buzan, Morten Kelstrup, Pierre Lemaitre, *et al.*, *Identity, Migration and the New Security Agenda in Europe* (London: Pinter, 1993).
24. Anthony D. Smith, 'National Identity and the Idea of European Unity', *International Affairs* (Vol. 68, No. 1, 1992), pp. 55-76.
25. Wæver *et al.*, *Identity, Migration*, ch. 4.
26. Ibid., ch. 7.

27. David Armstrong, *Revolution and World Order: The Revolutionary State in International Society* (Oxford: Clarendon, 1993).
28. Barry Buzan and H.O. Nazareth, 'South Africa Versus Azania: the Implications of Who Rules,' *International Affairs* (Vol. 62, No. 1, 1985–6), pp. 35–40 and p. 36.
29. E.H. Carr, *The Twenty Years Crisis* (London: Macmillan, 2nd edn, 1946), pp. 79–87; Hedley Bull, *The Anarchical Society*, ch. 9, esp. pp. 200–5.
30. K.J. Holsti, *Peace and War: Armed Conflict and International Order 1648–1989* (Cambridge: Cambridge University Press, 1991), ch. 5.
31. Ibid., chs 2 and 6.
32. Adam Watson, *The Evolution of International Society* (London: Routledge, 1992), p. 304.
33. Richard Little, 'Deconstructing the Balance of Power: Two Traditions of Thought', *Review of International Studies* (Vol. 15, No. 2, 1989), pp. 87–100.
34. Jervis, 'From Balance to Concert'.
35. Youssef Cohen, B.R. Brown and A.F.K. Organski, 'The Paradoxical Nature of State-making: The Violent Creation of Order', *American Political Science Review* (Vol. 75, No. 4, 1981), pp. 901–10.
36. Buzan, *People, States and Fear*, ch. 6.
37. Robert O. Keohane and Joseph Nye, *Power and Interdependence* (Boston, MA: Little, Brown, 1977).
38. Robert W. Cox, 'Production and Security', in David Dewitt, David Haglund and John Kirton (eds), *Building a New Global Order* (Toronto: Oxford University Press, 1993), pp. 141–58.

Index